ADVANCE PRAISE FOR
The Heart Moves in a Circular Direction

"*The Heart Moves in a Circular Direction* is raw and compelling, written from the soul." Jacquelyn Mitchard, author of *The Deep End of the Ocean*

"*The Heart Moves in a Circular Direction* is a journey through the raw landscape of childhood as a daughter struggles with her mother's mental illness. It is a powerful read, heartbreaking in its honesty and heartwarming in its exploration of the strength and fragility of the ties that bind." Ellen Kort, first Poet Laureate of Wisconsin

"This is a brave, deeply-felt, and quietly important book. It is a well-told story of trying (again and again) to grow up with a schizophrenic mother; and in the end it is a recounting of victory, and of redemption. The core of this book is the author's search for an authentic self…. she transforms a legacy of abandonment and suspicion into a life rich in trust, integrity, and love." Augustus Y. Napier, Ph.D. Author of *The Fragile Bond* and co-author of *The Family Crucible*.

"… the detailed story of how early powerful experiences are assimilated into the self … we (therapists) can learn again the value of patience, gentleness and creativity in our work." Sonia March Nevis, Ph.D. Gestalt International Study Center

The Heart Moves in a Circular Direction

The Heart Moves in a Circular Direction

A STORY OF HEALING

INGEBORG GUBLER CASEY

iUniverse, Inc.
New York Lincoln Shanghai

The Heart Moves in a Circular Direction
A Story of Healing

Copyright © 2007 by Ingeborg Gubler Casey

All rights reserved. No part of this book may be used or reproduced by any means, graphic, electronic, or mechanical, including photocopying, recording, taping or by any information storage retrieval system without the written permission of the publisher except in the case of brief quotations embodied in critical articles and reviews.

iUniverse books may be ordered through booksellers or by contacting:

iUniverse
2021 Pine Lake Road, Suite 100
Lincoln, NE 68512
www.iuniverse.com
1-800-Authors (1-800-288-4677)

Because of the dynamic nature of the Internet, any Web addresses or links contained in this book may have changed since publication and may no longer be valid.

ISBN: 978-0-595-41227-3 (pbk)
ISBN: 978-0-595-67881-5 (cloth)
ISBN: 978-0-595-85582-7 (ebk)

Printed in the United States of America

The information, ideas and suggestions in this book are not intended as a substitute for professional advice. Neither the author nor the publisher shall be liable or responsible for any loss or damage allegedly arising as a consequence of your use or application of any information or suggestions in this book.

This is a work of memory. It is based on my own memories aided by letters written by my mother, father and myself, as well as by court records and personal journals. In many cases, I have used fictitious names to protect the privacy of the individuals involved.

To My Parents, in Loving Memory,
Hans Gubler
1890–1969
and
Paula Langjahr Gubler
1907–1993

Hans and Paula Gubler, 1932

Contents

Acknowledgments... xv
CHAPTER 1   A Reunion..1
CHAPTER 2   A Phone Call...5
CHAPTER 3   A Promise...15
CHAPTER 4   A Decision..27
CHAPTER 5   Orphans...29
CHAPTER 6   Another Phone Call....................................34
CHAPTER 7   A Visit...41
CHAPTER 8   Memories of Home......................................45
CHAPTER 9   Hope..51
CHAPTER 10   Hiding..54
CHAPTER 11   Slipping Backwards....................................62
CHAPTER 12   Shopping..72
CHAPTER 13   On Our Own..75
CHAPTER 14   Rescuing Mama...79
CHAPTER 15   Easter Eggs...83
CHAPTER 16   Doing Onto Others.....................................87
CHAPTER 17   Homesickness...103
CHAPTER 18   Miss Rudikoff..109

CHAPTER 19	Searching	113
CHAPTER 20	Daniel	116
CHAPTER 21	A Test	121
CHAPTER 22	Unraveling	126
CHAPTER 23	Ken	130
CHAPTER 24	Birthing	136
CHAPTER 25	Dreams and Daydreams	138
CHAPTER 26	Awakening	144
CHAPTER 27	A Mother Bird	148
CHAPTER 28	Growing Up	153
CHAPTER 29	Family Therapy	156
CHAPTER 30	Going Deeper	159
CHAPTER 31	Falling Apart	163
CHAPTER 32	Healing	167
CHAPTER 33	Reckoning	171
CHAPTER 34	Gifts	179
CHAPTER 35	Balancing	183
CHAPTER 36	A Foot Sore	190
CHAPTER 37	Finding Home	196
CHAPTER 38	A Final Visit	202
Epilogue		205

Acknowledgments

During my years as a psychotherapist, I have learned much from my clients. I have been privileged to hear their dreams, hopes, fears and struggles. In our work together I have been reminded again and again that it is through telling our stories that healing begins. And though every story is unique, we share much in common. Through hearing the stories of my clients' lives, I have learned that whether we are blessed with well-functioning mothers or not, the tasks of growing up are the same for all of us.

I would like to thank the many people who have expressed their interest and support for my project as it has developed over the years. Sonia Nevis, an outstanding teacher of psychotherapy from whom I have learned so much, provided the encouragement and support I needed to start writing. Through the writing program at the University of Wisconsin-Extension, I was fortunate to connect with Laurel Yourke, who took an interest in my project. Through her insightful guidance, I turned my first unwieldy manuscript into a readable story. I also wish to thank Tom Barry who generously helped me with the cover design. Last, but not least, I want to express my deep appreciation to my husband Bob, who has read this manuscript in all its forms countless times. Whether it was a style issue, computer problem or question of punctuation, I am grateful to have had his encouragement and reliable help.

1

A Reunion

✦

1967

From the safety of my car, I studied Mama as she stood in the doorway of the county hospital. Next to me, my sister, Eveli, seemed in a trance as she stared at the same scene. Neither of us said a word.

The hospital—an ancient, red-brick building with bars on every window—evoked images of noisy inmates, crowded dormitories and dreary dayrooms. When she was first committed here, Mama protested angrily about being forced to live behind locked doors. Now, years later, she stood submissively, her limp arm gripped firmly by a husky matron. Her hair, once a deep auburn, now a sickly yellow, hung in long Shirley Temple curls. Her aging face and stooped body contrasted bizarrely with the little-girl hairdo.

Mama's appearance shocked me. Though it had been over ten years since I had seen her, I hadn't prepared myself for her aging. It was hard enough just to come.

I inched the car forward, stopping in front of Mama and the matron. In one swift motion, the matron opened the car door and deposited Mama onto the back seat, not releasing her arm until she was seated. Without a word, Eveli moved back to sit next to Mama. I drove away quickly, glad to be the driver, glad I didn't have to be the one in the back seat.

Mama acted as though we were strangers. Maybe she had wiped us completely out of her mind. Maybe that was easier than having two daughters who never visited, who never called. Maybe this was her way of showing us we no longer mattered.

Eveli asked questions, but Mama only answered yes or no. She acted like she didn't want to be with us. She didn't hug us, rub our cheeks, or tearfully tell us she had missed us. She didn't berate us or complain, cry or yell. She was quiet and distant, as though she was saying, "you wanted to separate yourself from me, okay, be separate." A vital connection felt severed. Even though I had chosen it, I was shocked. What were we to be to each other in this separateness? A chauffeur and passenger?

I had seen Mama act this way often, when she was wary and suspicious. It was her usual way with most people. But never with me. I was always the one she trusted. I kept my eyes on the road and wondered if the sweet, affectionate mother I knew in childhood was gone forever.

Earlier, when Eveli and I arrived at the hospital, we had checked in with Dr. Kunzler, the superintendent. He hadn't seen either of us since we were teenagers, but he recognized us immediately and invited us into his office. I thought we would finally get to talk about Mama like adults, but he only wanted to talk about us. He kept asking about our marriages, our jobs and Eveli's children as though he had all day.

Now, after many years of experience as a psychotherapist, I have come to understand Dr.Kunzler's concern. He knew we were patients also. Less obvious in our need than Mama, but with real emotional wounds, wounds we were only dimly aware of at the time. I think of him when young women talk to me of their worries about their own depressed, alcoholic, sick or psychotic mothers. Some of these daughters also think they're doing fine, as Eveli and I did. They seem puzzled that I'm more concerned about them than their mothers. They're certain they are fine, and I'm certain of the difficulties lying in wait.

When Eveli and I asked Dr. Kunzler how our mother was doing, he answered quickly that there had been no change, as though the subject wasn't worth discussing. He called the ward and told them to get Mama ready for an outing. This was what we had asked for, but I was still surprised that we would be trusted to take Mama off grounds. I was expecting him to tell us it wasn't a good idea, or at least to call Daddy to see if we had his permission. Maybe he thought that since I was now a psychologist, I would know how to handle Mama. I was leery. I wished the hospital had a visiting room.

I had stopped visiting Mama during my sophomore year in college. Before that I sometimes accompanied Daddy when he took Mama out for lunch and shopping. But every outing ended the same way: with Mama crying about being forced to return to the hospital, a place she hated, or, worse, Mama angrily blaming Daddy for everything that had happened to her. Her tears and complaints left me in turmoil for days. When I could bear it no longer, I cut off all contact with her.

After that, I tried to block her from my thoughts. I moved through my life pretending I had no mother, as though I owed her nothing. But every so often a wave of guilt engulfed me. How could I not visit or write or call in a year? Two years? Three?

The years went by, yet I felt no more capable of facing her. But if I never tried, what kind of person did that make me? Not worthy to be a member of the human race. I couldn't stand my own thoughts and feelings, so I'd slam a steel door on them. I could almost hear it clang. Then nothing. Numbness. And I could resume my life.

During those years, Eveli had moved to California and started raising a family. By the time she returned to Wisconsin for a visit, I had finished grad school. I longed for her to tell me she understood the decision I had made years before. I knew it sounded selfish. I wished she would tell me it was okay. She had done no better—going off to California and not coming back for ten years. Of course, she had a better excuse: four children.

Whenever we were together, we both avoided talking about Mama for as long as we could. We didn't want to ruin our good time. But a couple of days before Eveli was to fly back to California, we acknowledged that she was on our minds. Talking about Mama usually filled me with dread, but in this conversation we realized something had changed: we were adults now. We owned cars. We knew how to drive. If we wanted, we could visit her on our own. We didn't have to wait for Daddy to take us. We didn't need anyone's permission. Alone I lacked the courage, but with Eveli, it suddenly felt possible. And so we decided to visit Mama—on our own, for the first time, as adults.

The hospital lay just a few miles outside of town, but with Mama in the back seat refusing to talk to us, the drive seemed painfully long. Once in town, I drove around the courthouse square slowly. I hoped we could ease into a normal visit of lunch and shopping. I pointed to the Chocolate Shop. "Should we have some lunch?"

"I don't want any." Mama's voice was flat.

"How about a cup of coffee? Or some ice cream?"

"I don't need any."

"Eveli, aren't you hungry?" Eveli didn't answer. I wondered how we would visit if we didn't get out of the car. "How about going into a few dress shops? We could browse around."

"No, I don't need anything. I don't need to go into dress shops. I'll just go in the drugstore by myself."

"We can go in with you. I'll park." Desperately, I wanted to reinstate the familiar ritual of past visits, but it wasn't working.

"No, no, it's all right. I'll go in by myself. I'll just be a minute."

"But we can go in, too. I need to come with you."

"Oh, what does it hurt?" Eveli cut in. "If she wants to be by herself, what's wrong with that?" Eveli sounded irritated.

I wanted to remind Eveli about the time Mama took off for Washington, D.C., and two F.B.I. agents had to bring her back. I imagined Mama slipping out the back door of the drugstore and heading for the bus depot. I was sure that I, the psychologist, would be blamed. I could hear Dr. Kunzler yelling, "You did what? You let your mother go into a store by herself? You shouldn't have let her out of your sight." Eveli didn't seem to realize we were responsible. But if I brought it up, she would only say, "So what? So what if she runs off? Wouldn't you run from that god-awful place if you could?" I wasn't brave enough to start a fight with Eveli, not with Mama in the car.

I gripped the steering wheel, trying to follow Mama with my eyes as she disappeared into the store.

"For heaven's sakes, relax. Where would she go, anyway?" Eveli chided. A worse scenario unfolded in my mind. What if Mama never came out? What if she just stayed in the store? We would have to go after her. She might pretend she didn't know us. We would tell her it was time to go back to the hospital, and she would say we had no right to take her back. Then we would have to coax her quietly, hoping to avoid a scene. But she wouldn't care about embarrassing us. She would yell for the manager and protest that we were mistreating her until everyone in the store would notice. They would think we were abusing our elderly mother. We would have to drag Mama into the car while she kicked and screamed, "You're not taking me back there. I refuse. I refuse to go." I had already lived through one scene like that, and I didn't want to go through another. Being a psychologist didn't help one bit.

All this time, Eveli was chatting, telling me there was nothing to worry about. Finally, Mama emerged from the store clutching a small bag. She climbed into the back seat while Eveli smirked at me. I said nothing. I just wanted the visit to be over.

2

A Phone Call

♦

1969

My father had prepared for his death. To cut costs, he chose cremation. His ashes were to be stored at a funeral home close to the county hospital where Mama had been committed. At a nearby cemetery, he selected a burial plot and erected a headstone engraved with both their names. When Mama's time came, his ashes were to be placed in her coffin.

Time and again, Daddy tried to explain these preparations to me. But I was young—not yet thirty-one—and I couldn't bear to listen. A few words and I would be in tears.

I tried to be mature and rational. But it never worked. My will was a thin, weak thing, easily broken by the rush of my emotions.

Daddy was used to my tears, if never quite comfortable with them. Since my early teens I had been a crier. Sometimes I cried for no reason at all, at least not one I could name or explain. And sometimes I couldn't stop.

My crying bouts worried me. As I grew older, I worried that I was turning out like Mama. In our family Mama cried; Daddy didn't. She could cry for hours, sometimes sorrowfully, sometimes angrily. Each time I cried I worried that Mama's craziness had already taken hold of me. Somewhere deep inside, in a place I couldn't reach, it was gathering force year by year, until I turned thirty-eight, the age Mama had been when she first went to the hospital. Then it would rise up and take me over. Just like Mama.

Of course, I had reasons to cry. Real reasons. Mama's mental illness for instance. It had been pronounced incurable. She had languished in that primitive county hospital since I was thirteen and would likely remain there for the rest of her life. I didn't know how to live with my guilt for abandoning her, yet I couldn't find the courage to act differently. These were all good reasons to cry.

But my crying bouts could be set off by any small thing—not necessarily thoughts of Mama—and so I never made the connection. It might have helped if someone had explained that to understand what my tears were about, I'd have to allow myself to cry. If someone had said that to heal, first I had to let myself grieve. But no one did, and despite the fact that I was a psychologist, I didn't understand how emotions worked, especially my own. Any surge of powerful emotion panicked me. I pushed it back down as soon as I could. There, somewhere inside, my grief accumulated, layer by layer, until I was packed tight as a tube of toothpaste. One little squeeze and out it oozed.

I oozed, then gushed, the day Daddy told me my Tante Gret, his only sister, had died. The torrent of emotion I released alarmed us both. Daddy handed me his handkerchief and tried to soothe me. I had never met my aunt—I was supposed to meet her on my first visit to Switzerland—so it seemed to Daddy that my grief was extreme. The more I carried on, the more worried Daddy looked. I suspected he was thinking, as I was, that, like Mama, I had a weak emotional constitution. And this must mean I had inherited her disease.

Looking back, I believe Daddy was only anticipating the pain I would feel when he died. He understood, in a way I couldn't, that Tante Gret's death was only the first of many losses for me. If I was this distraught over losing a relative I had never met, how much more would I suffer on losing him? And he wouldn't be there to comfort me.

After each conversation about his funeral arrangements, I dismissed all thought of his dying. I didn't want to imagine losing Daddy, the only person I had ever been able to count on. Besides, I saw no reason to dwell on it. He would live to be ninety, I was sure of it.

Even though he was old enough to be my grandfather—he was forty-eight when I was born—I never felt I had an especially old father. He had always looked and acted young. At seventy-five he challenged me to a race across a beach. I gave it my all, but he kept up with me, until laughing and panting, we declared it a draw.

And when, a few years later, on a hot, humid day in August, he looked tired and walked slowly, I pretended not to notice, not wanting to admit he suddenly looked his age. I told myself it was only the heat.

I was in my office in the psychology building when the phone call came. I picked up the receiver nonchalantly and heard a stranger's voice. Before I had my bearings, he told me my father had died. His body was being transported to the crematorium. I gasped. My mouth froze and my thoughts raced backwards, wanting desperately to go back, to before, to a moment when this had not yet happened.

What I remember most about that moment is the sensation of dropping; everything inside me rushed down, down to my feet and into the floor. I felt as though my whole world dropped away in that long, unforgettable moment.

"I'm so sorry." Karen, our clinic secretary, had stepped quietly into my office. She stood behind me now, her voice, soft and sympathetic. "He called while you were in class, but I didn't want to be the one to tell you. Should I call your husband?" My husband, Ken, was in his last year of law school and could usually be found in the law library, only a few blocks away.

Through tears, I nodded. I knew I would have to call Eveli myself. I sat alone, staring out my office window, wondering how I could bear to say this terrible news out loud. I wanted to pretend it wasn't so, that no one needed to be told. I wasn't ready to lose my only real parent. I had to force myself to dial Eveli's number.

Eveli, surprised to hear from me on a Tuesday morning, started chatting cheerfully. She didn't know yet. I had to tell her, but my throat was too tight. I could let her go on and for her it wouldn't have happened. I could protect her for a few precious minutes.

"Daddy died," I interrupted. Gasping, she protested as I had. Now I was the impersonal voice of reality. "Yes, it's true. He's really dead."

After hanging up, I put my head down on my desk and sobbed. My office door pushed open slowly. Ken, my husband, stood looking at me with sympathetic eyes. He held out his arms as I stumbled into his comforting hug.

"Why did it have to be Daddy?" I sobbed as he held me.

I felt relieved to know Eveli, my big sister, was on her way. All through childhood I had looked up to her. She had given me my nickname, "Biby," soon after I was born. She declared "Ingeborg" too hard to pronounce, and soon everyone called me "Biby." She had always been more mother than sister, the one in charge whenever Mama was in the hospital. We both had blue eyes and long blonde braids, but she was sleek, strong, and smart, while I was soft and round—Mama's baby. As adults, we looked more alike. Both trim and athletic, our hair, darker now, was cut short. With our glasses, we looked equally intellectual.

At the airport, Eveli felt limp as we hugged. She looked dazed, like an accident survivor. I had been hoping for comfort, but saw she needed it more.

It had been two years since Eveli and I had made our futile attempt to re-connect with Mama. After Eveli returned to California I occasionally told myself I should make another effort, but I never followed through. The mere thought of seeing Mama again filled me with dread. I never discussed Mama with my friends because, the truth was, I was too ashamed—ashamed of her illness, ashamed of turning my back on her. I didn't understand why I was afraid to visit her. I accused myself of acting like a selfish child.

But after a certain amount of self-punishment, I excused myself. My own life was too full as it was. During the two years since our visit, Ken had started law school, we had moved into our own house—a small bungalow on a dead-end street with lots of other young families—and our twins, Brian and Evan, had been born. While pregnant, I started a new job managing the training clinic in the psychology department at the university. The salary was barely enough to pay our bills, but I loved being back on campus working with students. My flexible hours allowed me to spend some time at home with Brian and Evan, and this more than compensated for the low pay.

I was eager to share all these new developments in my life with Eveli, even though the occasion for her visit was a sad one. That evening we briefly escaped from our grief into the happy laughter of Brian and Evan, my darling ten-month-old boys.

The next morning, uncertain about exactly what we were supposed to do, we headed to Lake Geneva, the town where we had grown up. After Eveli and I left for college, Daddy moved into a rooming house owned by our long-standing family friends, Mary and Gordon. There he lived in a room with a tiny kitchenette, sharing a bathroom with other roomers.

I parked in front of Mary's rambling old boarding house, just a block from the lake. I looked toward the lake with longing, aching for the sustenance it had always given me. The water, not yet frozen, gleamed like shiny steel under the November sun.

We walked up the porch steps and rang the bell. It felt strange to stand there, knowing Daddy was no longer inside. Mary greeted us warmly, and I felt gratitude for her presence. I had always admired Mary, one of my former Sunday school teachers. A journalist and photographer, she had dared to wear pants, even to church, in an era when married women stayed home and wore dresses.

Mary consoled us as she poured out her own grief. "I begged him to let me take him to the hospital. I found him just three days ago, hanging onto the banister, like this." She bent forward and put her hand on her chest. "He was halfway up the stairs. I said, 'Please, let me take you to a doctor,' but he said no, he just needed to rest. That was the last time I spoke to him."

We followed her up to Daddy's room as she finished her story. How she didn't see him the next day. How she became alarmed when she knocked on his door but got no response. How she had gotten her keys and unlocked the door and found him in his bed.

Mary knew all about Daddy's plan to be cremated. Unlike me, she had probably been able to listen. Mary, Gordon, Daddy and others were all in a Christian fellowship group where they talked about things like that. On principle, they had all left the large church—where Mary had taught my Sunday school class—a number of years ago. First, there had been a fight about racial integration. Then, a fight about incorporating into a larger denomination. Daddy and his friends were the rebels who voted in favor of accepting the African-American family and against losing their autonomy to a larger denomination. In both cases they lost, and so they left, forming their own small group.

After letting us into Daddy's room, Mary left us. "I'll be downstairs if you need me." We stood in silence, gazing around the small room where he had lived for the last seventeen years. Newspapers and books covered the table. I couldn't bear to look at the bed, the place where Daddy breathed his last breath. Every object in the room, once so familiar, suddenly looked out of place. How could all these belongings—books, clothes, mementos of trips—continue to exist, but Daddy, their owner, be gone?

I opened a drawer and saw a stack of photographs. There he was, beaming with pride as he held Nicky, Eveli's first born, now fourteen, his first grandchild. He was sixty-five when the photo was taken. He looked youthful and vigorous, his hair still thick and black, his black mustache neatly trimmed, a playful smile on his lips.

A more recent photo showed his hair had grayed, but his eyes were still twinkling and happy. I felt a stab of regret that I hadn't taken his picture with Brian and Evan on his last visit. As I gazed at photos of my uncles, aunt and cousins, people I had never met, my regrets multiplied. Daddy wanted to take me to Switzerland, but I was always too busy, too afraid my career plans would get de-railed. Now that he was gone, I wondered when, and if, I would ever get there.

The last trip he took, in August, had been to Switzerland. He spent two months with his brother and some school chums, traveling to spots they had hiked as boys. He sent me postcards from each beautiful place, reminiscing about his youthful adventures. When he got home in late October, he called and said he wasn't feeling well. It was just a mild flu, he said. He wouldn't be coming up to see me as planned but would come the following weekend. It was the last time I talked with him.

Eveli and I gazed around the cluttered room, every inch filled with reminders of Daddy and our childhood. Neither of us could face the work of sorting and packing so we retreated to Mary's kitchen. She reassured us there was no rush. "We need a memorial service, don't you think?"

Of course we did. I hadn't even realized that we, as his survivors, were expected to plan it. I had no idea how. I had never even attended a funeral. It may seem strange that I could have avoided this for thirty-one years, but that was how it was for us. We grew up in a tiny fragment of a family with a mentally ill mother. Mama and Daddy were the only members of their families to leave Switzerland, so we grew up without grandparents, aunts, uncles or cousins. When Mama was home, she wanted no contact with anyone. We never attended a wedding, a first communion, a baptism, an anniversary party—or a funeral. I didn't even realize that what we sorely needed was a well-practiced ritual to contain our grief. We had nothing—no rending of cloth, no rosary to pray—so we floundered. This is exactly what Daddy knew was coming. And why, I now understood, he had tried to ease the way for us, by planning ahead, as much as he could.

I was glad Mary seemed willing to be in charge. Eveli and Mary talked about what needed to be done while I drifted into worrying about Mama. She was the dark cloud hanging over me, a cloud so ominous I was afraid to mention it out loud. Losing Daddy was hard enough, but losing him also meant that I would have to face her again.

Eveli and I left Mary's as the November afternoon was fading. Ahead of us, the lake shimmered under the last rays of light. The water pulled me like a magnet, just as it had when I was a kid. The lake was the best part of growing up here. I had a favorite spot, where, sitting on the broad trunk of a willow tree that stretched out from the shore, I spent hours, gazing at the water and thinking my own thoughts.

"Mind if we drive this way?" Without waiting for Eveli's reply, I headed toward the lake, then along the shore line. I wanted the comfort of being close to the water. "Let's just drive up to Oak Terrace as long as we're here, okay?" It was the last place we had lived together as a family.

Eveli frowned. "What for?" It was a familiar struggle between us. I liked to reminisce; she resisted going back.

"Please."

Eveli sighed. "Oh, okay, but let's not drag it out."

I steered up the hill toward Oak Terrace. I always loved the address. To me, it sounded like an elegant estate even though it was just a couple of apartment buildings set in a grove of trees. We moved there in the summer of 1950, just before I started seventh grade, the summer we were waiting for Mama to come home from the hospital.

Before moving into Oak Terrace we had lived in a makeshift apartment on the backside of an older house. Hoping more pleasant surroundings would aid Mama's adjustment, Daddy rented the Oak Terrace apartment, the best he could afford. Our frequent moves from one cramped apartment to another had been the cause of many bitter arguments between Mama and Daddy.

I parked in front of our former home. So much had happened in the seventeen years since we moved out. The building looked smaller and shabbier than I remembered.

"Look, they've converted the garages into rooms. Would have been nice to have another bedroom." When we lived here, Eveli and I shared the only bedroom while Mama slept on the sleeper sofa. Daddy often slept in his office downtown. Even though we couldn't see inside, I could easily picture our old living room. Mama and I spent many hours there, sitting on the couch together while she told me stories about the county hospital. After school, I used to go straight home while Eveli went to her job at the phone company. Since Daddy was usually out of town on business, Mama and I had lots of time alone. That's when she let me into her secret world.

At twelve, I was Mama's perfect partner. Still young enough to suspend my disbelief, I had no reservations about accepting her world. Only by believing could I be close to her, and that was what I wanted more than anything. I wanted to think of her as smart and powerful and outwitting everybody. I could remember our conversations as though they happened yesterday:

"I'm going to tell you something very important, Biby. It's about Hitler—Adolph Hitler." Her voice sounded urgent, but her eyes shone with pleasure.

"Hitler? He's dead. Didn't he die at the end of the war?"

"That's what everybody thinks." She laughed. "He wants us to think that. He's clever and he's hiding."

"But the building he was in, didn't it blow up?"

"They never found his body. No one ever found his body. He escaped and now he's hiding. He's fooled everybody but me."

"How did you find out?"

Mama laughed again. "I told you, Biby. I know things that other people don't."

"Shouldn't the government know? I mean shouldn't you tell them so they can capture him?" The idea of Hitler still being alive scared me, but I loved being in Mama's world. I felt so grown-up there.

"No, no Biby. We're not in danger. Not just yet. He's not ready to come out. He's hiding in South America, and I know how to find him."

"You're not going after him, are you?"

"No, no Biby." She laughed again.

I loved for her to be happy.

"I don't have to go. All I have to do is to tell the right people. They'll do it."

"Who are they?"

"The State Department in Washington, D.C. Secretary of State Dean Acheson, he's the one. I have to go in person."

"Couldn't you just mail a letter?"

Mama laughed even harder. "You wouldn't say that, Biby, if you knew, if you only knew." She shook her head over my naïve trust. "Lots of people would like to know this. And they're the wrong people. Absolutely wrong. Things would get very dangerous if the wrong people found out. I'm being watched, you know." She leaned toward me and whispered. "That's why I must be very careful. Don't worry, Biby. I'll get the information to Dean Acheson at the right time."

I was special, one of the right people, and I loved it. But it hurt me to hear her cry about her years in the hospital—being separated from Eveli and me, missing our school plays and birthdays. Mama cried about this almost daily. It made me sad to hear her. I couldn't understand why she had to keep going over it. It was past, she was home, and I wanted her to be happy.

It was even harder when she blamed Daddy. I didn't believe he had done anything to hurt Mama, but I couldn't defend him without losing her trust. In my heart, I believed she would eventually discover that he had not been in cahoots with her enemies, as she claimed. She would forgive him, and we could all be happy together.

Sometimes Mama talked about the wonderful life we would lead after she delivered her secrets. She would be paid handsomely, of course, and we would move out of our one-bedroom apartment into a beautiful house with a garden. There, I would have a birthday party with a beautiful cake and a swan sculpted of ice cream. I wanted to talk more about my party, but most days Mama was not in the mood. She preferred dwelling on the wrongs done to her or the dangers she sensed.

Mama's world of good and evil, like the world in my Superman comics, made perfect sense to me. There *was* evil in the world. This could be the only explanation as to why she had been locked up in that jail-like hospital when she had done nothing wrong.

Daddy squirmed when I asked why Mama had to stay in the hospital so long. He would sigh and say she had been worn out and needed a long rest. Then he would stick his head back into his newspaper. His answers left me confused.

Mama was not confused. She knew exactly why she had been locked up. Her enemies needed to keep her quiet. She knew too much. Mama's answer gave me hope.

Weekends, when we were all home together, Mama turned quiet. Being a model housewife served as her cover. She kept a spotless house and served delicious meals. She wasn't lying. Not exactly. She was keeping her secrets to herself and pretending to be content to distract Daddy and Eveli. They couldn't be trusted.

I followed her example and acted my part as the perfect daughter. It wasn't hard. I wanted so much to please Mama. I wasn't even tempted to do anything that might upset her. School was easy. I brought home good grades with little effort. After school, I preferred coming straight home. I knew Mama would be waiting.

But shortly after I started eighth grade, I came home one day to an empty apartment. On the kitchen table, I found a note that read:

> Biby,
> I won't be home for supper. I've gone on a little
> trip to Washington, D.C. for a few days. You and
> Eveli can heat the soup in the refrigerator. Don't
> worry about me. I'll be home soon.
> Love, Mama.

So she had done it! She had taken her secrets to Washington! I was excited and only a little sad to be left out. This way, I couldn't be tricked into giving away vital information. I forgave her. I only hoped she knew how loyal I was.

"Hi, Kiddo, where's Mama?" Eveli, a senior in high school, was home earlier than usual.

"She's not home."

"I can see that." Eveli sounded annoyed. Then she saw the note. "Oh, my God. Did you know about this?"

"No," I replied truthfully.

"You did, too, didn't you? You should have told someone. You should have told me or Daddy."

"I didn't know, honest. Besides, what's wrong with her going?"

"Oh, for Pete's sake, don't you understand anything? She'll get in trouble. Now they'll send her back to that god-awful hospital."

"But she knew important things. She had to go."

"You actually believe that stuff?" She stared at me in disbelief. "You poor kid! How could you believe that crazy stuff?"

I wondered if Eveli could be right. But I brushed my doubts aside. Mama hadn't shared her secrets with Eveli. Only with me.

When Daddy came home, he was crestfallen. "It's a shame, a darned shame. Just another month and she would have been off probation. Now they'll send her back."

My heart sank, but I clung to hope, still wanting to believe in Mama. I prayed she would get through to the right people, the ones who would protect her.

"Where did she ever get the bus fare?" Daddy mused. "She must have saved it bit by bit from the household money." He shook his head and laughed. "I have to hand it to her. She's clever."

The next night, he told us Mama was back in the county hospital.

"That fast? They put her back that fast?"

Daddy laughed sadly, shaking his head. "Yah, yah, she went to Washington all right. She went right to the State Building and asked to see Dean Acheson himself. It didn't take them long to find out who she was and where she came from." Then he laughed out loud. "So two F.B.I. agents had to fly with her all the way back to Wisconsin! Yah, I have to hand it to her—who would have thought she'd get that far?"

3

A Promise

✦

1951–55

Mama wrote sad letters from Green County Hospital, begging me to visit. I wasn't allowed to see her because Dr. Kunzler, the superintendent of the hospital, believed children shouldn't see parents who were mentally ill. To me, at age thirteen, this made no sense. I begged Daddy to get special permission, so he told Dr. Kunzler I was mature for my age. By the time Dr. Kunzler gave in, I had turned fourteen.

On the morning of the visit, I chose my outfit carefully: a white blouse, a blue plaid skirt, a blue ribbon in my long pony tail. I cleaned my white buck shoes carefully. If my shoes weren't clean, if my outfit didn't please Mama, our day could be ruined.

Daddy, talkative as usual during our hour-long drive, turned strangely silent as we approached the hospital. In the distance, a white arch over the road gleamed in the sun as though leading to an elegant country resort. But as we came close, I read the words on the arch: "Green County Insane Asylum." I gasped.

Daddy glanced over at me with a concerned look on his face. "This county is a little backward. The people here don't keep up with modern thinking."

As we drove into the complex of buildings that made up the hospital, I studied the place Mama hated so. On first glance, it didn't look bad. Just some old buildings, their red bricks blackened with age, sort of like a really old high school. Then I saw the bars on the windows, and the heavy chain link enclosing the balconies. The place looked deserted. Not a single patient was outside enjoying the beautiful fall day. I wondered if they were ever allowed outside.

Mama stood waiting under a carport, her arm gripped tightly by a husky matron. Her face lit up when she saw me.

As soon as the matron deposited Mama into the back seat, I climbed in next to her. After hugging me close, Mama sat back, gazed into my face while stroking my cheeks and hair. "I'm so grateful you came to see me, thank you, thank you." She clutched me tightly again, pressing her cheek against mine. After a few minutes, I wanted to shake myself free, but I couldn't disappoint Mama, so I let her pet and stroke me as much as she wanted. It was the least I could do.

After lunch, Mama proceeded from shop to shop, picking out things she needed and fingering fancy lingerie, while Daddy and I trailed behind her. When Daddy announced that it was time to go back to the hospital, Mama ignored him.

"Paula, you don't want to miss supper."

"I don't care about supper," she snapped.

I tensed, fearing she would start a fight right in the store.

"Come on, Paula. It was a nice day, wasn't it?" Daddy sounded nervous. I hated having to end Mama's happy afternoon, but I knew Daddy would get in trouble if we didn't get her back on time. I was relieved when Mama yielded and followed Daddy out of the store.

In the car, she sat close to me, rubbing my cheek with the backs of her fingers and chanting, "It's not fair, it's not fair. I don't want to leave you. They're keeping me away from you."

Daddy drove excruciatingly slowly, I supposed to give Mama more time with me. But it only seemed to make the drive back torturous. Mama was getting louder now, crying and sobbing as she recited the wrongs done her. I dreaded what was coming.

By the time we pulled under the carport, Mama's voice had become a whimper.

When the matron stepped forward, Mama protested loudly once again. "I can't stand to go back in there. Hans, do something, please."

"Paula, you know I can't. Don't make it harder."

The matron opened the car door, seized Mama by the arm, and pulled her out roughly. Mama submitted meekly. The matron allowed Mama to stand and wave as we drove away.

As Mama disappeared inside the locked doors, a part of me followed her into that mysterious building. I tried to imagine living there month after month, knowing I could never go out for fresh air, unable to escape. Silently, I vowed to get her out as soon as I could.

During the next few years, I saw Mama only occasionally, but we continued to write frequently. Whenever I saw a pink envelope in the mail box, I felt a rush of hope. She always thanked me for whatever I had sent; then made new requests. She asked for yarn to knit us socks and sweaters, as well as shampoo, toothpaste, or stockings. But most of the letter was about her misery, her ache for us. Always she begged me to talk to Daddy about getting her released.

When I asked Daddy when Mama would be coming home, his answers were vague. The best he had been able to do was convince Dr. Kunzler to allow him to bring her home for a few days each Christmas. As the years went by, the idea that Mama would stay confined in that wretched place for the rest of her life became an unspeakable possibility that hovered over me like a shadow. Daddy never said so directly, so in my heart, I kept alive a tiny hope that someday something would change.

Then, in my first year at the university, I noticed an article about a new psychiatric hospital opening close to campus. They were holding an open house, so I decided to look the place over. Perhaps I could get Mama transferred. I had nothing to lose by trying.

At the new hospital, I felt encouraged to see big glass windows with no bars. I wandered through the arts and crafts area, the dining room and the gleaming halls. I admired the simple rooms. How Mama would love having her own room. Lack of privacy was her chief complaint.

I summoned all my courage, walked to the front desk and asked for an appointment with one of the psychiatrists. "Is it an emergency?" the receptionist asked. I didn't know what to say. It felt like an emergency to me, one that had lingered for years.

"I'd like to come as soon as possible." I was afraid if I said more, she would tell me to come back with my father or something equally impossible. Instead, she told me to take a seat and wait until the psychiatrist was free.

The psychiatrist sat behind his desk with an unsmiling but not unkindly face. He looked at me with a puzzled expression.

"I'm not here for me—it's my mother. She's in a county hospital and not getting any help. It's a terrible place. There are bars on the windows, and she doesn't get therapy." I tried to read his face. He said nothing, so I kept talking.

"She was at the state hospital before. That wasn't so bad. She could talk with the chaplain and go to the craft room. She made all kinds of stuff—wooden plates and napkin rings with designs on them. She's really creative and needs to do artistic things. They don't have anything like that where she is now. She says it's so noisy, she can't even knit. She used to make all our clothes."

"How long has your mother been there?"

"At Mendota for two years, then they transferred her. I don't know why. Then she came home. She was really doing well—she had just about made it through her probation, but then she went off to Washington without telling anyone. So they sent her back to the county hospital, and she's been there ever since. Locked up. That was four years ago. Please, you've got to help her."

"The person you really need to help is yourself."

"Me?" He didn't seem to understand what I'd said. "I'm okay. I'm going to school. I'm fine."

"That's good, but you could still use therapy."

"What for?"

"You must have had a hard time growing up."

"Not really. She's the one who needs help, not me."

"You're not the one who can help her. You've got to help yourself—finish college, lead your own life."

"I am. But sometimes I can't concentrate because I worry about her. Couldn't she be transferred? Then I could visit her more often."

"I'm not sure that would be good for you. Anyway, this hospital is only for children. We have a better chance of helping people if we can help them before they've been ill for many years like your mother. I'm afraid there's not much anyone can do for her now."

I almost ran out of the building. Not much we can do for her! What did he know? He hadn't even talked to Mama. He didn't want to be bothered. I hated him. How could he tell me to forget my own mother? But I kept going back to his words, turning them over and over. Just the way my tongue always reached for the sore places in my mouth and rubbed, over and over.

At the co-op where I lived, Mama's latest letter waited: "... I miss you so. When are you coming to see me? I wait for the day we'll be together. I am so lonely here. I love you." I could barely stand to read it.

That night, I showed the letter to Daniel, my boyfriend. I had never told him about Mama. I was used to keeping everything about Mama a secret. But after my session with the psychiatrist, I had to talk to somebody.

"I can't stand to think about her in that place with those barred windows."

"Why doesn't your Dad move her to a better hospital?"

"He can't afford a private hospital. Besides, she shouldn't be in a hospital at all. She didn't do anything wrong. She never had a trial."

"Look, people don't just get locked up. There must be a reason." Daniel sounded impatient, but I was relieved he was asking questions, just as though this was a normal, everyday problem.

"They say she's mentally ill, but she's really okay."

"But what did she do?"

"She didn't do anything except go to Washington. They call it schizophrenia, but if you met her, you wouldn't notice anything."

"There's got to be some way to treat that."

"She used to get more therapy at Mendota, but now she doesn't even get arts and crafts." I was thankful for Daniel's interest. At least he wanted to understand which was more than I could say about the psychiatrist.

We reached no answers, but knowing I could talk with Daniel made it easier to get through the days. Night after night, I unloaded on him, usually crying in the process. His questions, logical and thorough, comforted me. They seemed to imply there was a solution. If we kept analyzing, we would eventually solve even this problem.

But one night, when I started crying, he turned to me abruptly. "Look, this has to stop. We've been talking about your mother every night for weeks, and we're going in circles. It just seems to make you more upset."

"I can't help it." I felt betrayed. I wasn't prepared for Daniel to give up so suddenly.

"You can too. You can decide to stop thinking about her. Let's face it, there's nothing you can do for your mother."

"How can you say that?"

"You've got to forget about her."

"Forget her? What are you saying?"

"We've got finals. We can't keep going over and over this."

"I can't forget her. I thought you understood. Could you forget your mother?"

"Look, if someone's drowning, and you try to save them, but they keep pulling you under, there's no sense in both of you drowning."

I felt he'd just slammed a door in my face. Daniel's solution, so cruel yet so logical, was just like the psychiatrist's. Neither of them told me how I was supposed to live with myself afterwards. I knew I would never again mention Mama to Daniel. I withdrew into myself, letting him think I was taking his advice while comforting myself with thoughts of Christmas when my family would be together, the first time in a year.

We had Christmas together only because of Daddy's persistence. He had finally persuaded Dr. Kunzler that a home visit at Christmas would do Mama good, and that he could manage her. We no longer had a real home, so every year Daddy scrambled to find us a place.

Daddy could barely contain his excitement when he told me what he had arranged that Christmas. Our past holiday dwellings had never been to Mama's liking—a sparsely furnished teacher's apartment, a modern ranch style house with a silver tree adorned with pink tinsel. But that year he had managed to borrow a lovely, older home across the street from his rooming house. The house belonged to Mrs. Nelson, a friend of Daddy's landlady, Mary. Mrs. Nelson, a widow, worked as a receptionist at a resort. She would be putting in long hours over the holidays and would stay in a room the resort provided. She had offered us her house out of the goodness of her heart, Daddy explained.

The house was beautiful—sunny windows overlooking the lake, spacious rooms with Oriental rugs, even a baby grand piano. Mama would love it. I wished Eveli would be there to enjoy it with us, but she was married now and living in California with her husband and baby.

I wanted Mama's entry to the house to go smoothly, so while Daddy drove over to pick her up, I bought a few fresh groceries and tidied the kitchen. I was doing my best to ignore my feelings—a familiar but confusing mixture of longing, hope and fear that overtook me whenever I was about to be reunited with Mama.

When I heard Daddy's car, I pulled aside the curtain and peeked out. Mama slowly emerged from the car, her long auburn hair peeking out from the hood of her winter coat. She stood waiting, looking frightened and vulnerable while Daddy got her bags out of the trunk. The years in the hospital had taken their toll. Mama was seventeen years younger than Daddy yet looked his age. She eyed the house warily, not moving until Daddy took her elbow and guided her toward the door.

As Mama entered the kitchen, I pushed my feelings aside. I had to concentrate on being the girl Mama wanted—a girl who wore clean white blouses and had no ambitions or desires, a girl without interest in boys, who had never done the things I had done.

Mama knew nothing about my real life. She didn't want to know. She never asked questions. I didn't care. It was better not to be the object of scrutiny like Eveli, who bore the brunt of Mama's criticism. I was Mama's golden girl. She had only been angry with me once that I could remember—when I was eight and lost a sweater she had knit for me. Even though I had been careful ever since never to repeat a mistake like that one, I lived in fear that Mama would discover I wasn't as good as I pretended.

Daddy ushered Mama in grandly, eager to show her the house. Mama embraced me, then stepped back to look me over. "Bibili, Bibili, I missed you so." She stroked my cheeks with the backs of her fingers. Suddenly, I felt small and shy, as though I was a six-year-old, rather than a savvy college girl. I held my breath as her eyes grazed over me. Would my hair be okay? I had grown it long again and wore it in a long bushy ponytail, just as I had when I was fourteen. Was I too fat? Once, when she came home from the hospital, she had immediately put me on a diet. She didn't seem to notice my glasses anymore, though she'd been dismayed when I first got them, not caring if I could see the blackboard or not. In her opinion, glasses ruined a girl's appearance. I was relieved to hear no negative comments.

"Well, Paula, what do you think? Isn't this a beautiful house? Mrs. Nelson was so generous to let us have it, and all to ourselves." Daddy went on about Mrs. Nelson, which I knew was a mistake. I was surprised Mama didn't blow up on the spot. Ignoring Daddy, she was moving silently from room to room. I held my breath. So many times, our Christmas reunions started off with Mama yelling at Daddy. But this time she took her suitcase upstairs without a word and settled into the front bedroom as though she had returned to a house she had lived in all her life. I could tell she felt comfortable. The house was decorated the way she would have done it, given the chance.

As Mama seemed to relax, Daddy looked triumphant. He had been trying to please her for years. Perhaps he had finally succeeded. I fell into a reverie, pretending the house was ours. Perhaps Mama and Daddy were seduced into a similar fantasy. Mama seemed happy to be cooking her favorite dishes and serving them on the widow's best china. The house was airy enough to nurture our fantasies, fantasies of inviting friends over and making believe we were a normal family. Ordinary fantasies, but risky for us.

"Paula, I've been thinking. It would be so nice to invite the Larsens. The people I've told you about. They've been so kind to me." Mama started clearing the table. "If you'd give them a chance, I know you would like them." He followed her to the kitchen. "Mrs. Larsen—Joan—has an artistic temperament, like you. She shows her paintings in the art show." Daddy believed Mama's breakdown was caused by lack of contact with educated, creative people. He felt guilty for isolating her in Delavan, the small town where she had her first breakdown.

Mama said nothing. Her face tightened. It was her way of saying, "I want no part of this."

But when Daddy wanted something, he persisted, and Mama finally gave in. Later that day, Daddy announced that his friends had accepted the invitation. "Paula, thank you. I know you'll like them. It's a shame more people don't get a chance to sample your wonderful cooking."

Mama, looking tense, said nothing.

When Mr. and Mrs. Larsen came, Mama stayed in the kitchen while Daddy and I went to the door. Our guests quickly made me feel at ease by asking about my classes at the university. We sat in the living room while Daddy bobbed nervously between living room and kitchen, muttering that he wanted to bring Paula out to meet them. After an uncomfortable length of time, Mama appeared in the doorway, Daddy behind her, pushing her into the room. She acted like a shy schoolgirl, only managing to say, "Pleased to meet you." There was an awkward lull before she murmured, "I've got to get back to the cooking," and retreated to the kitchen. I followed, asking if she needed help. "No, no, Biby, you stay out there. You talk to them."

As Mama set out the platters, Daddy proudly ushered his guests to the table. He poured wine and toasted his friends. Mama served the food. The Larsens complimented her cooking and tried to draw her out. Mama said hardly anything, so Daddy took over. He never had trouble talking.

After dinner, Daddy suggested we move to the living room. Mama started to clear the table.

"Paula, let this go a little while. Come sit with our guests."

"I just have to put the food away."

Daddy suggested I help, but Mama shooed me back to the living room. I knew it wasn't going the way Daddy had hoped, but I felt powerless to change anything. After a few minutes, Daddy excused himself and went to the kitchen himself. I could hear them arguing. I only hoped there would be no explosion. He came back looking exasperated. In the kitchen, Mama was banging pots noisily. We conversed nervously a few more minutes before the Larsens mentioned it was getting late.

"Paula, our guests are leaving. Please join us." Daddy rushed to the kitchen. This time Mama came back with him, but the Larsens stood to leave, thanking Mama many times for the wonderful meal.

Mama waited until she heard the car pull away before she turned on Daddy. "Who do you think I am?" Her voice, deep and guttural, sent a chill through me. I saw the pain on Daddy's face as he withered under her attack. "Treating me like a servant. You expect me to cook for your friends and clean up the mess while you sit."

"But Paula, I told you I'd clean up. I wanted you to join us."

"Ya, ya, that's what you say. You don't know anything about cooking and cleaning."

"I wanted a nice evening for you, Paula. Why couldn't you give them a chance? They're nice people."

"Nice to you maybe."

What were we thinking? How did we expect a woman who had been locked in an institution for four years to be a gracious hostess to people she had never met, to want to make friends? It seems ludicrous, but that's how badly we wanted to pretend there was nothing wrong with Mama.

Despite that evening, I still invited my college roommate to spend a day. Mama seemed more comfortable with this. She didn't have to converse. All she had to do was make lunch. She didn't complain when Wendy and I went skating. She had cocoa ready when we returned.

Wendy and I eventually drifted to the piano where we found some old sheet music. As Wendy's beautiful voice carried through the house, I could hear Mama singing along in the kitchen. But when we started singing "Lili Marlene," Mama waltzed into the living room, holding her skirt out with her hands. She smiled mysteriously, then giggled as she twirled toward us. I froze, hoping Mama would waltz back to the kitchen and leave us alone.

"I used to sing and dance. You didn't know that about me, did you, Biby? No, I never told you." She giggled again and twirled around the room, singing "la, la, la" to the tune of "Lili Marlene."

I went stiff. This was exactly why I had never brought friends home before.

Wendy looked at me, wanting guidance. But I didn't know what to do either. Praying Mama would stop, I moved away from the piano.

"You sing very well. And you dance beautifully, too," said Wendy. She sounded as though she was praising a five-year-old. Mama looked triumphant as she resumed twirling and singing. I watched helplessly.

It seemed we were forced to admire her for an eternity. I knew if I told her to leave us alone, things would get worse. We could only wait her out. Finally, she waltzed back to the kitchen, and Wendy gathered up her belongings. We said good-bye quickly.

I was relieved when Wendy left. At least Mama hadn't yelled or cried or talked about Hitler's secret hiding place. I would never risk introducing her to another friend.

The next day, I still hoped Mama and I could have a good time, so I suggested she teach me to cook some of my favorite things. I especially wanted to bake the Christmas cookies I remembered from childhood. I couldn't read the German script in her red leather scrapbook and feared I would never learn unless she showed me.

Mama laughed. "You think I'm going to show you how to cook so you don't need me anymore? So Daddy won't have to let me out of that place for Christmas? I'm not so stupid as that!'"

I was shocked. I wanted to swear I would never betray her, but I knew it would do no good. No matter how hard I tried, I couldn't stay little and innocent. I was growing up, and in Mama's eyes, that meant I was turning into the enemy. I didn't mention recipes again.

On what was to be our last day in the house, Daddy put down his newspaper at the breakfast table and cleared his throat. "Paula, you know we'll have to be getting back to the hospital today." When Mama didn't answer, he followed her into the kitchen. "It's been nice here, but Mrs. Nelson will be back tomorrow." He sounded nervous. I didn't blame Mama for resisting. Why did she have to be locked up anyway? If she could cook and serve meals for guests, didn't that prove she was sane enough to get along outside the hospital?

At lunch, Daddy mentioned once again that it was almost time to leave.

Instead of getting angry, Mama asked sweetly, "Couldn't we stay another day or two?"

Daddy squirmed. He hadn't expected this. He had as much trouble saying no as I did.

"I'll talk to Mrs. Nelson." By dinnertime, he had good news.

"Yah, she said we could stay, but she'll have to be here, too. She said she'll be working and not in our way."

We drifted into a second week, all of us getting more comfortable. No other guests were mentioned, so Mama relaxed. She was still enjoying cooking. We never saw the widow and only heard her briefly before she left for work.

But as the second week drew to a close, Daddy had to bring up the inevitable. "You know we have to be leaving, Paula. Biby has to go back to school, and Mrs. Nelson will want her house back. She's been very generous."

"Ya, ya, I know," Mama snapped. Daddy seemed afraid to take a firm stand, perhaps out of fear of the awful scene Mama could make within earshot of the widow.

In the morning, the atmosphere felt tense. After a silent breakfast, Mama and I packed our suitcases. When she was finished, Mama put hers on the bed and sat next to it.

"Should I carry that down?"

"No, no, Biby, you go ahead." I went down worrying about what might happen next.

"Paula, Paula, are you ready?" Daddy called up the stairs. "What's taking so long?" He sounded impatient. When she didn't answer, he ran up the stairs with me right behind. "Paula, we have to go." Mama, still sitting next to her suitcase, looked like a refugee who refused to be moved one more time.

"Paula, please be co-operative," Daddy begged. "The widow needs her house back." Mama sat silent, unmoving.

"It's been a nice Christmas. Don't spoil it. Biby has to get back to school. Please." But Mama wouldn't budge. Daddy, increasingly frantic, threw up his hands. "I give up." He went back downstairs. I sat by Mama, not knowing what else to do, wondering how we would get her to leave. Then I heard the widow charging up the stairs.

She marched into the bedroom, looking fierce as a hospital matron. "This is ridiculous!" She seemed to know exactly what to do. She picked Mama up by the elbow. "You're leaving now. Time to go." She steered Mama toward the stairs. Mama didn't resist. I grabbed Mama's suitcase. The widow held Mama tightly until she deposited her in the car.

Then she turned to Daddy. "I loaned you my house so you could spend Christmas as a family. What did I see? Your wife in the kitchen day and night, cooking three meals a day, washing up after both of you. Couldn't you help? Why didn't you take her to a restaurant? I never saw her get out of this house the entire time you were here. What kind of a vacation is that? If I had known how you were going to treat your wife, I would never, never have given you my house to do it in. Some enjoyment for your poor wife!"

I knew her indictment included me. I had been lazy and ungrateful, just like Daddy. I felt humiliated for him. According to the widow, not only had he been selfish and insensitive, he wasn't even man enough to get his wife into the car. Daddy tried to explain that Mama never wanted to leave the house, but the widow was in no mood to listen. We still had to get Mama back to the hospital, so Daddy started the car. I was in the back seat, afraid that if we didn't get moving, Mama would get out, and we would have to force her in again, this time on our own. I had no chance to say, "Thanks for the beautiful house. It was so generous, and we really appreciated it." The widow had her own fantasy of a family reunion at Christmas. Clearly, we hadn't fulfilled it.

On the highway, Mama's rage erupted. "You dirty dog! You tricked me again, treated me like a servant, expected me to cook and clean for you and your friends. Yah, your friends! What thanks do I get? Yah, I'm good enough to cook and clean, make money for you, and when you have no more use for me, you lock me up again. I've had enough of you, Hans Gubler! Enough of your dirty tricks!"

I withered silently. She aimed her attack at him, but I felt battered and bruised, as if she had directed it at me. I had eaten the meals and let her wash the dishes. Nothing could change that. I had heard it all before, but this time, after our almost idyllic Christmas, it hurt all the more. I wondered how Daddy stood it.

As we drove onto the hospital grounds, Mama grew quiet, drawing into herself as if shoring up her strength. She seemed distant as she hugged me good-bye, as though already detached. She went into her building without looking back.

4

A Decision

◆

1956

Back on campus, I threw myself into my own life and tried to forget our disastrous Christmas. Without making a conscious decision, I was following the psychiatrist's advice.

I didn't see Mama again until the following Christmas. After our experience at the widow's house, Daddy had decided to keep things simple by renting a suite in a motel. We drove together to pick Mama up at the hospital. When I saw her, my emotions stirred only faintly. Her embrace was quick and quiet. An invisible veil seemed to separate us.

Even Daddy was subdued. As we drove through Lake Geneva and passed the widow's house, I couldn't help but remember our Christmas there. It was as though it happened yesterday, yet I felt strangely detached from the scenes as they replayed in my mind.

At the edge of town, the motel parking lot was empty. The place looked lonely, but at least we would have no witnesses if Mama had an outburst. I dreaded her reaction as we carried our suitcases into the two-room suite. But she was surprisingly quiet. It seemed we had all decided to remain detached.

The day after Christmas, we didn't have a hard time leaving. None of us felt sad leaving the dreary motel rooms. Mama was eerily quiet during the hour-long drive back to the hospital, as though she knew what I was thinking.

I was in the back seat working up courage. For months I had toyed with the psychiatrist's solution, the one my boyfriend had endorsed. I knew they were right: I had to let go of Mama and live my own life. I had to tell Daddy this was my last Christmas with Mama. I had imagined it hundreds of times, each time thinking I was monstrous to even consider it.

At the hospital, Mama got out of the car without protest. She hugged me good-bye but didn't cling. It was as though she had already prepared herself for what I was about to do.

When Daddy pulled onto the highway, the time had come. If I put it off, I would never go through with it. I took a breath and blurted, "I can't go through another Christmas like this. I can't see Mama anymore." There, I had said the terrible thing out loud. The earth hadn't swallowed me. I only felt numb, as though what I had said was not quite real, like it was just an experiment. I couldn't look Daddy in the eye, so I glanced at him furtively. He looked sad and philosophical, a look of resignation I had seen before.

"I understand, Biby, it's all right."

Then I felt worse, knowing I was giving up on a dream we had kept alive together.

Looking back, I sympathize with my struggling teen self. Of course I had to do it. Of course Mama's emotional demands were too outrageous. Of course I had to use my energy for my own life. This is what I tell my young clients. But at the time, I felt purely selfish. I only wanted my own pain to stop. *My* pain, my helplessness. The pain of knowing each visit would be the same, over and over, stretching into infinity, each time reopening a wound that never would heal. I would rather have a death, I thought. A clean cut. Then numbness. No more tearful good-byes. No more feeling inadequate. That's why I did it.

5

Orphans

◆

1969

We held Daddy's memorial service the Sunday after his death at a small country church outside Lake Geneva. It was where Daddy's group met weekly for Christian fellowship. A fire was already blazing in the large stone fireplace when Ken, Eveli and I arrived. Mary and her husband, Gordon, were arranging chairs in a circle in front of the fire. They had already set up a table with refreshments on the side.

As people filed in, Eveli and I recognized a few familiar faces from our childhood church. Others we met for the first time that day. As we sat sharing memories of Hans Gubler, I felt comforted. One by one, his friends talked about what he meant to them. They spoke of his zest for living and his willingness to speak out on unpopular subjects. How, even after knowing him for years, they still called him "Mr. Gubler." Yet despite this formality, talking with him meant intimacy. Chance meetings over coffee led to long conversations.

Hearing them talk, I began to appreciate the life Daddy had built for himself in Lake Geneva. He had told me about his friends and activities, of course. I knew he volunteered at the local historical society, and that he went to evening discussion groups at the library. I knew he enjoyed his brisk, daily walk to the post office, frequently followed by a stop at a coffee shop. But until that day, I never saw the whole picture. His life, I was startled to realize, no longer centered on Eveli and me. He had not, as I had feared, lived in loneliness, aching for a family that no longer existed. These people, here in this room, had known and loved him.

Laughter rippled through the group when someone mentioned Daddy's attire. I had to smile remembering how, summer or winter, he always wore a gray business suit. The only concession he made to hot weather was to take off the vest that was usually buttoned tight under his suit coat. He never wore jeans or work pants. He didn't own any. Eveli and I had once tried to persuade him to wear shorts in the summer. He wouldn't. He was Swiss, and in Switzerland, businessmen wore suits.

The morning after the memorial service, I awoke before dawn feeling a sinking despair. For an instant I was puzzled. Why so despairing? Then, I remembered: Daddy was dead. The awful truth of it—fresh, raw, and unacceptable.

I felt grateful to hear Brian and Evan babbling in the next room. My ten-month-old twins made my purpose clear. I had to get up and take care of them. I couldn't lie in bed wondering if I had the will to face the day. As I lifted them out of their cribs their happy faces lifted my spirits. I felt soothed by their little hugs and cries of pleasure. While attending to their needs—changing, dressing, feeding—I didn't have to be absorbed in sorrow.

After Ken left for the law school, taking Brian and Evan to their baby sitter on his way, the house felt strangely empty. Not wanting to be alone, I woke Eveli. Over breakfast we agreed: we had to visit Mama.

As Eveli and I set out once more for Green County Hospital, I felt grim and determined. The fact that the place was now called a "hospital" rather than an "insane asylum" made little difference. It was still oppressive and painful to think of Mama being locked up there. We tried to chat, but not about Mama. Any topic but Mama. Why make ourselves feel bad before we had to?

Looking back, I wonder why we didn't unburden ourselves. Why didn't we talk about our feelings? We could have shared our guilt, our grief and comforted each other if only we had known how. But we didn't even know we were entitled to feelings. To speak of our own feelings would be selfish when Mama's suffering was so much worse. We could only consider *her* feelings—how she was doing, what she needed, and what we might do for her. No wonder we felt so helpless.

As we approached the hospital, I tried to imagine Mama's reactions to our sad news. Daddy was the only one who attended to her needs. Once a month, he took her out for lunch and shopping. Then he would visit me and talk at length about his latest attempts to get her better psychiatric care or to get her to a dentist, something she resisted fiercely.

Failing to find the familiar superintendent's residence, I finally realized it had been torn down. In the two years since Eveli and I had last visited Mama, a new administration building had been built where the superintendent's residence once stood. Inside, a clerk directed us to the dining room, which now served as a visiting lounge between meals.

Despite the many windows, the dining room had an oppressive aura. The steam tables were empty, but the room was overly warm from the heat of the kitchen. Vending machines lined one wall. We sat down at a table to wait for Mama.

It seemed like hours before a matron approached us. A large ring of keys dangled from her waist. "I'm sorry girls, but your mother won't leave the ward. She heard about your father on the local news this morning. She got terribly upset. We usually don't allow visitors on the ward. But if you want to come up today, the super says you can."

I wasn't sure I wanted to see the ward, the place Mama had described so bitterly, but there seemed no choice. Eveli was already following the aide. We walked single file behind her, then waited while she unlocked a heavy door. We followed her down a long corridor, up the stairs, and into a long room where women sat in a row looking out through windows backed by chain-link fencing. Evidently, this was supposed to be the sun room. The room was so narrow we practically had to step over the women's feet. I looked down at the floor, not wanting to stare. We proceeded through a dingy dayroom without furniture. Women wearing faded house dresses and vacant looks wandered aimlessly through the room. I couldn't help noticing a short, fat woman with gray hair that had been chopped off above her ears. She paced back and forth, rocking a large doll in her arms. I wondered if the death of a baby could have driven her crazy.

Past the dormitory, where beds lined the wall in military rows, the aide pointed to a windowless corner. "Your mother's over there, girls."

Mama sat inside a booth on a high stool, crying. The booth, with a waist-high counter and a back wall of cubby holes, was the ward's clothes station. All patients' clothing was kept there, with Mama in charge. Her job was to sort and hand out the clothing. Before sending it to the laundry, she marked each item with a black stamp, "WW4" for Women's Ward Four, and the owner's name in black indelible ink. Years ago, Mama cried bitterly about the black ink ruining her white lacy blouses. She would have preferred to wash them by hand, but this wasn't allowed on a crowded ward. Too dangerous. Now, as mistress of the clothes, Mama folded and stacked each garment. This protected the clothing from patients' destructive outbursts. Even Mama had ripped clothes when first sent to WW4, one of the few ways of expressing rage and grief here.

After being appointed clothing keeper, Mama stopped ripping clothes and devoted herself to keeping perfect order, the same way she had kept house. Dr. Kunzler told Daddy that if not for Mama, he would have had to hire somebody, because no other patient could have handled the responsibility. They didn't pay her, but at least the job gave her a special status. Inside the booth, she ruled her own small territory.

Mama looked up as we approached. Her hair, now white, hung long around her face. "I don't know them. No, I don't know them." She said it forcefully through her tears. "I don't have any daughters. You are nothing to me. You must be orphans."

I felt a stab in my heart. I had already disowned her, years ago. Foolishly, I believed that should protect me from the pain of rejection.

"We came to tell you about Daddy. He's …"

"He's not dead, no, no, don't tell me lies."

Eveli and I started crying while Mama kept repeating that we were orphans. She's right, I thought. We were orphans. Daddy was our only true parent. I longed for Mama to tell us it would be all right. I knew she couldn't. We would have to comfort her.

Despite her protests, we sat down. After exhausting herself in angry weeping, without apology or explanation, she suddenly switched her tone. "You should get fixed up better when you come to visit. Biby, you don't even have on any lipstick. You used to have your hair so nice and curly, like a little lamb. You looked better when I took care of you. Eveli, couldn't you find a nicer blouse? Don't come see me unless you can look nicer."

Mama had sewed our childhood clothing—play suits and dresses, all hand-embroidered with tiny flowers. While Mama continued to criticize our appearance, I drifted back to childhood, scenes as vivid as though they happened yesterday:

"This will look beautiful on you, Biby." Her eyes gleamed with pleasure as she held up my new dress.

When Eveli's turn came, she made a face. "Why can't I wear blue jeans?"

"Nye, nye, Eveli. Why do you want to wear those ugly things?" Mama reached for Eveli, but she darted off.

"I don't want to wear that stupid dress. None of the other kids wear dresses."

Mama was getting mad. Please, just wear the dress, I thought, too scared to say anything. Secretly, I admired Eveli, but I wondered how wearing blue jeans could be more important than making Mama happy.

When I turned back to Mama, I realized nothing had changed since our childhood. All Mama cared about was how we looked. Back then, her disapproval devastated me, but now, I felt a rush of energy. New and unfamiliar thoughts flashed through my mind, thoughts I didn't dare say out loud: "How can you talk about lipstick and blouses? Daddy just died. How dare you criticize us in our grief? All you ever cared about was us looking picture-perfect so you could imagine everyone staring at us, thinking how wonderful you were to have nice looking girls in beautiful outfits. That's all we were—extensions of you to show off. You never let us be ourselves. Well, I'm not your good little girl anymore. This is exactly why I broke away."

It took me a minute to realize I was angry. Never before in my life had I felt angry at Mama. I was too busy holding her together. I felt liberated even though I had said nothing out loud, not even to Eveli.

As we drove home in glum silence, our visit felt pointless. Nothing had been accomplished. Nothing except that I now understood Mama's terms clearly: to be acceptable, I had to act like a child. She only wanted the false self I had fought so hard to leave behind.

We wondered what to do next. Should I visit her? I didn't know if I could stand to, especially by myself. I envied Eveli's escape to California.

"Maybe you should just wear a little lipstick. That wouldn't hurt, would it?" Eveli was trying to be helpful.

Did she realize what she was asking? It sounded trivial, but I knew where it led.

"I will not! After all the years it's taken me to get free! If I let her, she would rule every choice I make. I can't live that way. She can take me or leave me the way I am!"

My vehemence surprised me. I felt betrayed by Eveli. She was supposed to be my ally. I wanted her on my side, not Mama's.

6

Another Phone Call

◆

1970

The pain of missing Daddy shrank ever so gradually until it was a small kernel buried in my heart. Tiny events, something as small as driving by a scene Daddy would have enjoyed, could make that kernel swell into a fresh wave of grief. But over the course of a year, those moments came farther and farther apart, until I could move through most days without dissolving into tears.

A year had passed since Eveli and I had visited Mama to tell her the sad news about Daddy. Thinking of going back to see her still filled me with dread. Nothing had changed. Yet I couldn't put it to rest. Who did she have except me? I kept telling myself I should be able to handle seeing my own mother. After all, I was not a child anymore; I was thirty-two, and what's more, a clinical psychologist. How, I wondered, would I ever find the courage to go back?

Sometimes, in desperation, I considered therapy. But how would it help? Therapy wouldn't change Mama. A therapist couldn't tell me anything I didn't already know—or so I thought.

I hadn't yet admitted that therapy scared me. Not easy to admit, considering I was in the therapy business myself. Therapy might unleash that dangerous part of me, the crazy part of me that I feared would go off like a time bomb when I turned thirty-eight.

When the phone call came, I was home with my twins, Brian and Evan, who were by then almost two years old. It was late afternoon, their irritable time. They were penned in their playroom, next to the kitchen, while I rushed around trying to get the essentials done before they clamored for attention. My rambunctious toddlers feared nothing, least of all my scolding. They constantly surprised me with new stunts, like climbing out of their cribs in the middle of the night and wandering through the house. One night I found them sitting on the kitchen floor happily stirring a pile of broken eggs, brown sugar and catsup. I was a failure at setting limits. Whenever I looked at their adorable faces, I melted. I let them do as they pleased, feeling helpless to do otherwise.

My difficulty controlling them embarrassed me. After all, as a psychologist, I was supposed to know what to do. I watched other mothers, amazed at their ease in keeping their children in check. What was I doing wrong? Over and over, I resolved to be firm but could never follow through. When they cried, my heart felt ripped in half. I couldn't stand the pain of saying no.

I turned to Flora, my babysitter, for guidance and support. Flora, a neighbor and an experienced mother, had miraculously appeared when I needed her most. Without her, my plan to combine career and children would never have worked. Leaving Brian and Evan every morning was hard, but deep down I believed Flora could give them better care. I was giving them the best gift I could—my sanity.

People clucked with sympathy when they heard I went back to work only three weeks after my sons were born. I didn't tell them I had planned it that way, that I was afraid I might go crazy if I stayed home with my own babies. In my head I held a constant debate as to whether this fear was baseless or not. After all, schizophrenia usually strikes in the late teens or early twenties. At least I had made it past that danger point.

But my measuring stick was Mama's life. At the age of thirty-one, Mama, like me, had two children and appeared to be a successful homemaker and mother. By the age of thirty-eight, she was committed to a mental hospital. Her diagnosis: paranoid schizophrenia. Now, at sixty-two, she had spent the last eighteen years of her life on a locked ward.

The contrast between our lives could not be greater, yet deep-down in some essential, indescribable way I continued to believe I was like her. Eventually, unless I remained on guard, my true nature would leak to the surface and destroy the life I had so carefully built. I had six more years to worry about the mental breakdown ahead. Only after I turned thirty-eight would I begin to trust my future.

When I was away from Brian and Evan, I ached for them, but being home with them for more than a few hours frazzled me. I usually felt I was just a step ahead of disaster. That day when the phone rang, I grabbed it quickly, hoping Brian and Evan wouldn't notice. Talking on the phone was their signal to increase uproar.

"Mrs. Casey?"

"Yes?"

"This is Green County Hospital calling about your mother, Paula Gubler."

My stomach turned to jelly. I prepared to hear that she, too, had died. Just like Daddy—suddenly. No chance to make it right.

The woman didn't seem to realize she had put me in a state of shock. She made no mention of the fact that I hadn't seen Mama for a year. No acknowledgement that in the last fourteen years I had only seen her twice.

"We're calling regarding your mother's teeth. They're in very bad condition."

So she wasn't dead. Just her teeth.

"Doctor recommends false teeth."

Why are they calling me? Then I remembered: Daddy was dead.

"Doctor thinks the infection affects her health. He says her teeth should all come out, under a total anesthetic. We would like the consent of a family member." She made it sound routine, as though they had been calling me about Mama's condition all along.

I wanted to push this new responsibility away. No one had asked if I wanted to be Mama's guardian. My life was hectic enough. Ken was still in law school. Working and caring for Brian and Evan took almost all my time. Grocery shopping, laundry, and settling Daddy's estate had to be squeezed in between. My hands were full.

I fully intended to say, "Yes, go ahead. I don't care what you do." But when I opened my mouth, something else came out. "I haven't seen her for a year. I'd better come down before giving consent."

"That sounds good. But be prepared, her halitosis is terrible. When can you come?"

I had expected her to say, "There's nothing you can do about her teeth. You may as well just get it over with." Being treated with respect surprised me.

"I'll try to come Saturday," I replied. I hung up wondering how Ken, who practically lived at the law library, would react to learning he had to stay home with the boys.

To my relief, Ken was positive. He had often tried to convince me to visit Mama as he thought it would be good for me.

I was the only one having second thoughts. Why, why had I jumped into this? Could I really go through with it? How would I get her to accept losing her teeth? I was certain my gesture would be futile. She would probably refuse to see me. If she did talk to me, she would make no sense. I had no illusions I could save her teeth. There was no point in trying to get her to the dentist. Daddy had tried. When he finally persuaded her to go, she refused to sit in the chair or even let the dentist look at her mouth.

Still, I had to go.

On Saturday morning, I felt sick. It was worse than facing an exam. Could I go through with seeing Mama? Alone? I toyed with backing out, but Ken kept encouraging me. Finally, I stumbled into the car, carried by momentum rather than will.

Alone in the car, I tried to imagine what I would say. How do you begin when you have turned your back on someone for years? Not just someone, your own mother. It should be so simple—visiting Mama. How could I explain why it was hard? *Not* seeing her—that was supposed to be hard.

I decided I needed a gift, a peace offering that would say, "I'm sorry." That first moment—that's what I dreaded most. At least I would have something to hand her, something to distract us both. I stopped at the shopping center, picked a pink robe, and had it gift wrapped.

The road from Madison to Monroe winds through rolling dairy farms. For me, it's the landscape of home, always comforting, always beautiful, even on a gray November day when clusters of golden oak leaves and white birches glistened in the mist.

When I passed New Glarus, a town settled by Swiss immigrants, tears flooded my eyes. The little town always reminded me of Daddy. He loved visiting it, eating Swiss food and speaking *Schweitzerdeutsch* with people from his native country.

Daddy tried to make Eveli and me practice *Schweitzerdeutsch* so we would sound Swiss when he took us to Switzerland to meet our relatives. *Schweitzerdeutsch*, he explained, was Switzerland's own language. The Swiss could tell if you were really Swiss by the way you pronounced certain words like "*Kuchechasli*," which meant kitchen cupboard. Daddy wanted to make sure I said these words right, way back in my throat.

He loved Switzerland, yet wasn't happy there as a young man. He had told me many times how he hated his job at a bank in Zurich. He stood all day in a booth counting out money to customers. "And Biby," he would say, "when I thought of doing the same thing every day for the rest of my life …," he slumped over and shook his head. Then he looked up and bounced to his feet. "This is not for me!" That's when he found a job representing a Swiss textile firm that brought him to America. He loved traveling and seeing new places. After a few years with the Swiss textile firm, he itched to start his own business. He starting importing fine Swiss linens on his own and showing them to wealthy women in their homes. He displayed them on their own tables, so they could see how the linens looked with their china. They would order two or three large tablecloths at a time along with napkins as well as dozens of guest towels and fine handkerchiefs to be monogrammed in fancy stitching.

Only he could have made this enterprise a success. He charmed his customers with his old world manners and entertained them with stories of his travels, often enjoying tea or coffee with them at the end of business. He never earned much. In fact, he worried constantly about money and never felt secure enough to buy a house. Daddy often expressed his regret about never buying Mama the house she longed for. We had wondered together if things might have gone differently if Mama had had the security of her own home.

By the time I arrived at the hospital, I had resigned myself to my fate. I would see Mama. It would go badly, and I could return home, absolved of guilt for another year or so. No one could accuse me of neglecting my mother. I checked in at the administration building.

There I learned that Mama had been transferred to the new building. I drove around to the new parking lot at the back of the grounds. As I parked, I looked the new three-story building over. I felt grateful to see large picture windows with no bars. These windows, I realized, were possible because of new medications, ones that were not available when Mama first came here. Inside, the ground floor offices of the new outpatient clinic were closed and dark for the weekend.

Upstairs, the nurse at the desk called out a friendly hello. The day room was light and airy, but the patients were the same as ever—dull and lifeless in faded housedresses. I recognized one woman from the old ward, still pacing and clutching her doll. I knew better than to search for Mama in the dayroom. She never mixed with other patients if she could help it.

"Your mother's in her room." The nurse smiled as she pointed down the hall. The room was large and airy with four beds, one in each corner. Mama was lying on her side with her arm folded up under her head, looking out the window.

"Hi, Mama."

She propped herself up on her elbow. "Biby, is that you?" Her voice was soft and normal, as though the break in our relationship had lasted only hours.

"Yes, it's me. I brought you a present." I thrust the package toward her.

"Thank you." She set it aside, barely glancing at it.

"You can open it later if you want," I offered quickly.

"Do you want me to open it now?" Her voice, kind and sweet, transported me back to the kitchen of our old house in Delavan, to polka music on the radio, Mama waltzing from sink to table, stirring a bowl balanced on her hip, the silver bracelets on her wrist chiming.

"It's okay. Open it later if you want," I offered quickly. I was surprised she was more interested in me than the present.

"How did you get here? Did somebody bring you?" She sounded puzzled.

"I drove."

"Yourself? You can drive?"

"Yes, I drove myself."

"You can drive? Whose car did you drive?"

"My own." It was as though she had just awakened from a twenty-year sleep.

"You're smart to be able to drive. Much smarter than I ever was. Where did you get a car?"

"I bought it. I have a job."

"You have a job?" She sounded incredulous.

"Yes, teaching at the university. I teach psychology."

"And you earn enough to buy a car? And you drove yourself? How did you know the way?"

"It wasn't hard." I felt embarrassed to be praised for such ordinary accomplishments. Ordinary perhaps, but impossible for her.

"You were good to come see me. You're such a good girl. You always were."

I hadn't expected this. Tears welled in my eyes. I was rapidly slipping back into being her little girl. She was calm, not crazy, looking right at me, listening to me, seeing me. I had forgotten how much I longed for this.

"You always were a good girl. I'm sorry I was such a bad mother, sorry you had it so hard. I didn't want it to be that way. I wanted you to have everything nice. I hope you'll forgive me. I hope you're happy and having it better than I did."

Through my tears, I jumped at my chance to talk with her. "Yes," I said. "Yes, I'm happy. I'm married and have two children, and I like my job."

"You're married? You have children? And a job, too?" She sounded in awe. "You're a lot smarter than I ever was. You certainly are smart to do all that. Children and a job. And driving, too."

I glowed. She had seen and heard who I was and declared her approval. I had given up hoping for her blessing so long ago I had forgotten I ever wanted it. I wanted her to keep asking questions until we had talked about everything I had done in the last fourteen years. But I was afraid to be that greedy, so I asked her about her job in the clothes station.

"I had to stop. I got a foot sore and couldn't stand so much."

"Is it better now that you're resting?"

"No, no, it's not. It's not healing because my blood is weak, and now they want to take all my teeth." Leaning forward, she grasped me by my wrist and pleaded, "Please, please don't let them. Promise me you won't let them do it to me. I would die."

"Die? From having your teeth out?"

"Yes, I would die. From loss of blood. I would bleed to death."

Just as the nurse had warned, Mama's breath was terrible, her teeth, yellow and slimy. I didn't care. All that mattered was that she was talking to me.

"You wouldn't die, you ..." She cut me off.

"No, Biby, you don't know what they're like here, what they've done to me. No, no, please, please don't let them."

I wanted to explain that eventually she would have to have them out, or they would fall out. But logic would go nowhere. Should I just overrule her and then try to comfort her as best I could? Or should I respect her right to make her own decisions? I feared she might die from the shock of waking up with no teeth. She might not want to live. I didn't want to be responsible for that, not now.

"I won't let them. I promise. Not unless you change your mind."

"Promise you won't let them. I can't trust anyone here. Please promise me."

"I promise, I promise. It'll be okay."

"Oh, thank you, thank you so much. I'm so grateful. Thank you."

I was embarrassed. It should, after all, be her right to decide even if she had been locked up against her will for the last twenty years. The only thing that mattered to me was a chance to visit her again. I didn't care if she had rotting teeth and halitosis. I would promise anything for another conversation.

"I'll come back as soon as I can. Two or three weeks."

Driving home, I went over what had happened again and again. Word for word, I replayed our conversation. I could barely contain my elation. She wasn't crazy! Mama wasn't crazy anymore! And she wasn't even angry! She didn't blame me for not coming all these years. She even said she was sorry. I was always the one who had said sorry. Sorry, sorry, sorry ... over and over again ... Sorry I didn't wear the right thing. Sorry I didn't do the right thing. Sorry you're in this hospital and I can't get you out. Sorry you're so unhappy and I can't help. Sorry your life is so wretched and mine so good.

"I'm sorry I was such a bad mother ... You're smarter than I ever was ... I hope you're happy ..." Her words rang like silver bells tinkling in the wind.

7

A Visit

◆

1970

Two weeks later, I was driving back to see Mama and bubbling over with happy fantasies about taking her shopping, having picnics with Brian and Evan, maybe even moving her into her own apartment. I was still trying to understand what had happened. I had read about spontaneous remissions of mental illness—catatonic schizophrenics who rise up from their stupor to help evacuate others in a fire, only to sink back into catatonia once the emergency was over. But this was different. Even between hospitalizations, Mama had never been this normal—actually interested in my life and sorry for what she had done.

Maybe she had never really been schizophrenic. I had read an article about paranoia developing from grief that is too big, too terrible. I had always resented the smug attitude of Mama's doctors who proclaimed with god-like certainty that we couldn't expect her to get better. They insisted schizophrenia is incurable. But maybe Mama just went crazy with grief for awhile.

She had a lot to grieve. Losing her mother at thirteen. Then, a mean stepmother who drove her out of the house. Leaving home to go to work at fifteen. Her father didn't even want to see her before she left for America. Then, more disappointment in her marriage. But perhaps, after all these years, she had finally let go of all these losses.

I parked by Mama's building and hurried up the stairs, eager to see her again.

The nurse at the desk smiled. "Good morning. Here to see your mother?"

"Yes, and I'd like to take her out for lunch. Is that okay?" I was prepared for denial.

"It's certainly all right, but I don't think she'll go. She's depressed. We haven't been able to get her to do anything, not even go down for meals. You can try though. You never know."

My heart sank. Depressed? Not just when we've started talking. It's probably just this place; anyone would get depressed here.

I found Mama curled up on her side, looking out the window.

"Hi, Mama." I tried to sound cheerful.

"Biby? Is that you?" She lifted her head slightly but didn't turn. Her voice sounded heavy and flat.

I pulled a chair close to the bed. "I brought you some magazines."

"Thank you, dear." She answered slowly, as though talking was an effort.

"I thought we could go downtown for lunch. And shopping. You must need a few things."

"Not today, dear."

I fought to keep from sinking. The weight of her voice pulled me down. "We could look in some dress shops."

"I can't go with you, Biby."

"Why not?"

"They won't let me."

"But the nurse said it was okay."

"That's what they tell you. I know better. They'll make it hell for me if I go."

"Who will? What do you mean?"

But Mama turned quiet. She wasn't going to give me any more answers.

I sighed and slumped into my chair. She was back to craziness, at least for now. It was futile to argue. Once she had a fixed idea, she wouldn't budge.

She had been this was way often when I was little, back when I was her little rag doll, always willing to sit in her lap and let her stroke me when she needed comfort. But no matter how hard I tried, she got sadder and sadder, crying as she did the housework. I used to find her staring into space, rubbing her cheek with her fingers. "Mama, Mama, what are you thinking about?" But she wouldn't answer. She was off in her own dream world. At other times she would be so busy poring over astrological magazines or writing long letters she hardly noticed me. I hated being ignored.

That's when I would flee to the marsh near our house. Running down the hill to the creek, I felt better. I sat on a rock with my feet in the water, staring up at the sky. The way the wind pushed small fluffs of cloud across the sky fascinated me. Down by the marsh, I no longer cared that Mama wasn't paying attention to me. No one could boss me. Not Mama. Not Eveli. I felt wonderfully happy in my own daydream world.

What if I lived all alone in the marsh? I would eat watercress out of the creek and make a nest of leaves. I would find a cave no one had ever found, a secret cave, dry and warm, its entrance hidden by weeds. I would push them aside and crawl in. It was dark inside. Piles of soft pine needles lay in the corners like beds. Someone already lived here. A band of orphans. They were watching me. I wanted to let them know they needn't be afraid of me. We didn't talk out loud. We communicated through mind language. They were dressed in old clothes, patched and ragged and too big. The oldest, just a little older than me, was the leader. The littlest was just barely walking and talking. They left the cave only at night to look for food. They needed to hide because they were in danger. The leader asked me to bring them something to eat, then made me promise I wouldn't tell anyone about them. Their trust made me feel important.

    I ran home and tiptoed through the back door. The coast was clear. I opened the icebox quietly and grabbed the jam. "Is that you, Biby?" Mama called.

    "I'm just getting a snack."

    "Don't eat so much now. You'll ruin your appetite." Mama usually let me do what I wanted, but I had to be careful not to upset her.

    "I won't." I slipped out the door with two jam sandwiches and ran back to the orphans. When they saw me, their eyes lit up. They hadn't had bread and jam in a long time. The leader fed the littlest orphan first. I did the chewing and swallowing, but it was really the little orphan who ate. The two sandwiches were just enough for all the orphans' supper.

    I asked if they'd seen Michal, our black cat who hunted mice in the marsh.

    "Does he have a little white star on his chest?"

    "Yes, that's him."

    "Sometimes he sleeps in the cave and keeps us warm."

    Thinking of Michal cuddled up with the orphans made me happy. I wished Michal would cuddle with me in my bed, but he preferred Mama. When he came home with a crippled mouse in his mouth, he dropped it at Mama's feet. When it tried to hop away, Mama would cry out. Then Michal walked between her legs, rubbing against her and waving his bushy tail like a banner, all the while purring loudly.

    "Michal, you naughty pussy," she would say, pouring him a dish of cream.

    We took Michal in when he was just a kitten. Mama found him mewing on our back porch.

    "Poor little *busseli*, out in the cold. Have you no home?" He was an orphan, it was clear.

    When I left the marsh, I pretended my orphans were with me. We scouted for things they could use—a rug put out for trash, vegetables in backyard gardens. Probably no one would notice if I picked one or two.

After the tomatoes ripened, I grabbed a big one from the garden on the corner. I ran to the marsh and gathered the orphans around me. As I bit in, the sweet juice ran down my chin. I knew the orphans found it delicious.

By the time I got home, my deed had been reported. Mama was shocked. "Biby! Why did you do it? Aren't you getting enough to eat?"

I hadn't planned on getting caught. Now the worst had happened: I had upset Mama. I hung my head and tried to look sorry.

Mama said I should never do it again and gave me a hug.

I was relieved I didn't have to explain. I needed to keep my orphans secret. When I first found them, I feared Eveli or Mama would know I was hiding something. I thought my secret would show on my face, just as if I came home missing a tooth. But no one asked questions. Hiding my orphans turned out to be easy as long as I didn't steal tomatoes.

Throughout my reverie back into childhood, Mama didn't move. She was still lying on her bed with her arm tucked under her head. I gazed out the hospital window at the empty fields and old barn, remembering the cows once kept there, milked and tended by the patients. A newspaper report once criticized the county for making a profit from their labor, so they closed the farm down. Too bad they couldn't have used that money to improve the lives of the patients by providing better food, dental care, and real therapy.

Mama forced a thin smile when she saw me gazing at her. It was all she could manage. I reached into my purse and fingered the envelope holding pictures of Brian and Evan. I had slipped them in at the last minute, hoping there would be a chance—the right moment—to show her. I yearned to say, "Look, Mama, this will cheer you up. These are your grandsons." I wanted her to hold the photo and say, "They're darling." Then I would glow with pride. "I'll bring them down as soon as the weather's nice, but you may have to help. They're always running in different directions." But today was not the right time.

I suddenly felt very tired. I was out of ideas, out of energy. I got up to leave. Mama hadn't mentioned her teeth.

"They didn't try to take your teeth out, did they?"

"No, no they didn't. Thank you, Biby. Thank you very much."

"Should I bring you something next time? Do you need anything? Shampoo? Toothpaste?"

"It's all right. I don't need anything."

"I'll see you in a couple of weeks."

8

Memories of Home

◆

1942–46

As I drove home, fatigue crept over me. My past was suddenly with me again. When I left for college, my childhood no longer felt relevant. I was rushing headlong into my own wonderful future, a future I was certain would bear no resemblance to my past. But now my memories came flooding back, almost more real than my present life.

Before we moved to Lake Geneva, we had lived in Delavan. Mama hated our old house there, but I loved it. It was the only place Daddy and Mama could find during the housing shortage of the World War II years. It was a roomy old place in a small town, close to a marsh with cattails and wild places where I could escape and feel free.

Mama made the house beautiful. She hung white lace-trimmed curtains in the living room windows and laid white shag rugs on the floor. Our furniture was mostly secondhand, refinished and decorated with stencils by Mama. Daddy hung a hammock on the front porch where I loved to swing and sing to myself.

"Paula, you make everything look like a million," Daddy praised her. "And for just pennies!"

Mama complained about the old coal furnace. She had to feed coal into the furnace throughout the day and hated getting black dust on her hands and clothes. One day, the furnace blew fine black soot through the house. It settled on the woodwork, the walls, the white organdy curtains, and the white shag rugs. I ran from room to room, laughing, surprised to see everything turned black. Mama cried. I tried to comfort her. Nothing really bad had happened. The furnace didn't blow up. But Mama, still crying, tied her hair up in a scarf, took down the curtains and put them in the sink to soak. She cried as she washed the woodwork, the walls, the floor and the furniture. She washed the white rugs in the bathtub and hung them on the line. She starched, ironed, and re-hung the curtains. It took three days, and she cried the whole time. She didn't let Eveli or me help; she sent us out to play.

When we came home, I wanted to tell Mama about our Monopoly game at the neighbors', but she made a face. She didn't like our neighbors, though she never kept us from playing there. She peeked through the curtain as our neighbor climbed out of his truck. "Look at that belly." She wrinkled her nose in disgust. "That's what he gets for eating potato chips and candy."

Mama didn't think much of any of the neighbors, except the elderly Reynolds sisters, who kept their house and yard almost as clean as Mama's. Mama never visited with anyone, which worried Daddy.

"Paula, Paula," he said one day, "you should get out more. It isn't good for you to be by yourself all week with only the children. You could make the effort, you know. Invite some ladies for coffee and cake. You bake such wonderful cakes."

"I don't have time." Mama looked annoyed.

"It doesn't have to take long. Just an hour. For a little visit. You could have Mrs. Kubly or Mrs. Huebner. They'd love to see you. Or Mrs. Schneider." He listed all the Swiss people we knew.

"Mrs. Kubly doesn't have time for sitting around drinking coffee either. I don't want to bother her. Besides, how am I supposed to get out there?" The Kublys lived on a dairy farm at the edge of town.

"Paula, Mrs. Kubly would love to see you. Call her. You can't just work all the time." Daddy sounded frustrated.

Mama stamped her foot. "Now I've made a mistake. How do you expect me to talk and cook at the same time?"

Mama didn't like mistakes. If her soufflé fell, she scolded herself: "I shouldn't have opened the oven so soon." Hours later, she was still upset. "I don't think those eggs were fresh. Ya, ya, that's what it was. I should have gotten fresh ones."

Sometimes Mama reminded Daddy that she attended Red Cross meetings to knit socks and sweaters for servicemen. Mama, the best knitter in the group, often helped the others. When she brought home an award, Daddy was proud of her. But even there she didn't make friends.

"Those women only care about playing bridge. They drink coffee and smoke cigarettes. I'm doing all the work. When they make a mistake, they come to me. I'm good enough for that, for fixing their mistakes."

One Friday night, Mama put supper on the table without a word. Eveli and I could tell she was mad, but we were too scared to say anything. Daddy kept asking, "Paula, what is it? Tell me." But she just glared at him. Eveli and I ate as fast as we could and then scrambled out the back door. We barely got off the back porch when we heard Mama explode. Her voice was so deep and guttural I barely recognized it. It was hard for me to believe it was my own sweet Mother yelling those terrible things at Daddy. Eveli and I shrank into the back wall, glad to be out of sight. We could hear every hateful word.

"You aren't fooling me, Hans Gubler. I know you're running around."

"Paula, that's nonsense."

"Don't tell me any more of your lies. I'm slaving away all week, trying to save every penny in this old house, while you're out having a good time with other women. It's criminal what you're doing to me, Hans Gubler."

"Paula, please. It's for you and the children. That's why I'm gone. It's not to run …"

"You're not going to get away with it, Hans Gubler. No you're not. I have helpers, too. Important helpers. You think you can just go do whatever you like? Oh, no. I'm finally wise to you."

"Please, Paula, be reasonable. Think of the children." But Mama wouldn't listen.

A few days later, when Mama was buying groceries, Daddy came home in the middle of the morning. We ran to him, surprised to see him. But he looked troubled, not happy as usual. Then he squatted down and said, "Mama has to go to the hospital."

"But she isn't sick. She went grocery shopping."

"She needs a long rest."

That didn't seem so terrible. Daddy went to the hospital once. Mama took us to visit him, and we brought him oranges.

"We can bring her oranges, can't we?"

Daddy laughed.

"Why are you laughing? What's so funny?"

"It's not that kind of sickness, Biby."

"Why can't she rest at home?" Eveli asked. "We can take care of her."

"No, no she has to go to the hospital. I need both of you to be good. The Reynolds sisters said you could stay with them while I take Mama there."

"Why can't we come? We'll be good," Eveli protested.

I didn't like the idea either. I had never been away from home before, ever, and I had never been inside the Reynolds sisters' house. I held Daddy's hand as we rang the doorbell. Inside, the house was clean but smelled funny, not like our house. It was quiet except for a clock ticking and chiming in the living room.

At supper, I didn't want to eat the strange smelling food. The kindly sisters didn't force me. They brought out a special treat for dessert—chocolate pudding. But I had never tasted it before. It looked dark and slimy. I didn't want to put it in my mouth.

"You baby. Try it. It's good." Eveli sounded ashamed of me.

I sealed my mouth shut. Mama wouldn't want me to eat it. I didn't care if Eveli called me a baby.

At night, I lay in bed next to Eveli, smelling the unfamiliar sheets and listening to the clock chime downstairs. "I want to go home," I whimpered.

"Come on now, go to sleep, it isn't so bad here." But the waver in Eveli's voice sounded as though she was scared, too.

The next day, when Daddy came for us, we threw ourselves on him. "Please Daddy, take us home. We'll be good. We promise."

"All right, but Mama isn't home, so we'll all have to pitch in, okay?"

"Yes, yes!" We jumped up and down. We'd have promised anything.

Somehow, Daddy managed to stay home and take care of us. I don't know what we lived on that summer, because he didn't do any business for a month. Later, when I was grown up, he told me how dismal the conditions were at the state hospital. The war had been over for a year, but the wards still overflowed with shell-shocked soldiers. There weren't enough rooms, so extra beds lined every corridor. There was also a shortage of doctors, so Mama didn't get much attention. He couldn't rest until he got her out of there.

We begged to be taken along when he visited her. Finally, he said it would be allowed. Eveli and I waited on the big grassy lawn in front of the hospital while Daddy went into one of the buildings to get Mama. After a long wait, we saw them walking towards us, and we ran to meet her.

"Eveli, Biby, I missed you so much." Tears rolled down her face as she hugged us. She seemed so frightened. I wondered what they were doing to her in this peaceful-looking place.

We sat down on our blanket with a picnic lunch, but Mama didn't eat. She only looked at Eveli and me and stroked our faces.

After lunch, we walked Mama back to her building. I wanted to go inside, but children weren't allowed.

"Say good-bye to the children now, Paula." Daddy pulled her away and disappeared down a long white corridor.

I was surprised when, after growing up, I learned Mama had been at the hospital only five weeks. It seemed she had been gone a much longer time. When

Daddy announced her homecoming, we jumped up and down, shouting, "Mama's coming home! Mama's coming home!" We could hardly wait.

"Remember, you have to be good girlies," Daddy warned. "We don't want to wear Mama out so she has to go back. Do everything she says. We don't want to upset her."

I vowed to keep Mama so happy she would never go back.

But soon Mama and Daddy were fighting worse than ever.

"You, Hans Gubler, you and your dirty, rotten cronies, you did this to me. You locked me up in that dirty, rotten, stinking hole."

"Paula, you know that's not true."

"It's not a hospital. It's a prison. I was locked up like a criminal."

"Paula, I got you out. As soon as I saw the conditions …"

"You shall pay, Hans Gubler. You've played dirty tricks on me for the last time."

Daddy sighed and shook his head. Mama cried.

When Daddy was gone on business, Mama turned to me with her complaints.

"Daddy's just a Mama's boy. He wants everything his way. He doesn't care how hard it is for me all week with that coal furnace. He won't do anything. He just makes excuses. I should never have married him. I shouldn't have had children. I should have known better. I wasn't meant to be a housewife and mother."

I could hardly believe my ears. I thought Mama loved me more than anything. Could she really mean she didn't want to be my mother?

Mama kept right on talking about the lawyer she hired. She planned to get a divorce. I longed for her to say something nice about Daddy. I couldn't bear the thought of not living with him.

Finally, I asked, "Will Daddy be all alone? Can we visit him?"

"Don't worry about him. He can take care of himself." Mama was upset that I took Daddy's side, so I stopped asking about him.

That fall, Eveli and I had only been back in school a few weeks when trouble started again. I knew something was wrong the minute I stepped into the house. Two big suitcases stood in the front hall. Mama lay on the couch crying while Daddy paced back and forth. He stepped toward Mama.

"Paula, I'm leaving now. My suitcases are packed."

"I didn't mean you should leave just yet." Her voice was muffled in tears.

"But I can't live here anymore. We're divorced now."

"Don't leave me alone just yet."

"What do you expect me to do? What do you want?" Daddy sounded exasperated.

"Just stay awhile yet. For the children."

Daddy sighed. "All right, Paula. For the children."

The next day after school, Daddy was waiting for me.

"Mama had to go back to the hospital. This time she's going to stay longer. We want to make sure she's well before she comes home." He watched me closely as he continued. "I'm going to take you stay with *Goeti* and *Goetili*."

My godparents—*Goeti* and *Goetili*—ran a dairy in a nearby town.

"Eveli is going to stay here with the Huebner's. You're only in third grade, so it won't be as hard for you to switch schools."

I could tell Daddy expected me to protest, but the plan suited me just fine. It sounded like a great adventure. I knew I was supposed to feel bad, so I tried, for Daddy's sake, to look sad. I wondered why tears didn't come. I wanted to feel sad about Mama going back to the hospital. But she was so happy in the morning before I left for school, I was sure something good was going to happen. This must be it, I thought. The good thing was that I was going to live with my godparents in their big house in the country.

Suddenly, I remembered our cat. "What's going to happen to Michal? We can't leave him here by himself."

"Yah, yah, Michal." Daddy sounded sad. "I called, but he didn't come. Don't worry, he's out hunting mice. He'll be all right."

But I did worry.

"Michal, Michal, my first cat, little orphan of the night, what ever became of you? Did you fend for yourself all winter in the marsh, eating mice for your supper and sleeping with my orphans in nests of dried leaves? Or did you come back again and again to the empty house to stare into empty windows, remembering when you slept safe and warm inside?"

9

Hope

1970–71

After my disappointing visit with Mama, I longed for the comfort of my present life. I pulled into my driveway, eager to see Brian and Evan. They greeted me at the door with happy shouts. I savored their hugs, grateful to feel loved and needed.

When I look back at that day, I wonder why I didn't put down my head and sob. What I most wanted—Mama's interest and attention—had slipped away as quickly and mysteriously as it had appeared. But if I had let myself start crying, despair might have washed me away.

By the time of my next visit, I had talked myself out of feeling sorry for myself. My mind was filled with fantasies of a better future. I was determined to reawaken Mama's interest in living and coax her out of her room. Then we would have that picnic with Brian and Evan. No need for despair. Wouldn't anyone be depressed at suddenly discovering that, somehow, years of their life had slipped by? I had to give her time to grieve all those years she spent in the hospital while Eveli and I grew up without her. Then we would talk.

I brought magazines and felt encouraged when she browsed through them.

"Look, Biby, here's a picture of you." She pointed to a photo of a little girl with long blond braids.

"No, it's not really me. I used to look like that, but it's not me."

"Yes, it's you, Biby. It's you." She cut it out and put it in a box with other clippings.

After two more visits, she consented to accompany me to the dining room.

"We'll bring the coffee back to the room, won't we?" She repeated her question all the way down the stairs, as if to ward off her fears of the world outside. Back in the safety of her room, we continued looking at magazines as we sipped our coffee. She was getting interested in clothes again and pointing out fashions that appealed to her. When she asked for lace and embroidery thread, I felt encouraged. On the next visit, she showed me an old blouse she had decorated with the lace I brought, then asked for white thread to tat her own lace.

I was so focused on bringing Mama out of her depression that I wasn't aware of reverting to my old childhood ways. It felt so natural. As a child I took pride in being the one who could soothe and comfort her. I learned to automatically censor every action, every word by asking myself one question: would it upset Mama? Even in the first grade when we were given the choice of making a lion or a lamb for our March calendar, I felt guilty for longing to paste yellow yarn over the lion's big mane. I knew Mama would prefer the lamb. I dutifully chose the lamb and, after presenting Mama with my offering, felt like a phony. I was only pretending to be the sweet girl she wanted.

There was my true struggle—to let myself be *both* lion and lamb. My lion had been banished, and I had yet to realize how much I needed those lion qualities if I was to hold my own with Mama.

By spring, Mama was giving me lists of things to buy. I was glad to do it, even though she showed more interest in what I brought than in talking with me. I brushed aside my disappointment. *What matters*, I told myself, *is her interest in something.*

"Biby? Is that you? Oh, I'm glad you've come. Did you bring the pink thread?"

"You didn't say anything about pink thread. Here's the other stuff you wanted."

"But I wanted pink thread," she whined. "Now I'll have to wait until you come again. Couldn't you go back and get it?" She was close to tears. I was trying my hardest to please her. How could she expect me to read her mind?

Two weeks later, when I brought the pink thread, she wondered why I hadn't brought a white polyester pants suit she had seen in the paper.

"Well, if you like, I can look for it in Madison, and ..."

Her face changed as though she had suddenly remembered something important. "I can go downtown with you today." She pronounced it solemnly, the way she used to announce her horoscope. Then she leaned toward me and whispered, "Do you have any money?"

"Yes, of course I have money." I was elated. "Shall we go right now?"

She put her finger on her lips, signaling I should be quiet. "You have to be very careful of the people around here. They get jealous, and they take it out on me. We can't leave together."

I would have accepted any condition to get her out of the hospital and downtown. So, once again, I entered her fantasy world, just as I did as a seventh-grader. I felt special, just as I did then.

"Pretend you're leaving," she whispered. "Go down and start the car. I'll come down after they think you've left. I have to pack everything and bring it along."

"Why?"

She tapped her finger on her lips a few times and frowned, reminding me I had to whisper. "My lace, my embroidery—I can't leave it here. They'll rip it up. I'll meet you downstairs." She motioned me on, then added, "Don't talk to any of these people. Don't tell them who you are. Make believe you're a social worker."

I nodded, intent on proving she could trust me. I would carry out her instructions perfectly, just as I had when I was a kid. Once again, I was caught up in her excitement. Together, we were outwitting them—Mama's enemies.

10

Hiding

◆

1946–47

I spent the winter of my third grade year living with my godparents, *Goeti* and *Goetili* or Auntie and Uncle Frank, as my godmother instructed me to call them, in their big house in the country. Their dairy was just down the road. I never felt lonely or homesick. Auntie, a large, cheerful woman, invited neighbor girls over to play, and on Friday nights, she drove me to the theater where I met my classmates for a cowboy movie. I enjoyed all of it but preferred to be alone, roaming the fields with the dog and dreaming about my orphans.

Eveli had stayed in our old town with another family. She was in seventh grade and wanted to stay with her class. I didn't mind leaving my old third grade class behind, but I missed Eveli.

Daddy usually visited on weekends, and, during the Christmas holiday, Eveli visited too. Then in early March, I came home from school one day to find Daddy drinking coffee with Auntie in the kitchen. He looked happy, chatting and snacking with Auntie.

Daddy loved to talk. He never seemed to have trouble finding something to say, even to people he didn't know at all. Mama never talked to anybody if she could help it. She fidgeted and got mad if Daddy talked too long. When Mama wasn't with him, he talked on and on.

When I walked in, Daddy looked up and stopped talking. He smiled like he had a big secret. I wondered why he was visiting mid-week. He didn't say anything until I sat down, and Auntie poured me a glass of milk.

"How would you like to visit Mama?"

"In the hospital?"

"She's not in the hospital anymore. I picked her up this morning."

"She's home?" This was better than I had imagined.

"She's in Lake Geneva. We're going to live there now."

I wondered why no one had told me about this. I had planned on anticipating Mama's homecoming by crossing off days on the calendar, like Christmas or my birthday. Now it had already happened.

"When can I see her?"

"I'll take you right over and, if you like, you can stay there tonight. Mama says she's lonely."

If I like? Of course I'd stay with Mama.

"But if you'd rather finish out the school year here with your friends, I'll bring you back tonight. Otherwise, you'll have to start another new school."

I didn't care about changing schools or leaving my friends. I wanted to be with Mama.

Auntie packed my clothes quickly, and without saying good-bye to anyone else, I climbed into the front seat next to Daddy, the seat usually reserved for Mama or Eveli. As we drove away, I felt even more important when Daddy told me Eveli wouldn't be moving to Lake Geneva until June. She wanted to finish the school year with her class. For now, it would be just Mama and me.

"Did you know, Biby, that Lake Geneva was named after a famous lake in Switzerland? They call it 'The Little Switzerland of America.' Mama might feel more at home there, don't you think?"

I agreed, but I didn't need any explanation for moving. Living next to a lake seemed reason enough. Now we could go swimming any time we wanted. We wouldn't have to wait for the weekend when Daddy could drive us to the beach. And Daddy was right, Mama was never happy in Delavan.

"We can't let Mama work too hard now," Daddy went on. "She needs a lot of rest. That's why I've only rented a room. Just big enough for you and her. No cooking, no cleaning." On weekends, he explained, he would bring Eveli to visit, and we would all eat in a restaurant or have a picnic.

He made it sound like we were going to have a lot of fun, but I couldn't help but think of the fights Mama and Daddy used to have. I wondered what kind of mood Mama would be in when we got to Lake Geneva.

"I'm counting on you to keep Mama from feeling lonely," Daddy said. "We don't want her to get upset and have to go back to the hospital."

In my heart, I pledged to make Mama so happy she would never, ever go back. I was sure I couldn't fail. We loved each other too much.

Daddy didn't tell me the truth about Mama's condition. I was too young and he didn't understand it himself. Years later, he explained how he didn't want to accept the doctors' verdict: paranoid schizophrenic, incurable. Daddy clung to the hope that Mama would recover if she were home with her family and got plenty of rest. Because of her sensitive, artistic nature, he believed she felt oppressed in Delavan. Lake Geneva, he was sure, would offer her more cultural opportunities, even if the rents were so high we couldn't afford a decent apartment. Daddy didn't tell me the other reason we had to leave Delavan until I was grown up.

As we entered town, I leaned forward, eager to glimpse the lake. I had only visited Lake Geneva in the summer, when the water sparkled, and the sounds of bathers and speed boats filled the air. But now it was March, and the lake lay still as glass. No boats were moored in the harbor, and the beach lay empty.

We parked in front of a yellow brick house across from the lake. In the front foyer, a large staircase with a polished banister led to the rented rooms upstairs. Mrs. Vickers, the landlady, lived on the first floor with her two grown-up daughters.

I ran up the stairs, eager to see Mama after our six-month separation. Compared to Auntie, Mama looked small and delicate, like a breakable doll, the kind that wears a fancy dress and sits on a shelf. When Mama saw me, she started to cry.

"I missed you so much." She hugged me, then stepped back and looked me up and down. Something was wrong. "Nye, nye, Biby, you've gotten fat. That Auntie ruined you."

Feelings of shame flooded through me. No one told me I had gotten fat. If I had known, I would have tried to fix it. I wanted to shake the fat off immediately. I started to cry. I was failing already.

"Don't cry, Biby, don't cry." Mama caressed my long braids, smoothing a few loose strands of hair. "It's not your fault." She turned to Daddy and switched to her angry voice. "It's that woman's fault. Look what she did to my little girl. She doesn't know how to feed her. All that fried food and white bread."

Mama stroked my face and told me she was going to feed me the right foods, and that the fat would come off in no time. Guiltily, I remembered all the angel food cake and ice cream I had eaten at Auntie's. I didn't want Mama to know I enjoyed it. I wanted her to think Auntie had forced me.

Auntie's cooking was different than Mama's. Mama thought meat was unhealthy, but Auntie cooked it for almost every meal. Mama never bought white bread or packaged cakes. At Auntie's, the Omar bread man delivered fresh white bread three times a week, along with jelly donuts, angel food cake, and an Omar coloring book for me. Auntie didn't think we needed a special occasion for a treat, so she always kept ice cream in her enormous refrigerator.

I didn't mind giving up sausages and white bread. Only pleasing Mama mattered. We had no stove or refrigerator, so our meals were simple—cottage cheese and fruit or cereal and milk. We stored our leftover milk on the window sill to keep it cool overnight. Mama never bought cookies or cake, so there was nothing to tempt me. Whenever Mama felt in the mood, we walked downtown for a supper of soup. Sometimes she let me get an ice cream bar for dessert.

The school was only a few blocks away, so I walked there by myself. When school let out in the afternoon, I played by myself in the park across the street. I watched as workmen put up the pier, and fishermen went out in their motor boats. On warm days, I sat on the dock with my toes dangling in the water, wishing summer would come quickly so I could go swimming. From the dock, I could see the dirt path along the lake shore. Daddy had already explained that the path went all the way around the lake, all twenty-eight miles.

I stared at the path, longing to see where it led, wishing I could walk along it. Suddenly, I realized I didn't have to wait for anyone to take me. I could just explore. A rush of excitement came over me as I ran toward the path. I hoped no one would ask where I was going. The path cut between houses and the shoreline, separating the front yards from the lake. Piles of white boards lined the shore, waiting to be built into piers. The houses were closed and empty for the winter. Nevertheless I worried someone might appear and yell at me.

The next day, I could hardly wait for school to be out so I could get back to the path. I walked further, wondering how long it would take to get to Williams Bay, the next town on the lakeshore. I passed a wild stretch overgrown with woods, a good place for my orphans to hide and, perhaps, sneak food from the picnic tables of the summer houses. Then came a row of willows growing straight out over the water, their gnarled roots clinging to the shore, their broad trunks beckoning me to lie down and let my fingertips dangle in the water. I rested there, lulled by the gentle lap of waves.

Every day, I explored the path, resting on one of the willows before going back to our room at the rooming house. At first, I thought only of my orphans as I lay there gazing at the water. Then my thoughts returned to our old house in Delavan. My whole life was right there in my mind like a private movie:

Back in that old house, standing on the green couch, leaning against the soft cushions, nestled in the brown afghan, looking out the window at the tree with white blossoms, Mama's hands reach for me. Mama's hands turn, carry, and put me in the bathtub, wash and soap me all over. The soap stings. I cry and cry. She doesn't stop. She coos at me and fusses. She wants me clean. She stands me at the sink and pours water over my head. I cry, "The soap's in my eyes. It stings, it stings." I howl and wail; she doesn't care. She wants my hair clean. Shiny and beautiful. She pours chamomile tea on my hair. "This will make it shine like gold," she says. She sounds happy. I want her to be happy. She wraps me in a big towel and combs out the tangles in my hair. When the comb gets stuck, she pulls harder, and I pull my head away and scream. She holds me tight in her hand. She wants those tangles out. She scowls. She won't smile until my hair is all brushed and smooth. She puts me in the sun in the backyard with my hair hanging damp on my neck "The sun will bring out the highlights and dry you up good."

She strokes my cheek with her fingers and looks into my eyes. She murmurs sweet words, but she looks sad. I don't know why. I want her to be happy. "Don't be sad, Mama." I rub her cheek with my fingers. She gives a little laugh, then looks sad again. I want to play, but when I start to move, she pulls me back and holds me. I go limp. I have to stay with her.

My story went on and on, just like the orphans' story, circling over the same things, over and over. I wanted to remember everything that had ever happened to me and put it in the right order. I didn't question why I wanted to remember; I only knew it felt good. Somehow I knew my memories, like piano pieces, needed practice, and I wanted to keep mine forever. They were just for me, not something I had to surrender to Mama or Eveli. They were my own private lullabies that I could sing to myself whenever I wanted.

After my reverie on the willow, I ran back along the path. As I got close to the rooming house, my thoughts shifted to Mama. I worried about her. It didn't seem to me that there was enough to keep her busy. I was used to seeing her manage a whole house, keep up the yard, shop, cook, and bake. Here we only had one room with a bed, a dresser, a table, and some chairs. When I came home from school, she was knitting. After my snack of milk and graham crackers, she knit again while I went out to play. After supper, I sprawled on the bed with a volume of the Bobsey Twins borrowed from the landlady's bookshelf in the hall. Mama kept knitting. I didn't know if she was happy or not, but at least she wasn't crying like in Delavan.

I knew I was different from Mama. She was delicate; I was plump and sturdy. Her eyes were hazel and her face pale; I was rosy-cheeked and blue-eyed like Daddy. Her graceful white fingers made the knitting needles fly, turning out row after row of even stitches that magically turned into perfect sweaters, socks, and mittens. My clumsy fingers worked slowly, and my stitches were lumpy and crooked. She took one look at my work, ripped it out and did it for me. I sat on her lap playing the baby, while she stroked my cheek with the backs of her fingers. She cooked; I ate. She talked; I listened. She cried; I comforted. Mama was my opposite, and I loved her.

Of course, Mama and I had more in common than I knew. We both performed well in the real word; I was a good student, and Mama cooked, knit and sewed despite being taken over by inner voices. But we both *lived* in imaginary worlds: mine was created from fantasies, while hers was a mystery I could only sense, never fully know.

I tried to make sense of Mama's ideas and moods as best I could. I didn't understand why Mama kept saying mean things about Auntie, or why she gave Daddy angry looks when he told her she should be grateful for all Auntie had done. I only knew I couldn't stick up for Auntie when Mama made jokes about the tiny red lines that webbed Auntie's plump cheeks or the flowered cotton housedresses she wore. Mama would never wear such ugly clothes, even to clean house.

Mama was proud of her clothes. She wore long, full skirts and white blouses trimmed with lace, never tailored suits or high heels. She knit her sweaters, socks, mittens and hats out of red yarn, embroidering them with white wool flowers and trimming them with white crocheting. She never went to a beauty parlor to get a permanent like Auntie and warned me never to go.

"They'll tell you lies, Biby—anything to get your money. They just want to make you look ugly by cutting your hair short like all these American women." Mama wore her hair long and loose, letting it fall in natural waves over her shoulders. In Delavan, she gathered rain water in pails to wash her hair. Then she would rinse it with chamomile tea to bring out the highlights.

Mama thought American styles ugly. She made fun of Auntie's fur coat, and how important Auntie acted when she wore it. She was just a farmer's wife, Mama said. Auntie had wanted her husband to be a professor of dairy science at the university, so she could live in Madison. But they didn't hire him, so Auntie had to live on the farm and drive a dairy truck. Mama snickered when she told me the story.

But Auntie never looked unhappy to me. She pitched right in with the men, lifting heavy crates of milk bottles and driving the truck. Sometimes she would take me along when she delivered milk and collected money. She showed me how to count out stacks of dimes and quarters before rolling them in red and green papers to take to the bank. Auntie seemed happier than Mama. But of course I couldn't say this. That would have upset Mama.

One evening, when Mama sat knitting and I was curled up in bed reading, I heard the front door open and footsteps on the stairs.

"Yoo-hoo, anyone home? Yoo-hoo!" I immediately recognized the high cheerful voice.

"Auntie!" I jumped off the bed. "It's Auntie!" I hadn't seen her since I had left her house so suddenly some weeks before. I was set to run to the door, but Mama put her finger to her lips and raised her eyebrows to silence me. She motioned me back with her hand and climbed into bed next to me, pulling the blanket up to our chins, all the while holding her finger to her lips. She was smiling, so I thought we were playing a game of surprising Auntie. I didn't know how we were going to get Auntie to look for us if it was supposed to be hide-and-seek. I couldn't ask any questions because Mama kept moving her finger to her lips, meaning I must not make a sound.

Auntie continued to call, "Yoo-hoo, Paula, Biby, are you there? Yoo-hoo!"

I wanted to run to the door and say, "Yes! We're here! Come in!" I wanted to show her around the house and take her to the lakefront park in the fading twilight.

Mama seemed to be silently laughing as she listened to Auntie. I wondered when Mama would stop the game. I heard the brightness in Auntie's voice fade. I could tell she knew we were inside. I knew she was hurt because we weren't opening the door. I didn't like the game.

But Mama would be unhappy if she knew I cared about Auntie. This was a loyalty test. If I didn't pass, Mama would be upset with me. I wished Mama didn't have to be so mean.

We heard Auntie's footsteps, then the front door closing. Mama broke out laughing. It was the first time she had laughed in a long time.

"Yoo-hoo. Yoo-hoo," she sneered as she made her voice sound like Auntie. She giggled, then did it again and again.

I had to pretend I thought it was funny, too, so I chanted, "Yoo-hoo," and giggled with her. I knew Auntie would be hurt if she heard us. I imagined Daddy scolding Mama: "Paula, how could you? After all she's done for us. You could at least try to be nice. This is no way to treat people."

But I could imagine Mama's response. "Humph. These are your friends, Hans Gubler. These are no friends of mine. Don't expect me to play up to your cronies."

I knew I wouldn't tell Daddy or anyone else. I was too ashamed.

Even now, many years later, I feel tears of regret as I think of the good-hearted woman who was kind to me and to whom I could show no gratitude. I still long for my eight-year-old self to jump off the bed, run down the stairs, and call out, "Wait, Auntie, come back! It was just a game Mama wanted to play. I was hiding just to go along with her. I want to see you. I didn't really mean it. I never told you ... thank you, thank you for taking care of me."

11

Slipping Backwards

◆

1947–48

Growing up, I loved spending time alone—by the lake, in the woods, or lying on the living room floor looking out the window. I never gave up my habit of reviewing memories, although as I got older, I no longer had time for long, daily reflections. But whenever I felt the need for comfort, I turned to my old childhood pastime. It was my anchor in times of turmoil, my reassurance amidst emotional upheavals.

If I had been using this great store of memories to more advantage the year I re-connected with Mama, I might have understood more quickly what was happening. When Mama whispered her instructions, I might have noticed the stirrings of childhood emotion, the thrill of once again being invited into her conspiracy—the two of us against the world.

I was only eight when Mama first began confiding in me during our evenings together in the rooming house. Eveli joined us when school let out for the summer, so our private conversations had to be put on hold. We spent our days at the beach or in the air-conditioned movie theatre, searching for relief from the heat.

At the end of the summer, when Mama and Daddy searched for an apartment we could afford, they found two. The first was spacious and airy with sunny windows overlooking a full backyard; the other was adequate but cramped and dark. It had one advantage: a lease. A lease would have allowed us to stay on through the following summer at a rent we could afford. But Mama had her heart set on the spacious kitchen and sunny windows, and so Daddy gave in.

The larger apartment was ideal for us because one bedroom had its own separate entrance and bathroom. That was Daddy's room. Mama and Daddy were still divorced, and although Daddy wanted to remarry, Mama had not yet consented. Since we were the only people in the house—the upstairs apartment stayed vacant all winter—it felt like the house was our own.

When we first moved in, Mama's mood picked up. She seemed happy to have a home to take care of again. We were all happy to stretch out and eat home-cooked meals once again, even if a shadow was hanging over us.

"Yah, yah, this was a nice breakfast, Paula." Daddy sipped his coffee. Mama poured more while Daddy read his newspaper. "Very nice. But you know we'll have to move out in the spring." Mama avoided his eyes. She was plumping up the bow on her tea cozy, a white quilted dome that kept the coffee pot warm. Mama had embroidered it with pink strawberries. "Paula, you understand that, don't you?" Daddy had been in favor of the apartment with the lease.

"Ya, ya, I know." Mama sighed and started clearing the table.

I wished Daddy didn't have to keep reminding us. It upset Mama. I wondered if Eveli even noticed. She was so busy with her new eighth-grade friends. Suddenly she was wearing a bra and going to dances. She certainly didn't want to spend any time with me, a mere fourth-grader.

By spring, Daddy's warnings became urgent. Just as he had feared, Mama refused to look for a new place. "You could pay the rent here if you wanted," she hissed. "I know you have more money than what you let on, Hans."

"Ach, Paula." Daddy stamped his foot impatiently. "Must we go through this again?" Mama acted like she didn't hear him. "I can't waste time on this. I've got to get going with my business." But Mama still wasn't listening. "All right, Paula, you win. I'm going to the office."

Later, when he came home for supper, he looked more cheerful. "Paula, we don't have to worry. Mrs. Baumbach let me have one of her apartments at a good price. After this, we won't have to move again."

"Hmmph. *Mrs. Baumbach.*" Mama sounded like a kid as she mocked Daddy's voice.

"Paula, please. She's doing us a kindness."

"Doing you a kindness, maybe. Mrs. Baumbach is doing no kindness for me." She disappeared into the kitchen. Mrs. Baumbach, a realtor, had rented Daddy his office. It was the front room of a once grand old house near the lake, a room large enough to hold Daddy's desk and work table as well as all his supplies and samples.

Our new apartment was the back half of the second story of the house. There was a tiny living room, which also had to serve as our dining room since the kitchen was a narrow galley, barely able to hold two people at the same time. On the other side of a dark corridor were the two bedrooms and a bathroom. There were also a back staircase, but we weren't supposed to use the stairs except as an emergency fire escape.

Mama packed and left the apartment she loved in obedient silence. She didn't explode until all our belongings were crowded into the new place.

"You dirty dog, Hans Gubler, you expect me to move into your dirty apartments and clean them up, one after the other, you and that Mrs. Baumbach. Ya, ya, I know all about her!"

"But Paula, she could have rented this for much more. It's only a block from the lake."

"I know what's going on between you and that divorcee."

"Please, Paula, not in front of the children ..."

"She must be laughing, thinking how stupid I am to clean up her filthy apartments so she can make more money. Ya, I was stupid all right, stupid to marry you! I won't make that mistake again." She sobbed bitterly, and Daddy shook his head helplessly.

Their marital truce over, Daddy now slept in his office on a roll-away bed. He was out of town most of the summer on business anyway. Mama kept crying as she went to work on the new apartment. I knew she felt cooped in without a yard or even a porch of our own.

I claimed the stairwell as my play area, spreading out my paper dolls and menagerie of tiny figures on the steps while Mama cleaned and cried. Eveli, after trying to coax me outside, complained to Mama. "Look at her, she hasn't been outside in three weeks! It's summertime, for Pete's sake, and all she does is play with those stupid paper dolls. It isn't good for her. Make her go outside!"

I cringed. I knew Eveli was right. I couldn't explain why I didn't feel like swimming or doing anything else. I supposed I was lazy or bad in some way.

"Oh, leave her alone, she's a good girl. She'll go outside later. Do you want to go swimming, Biby?"

I shrugged. "When the water warms up."

Mama signed us up for swimming lessons with the Red Cross, and on the morning of my first class, I went. It was cool and gray, and I had to force myself into the water. I wondered why swimming wasn't as exciting as when we first moved to Lake Geneva.

If I had understood then what I understand now, I would have said to Eveli, "Can't you see our mother's sad? It makes me feel sad too. I can't go outside and leave her alone. I have to make sure she's okay."

Since Eveli was now spending as much time as she could with her friends, I spent my days alone with Mama. When a stray cat appeared on our front steps, Mama's mood brightened. I followed as she carried down a saucer of milk. "Poor *buseli*. Just skin and bones." The skinny gray cat lapped hungrily. "And having kittens, too."

"Kittens? How can you tell?"

Mama laughed but wouldn't answer. "Can we keep her, please? And the kittens too?"

"Maybe." I could tell Mama wanted the cat as much as I did. "If she has a home, they're not feeding her much." We checked again after supper. The cat was waiting patiently under the porch, so Mama carried her upstairs.

"Poor Smoky. We'll have to fatten you up." Mama had already given the skinny gray cat a name. Mama lined a box with old towels and set it in the closet for Smoky's kittens. Then she carried Smoky out to the kitchen and fed her.

A few days later, Smoky let out a sharp cry of pain. I ran to the bedroom where Smoky lay in the middle of Eveli's bed, a circle of blood spreading around her on the tufted bedspread. The cry scared me, but now Smoky was purring and licking something. It was a mouse-like thing with closed eyes and flat ears. I had never seen anything so newborn—so helpless, it scared me. But Smoky seemed to know what to do. There were three kittens altogether. I worried Mama would be mad about the bedspread. I didn't want anything to spoil the magic of the kittens.

"Oh, Smoky! Must you have your kittens right on the bed? After I made that nice nest for you?" she said. But it was only pretend scolding. I watched Smoky lick each tiny kitten clean. Then, taking one in her mouth, Smoky jumped down to the closet, leaving the other two behind. I stayed on the bed to guard them.

"Don't worry Smoky, I won't let them fall." They were mewing and wiggling, trying to find their mother. Smoky came right back, and when all three were in their box, Mama took the bedspread and washed out the stain.

"Let Smoky alone with her babies. You can play with them when they're bigger." But when Mama went grocery shopping, I crept into the closet and watched the kittens nurse, their tiny paws kneading Smoky's belly as they sucked. Smoky purred with contentment. I was eager to tell Daddy—afraid they would be all grown by the time he got home.

Despite the excitement of Smoky's kittens, Mama sank deeper into her depression. Whenever she talked, I was glad. It was better than watching her pace and wondering what she was thinking. She never talked to Eveli or Daddy, so when she talked to me, I felt important. I wanted to understand. Why she had been sent to the hospital, for instance. I wished she would explain everything but she would only give hints. I hoped if I proved trustworthy, she would give me complete answers.

I understood why Mama had to be careful. She had been betrayed so many times. No wonder she didn't trust people. Mama had given up on Dr. de Werdt, the psychologist she used to see. She mentioned she might talk to the new young minister of our church. She thought she could trust him.

At first, I was jealous. I hated to be left out. Rev. Hoffman would hear what Mama was thinking, and I wouldn't. If only she could see that I was more loyal, more trustworthy than anyone else. But I was only a kid.

She stayed at Rev. Hoffman's a long time, and when she came home, she was calmer. I wanted to know what they had talked about, but she wouldn't tell me. She went again two days later, then again every day, three days in a row. The last time she came home upset.

"That Rev. Hoffman, I thought I could trust him. But he told nasty lies about me behind my back." Another betrayal. My heart sank.

"But what did he say? Who did he tell?" Mama wouldn't say more but acted as though she was in danger. I wondered if there was anyone in the world who could help us, anyone we could trust.

A day later, Mama told me the only person she could trust was Father Barnes, the Episcopalian priest. I wondered if this meant we would have to go to the Episcopalian church. I only hoped Father Barnes wouldn't betray Mama like the others had.

Mama seemed agitated all the time now, and I didn't know why. She never talked about her special powers anymore. Only the danger she was in.

"Biby, if anything happens to me, I want you to run as fast as you can and get Father Barnes. Will you do that?" She looked at me intently. I nodded. Of course I would. I would do anything to help Mama.

"But what could happen?"

"These people have it in for me. They want to make it hard for me." Then she cried. She refused to give any more details. She only repeated her instructions. The danger seemed closer.

I practiced running down the street to the Episcopalian parsonage. I went up to the door and stood there without knocking. I wanted to make sure I knew exactly where to go. Mentally, I rehearsed running down the back stairs of our apartment and through the downstairs neighbor's apartment just in case I couldn't go down the front stairs. If the danger came, I wanted to be ready.

When the moment arrived, I recognized it instantly. It was a hot, muggy morning, and I hadn't felt like doing anything. Mama let me get back into my pajamas and crawl into her bed.

"You faker," Eveli scoffed.

"Oh, let her rest a little," Mama replied. I felt safe in Mama's bed, daydreaming. Suddenly, I thought I heard strangers. I opened the door a crack and heard Mama saying "No, no, you're not going to take me, not like this, not in front of the children." My heart started to pound. This was the danger! They were taking Mama. I wanted to rush out to the living room and beat them with my fists and tell them they had no right. But I knew it was more important to get to Father Barnes. I had made a promise. I pulled on my shorts and T-shirt, and when I heard someone coming, jumped back under the covers. Eveli pushed open the door and stood looking white and shaken. I didn't know it at the time, but she had just witnessed men from the state hospital strap Mama into a straight jacket.

"You'd better get dressed, kiddo. They're taking Mama to the hospital, and we have to go with the social worker. I'll pack our clothes."

I wanted to tell her not to worry, that I was going to get help, but I had to keep my plan a secret. I gave her just enough time to get down the hall and into our bedroom. I pretended to go to the bathroom, but instead slipped down the back stairs. I pushed open the door at the bottom of the stairwell, ran through the downstairs neighbors' living room as they gawked at me and out their front door. My heart was pounding as I ran toward the parsonage. The sidewalk felt hot on my bare feet, and after being in the dark bedroom, the mid-day sun made my eyes blink. This was the moment I had practiced for, the chance to save Mama. Just as she had warned, something terrible was happening, and it was up to me to save her.

I rang the bell over and over. It seemed an eternity before I heard someone walking slowly toward the door. "Please, please, hurry," I thought. "Don't you know this is an emergency?"

A plain looking woman in a dark dress opened the door. Was she a maid or Father Barnes's wife? I didn't know if Episcopalian priests had wives or not. "Please, I have to see Father Barnes right away." She looked annoyed, like she was going to send me away, so I kept talking. "Please, it's an emergency." She told me to wait on a bench. The foyer of the big stone house was dark and felt cool after my brief run in the sun. I wondered what could possibly take so long. Finally, a slightly rounded man in a black suit with a stiff white collar and a grave face came down the hallway. I jumped up the minute I saw him. "Please, you have to come right away. My mother needs you. She told me to come and get you."

I had imagined this part in my many mental rehearsals. Father Barnes was supposed to look alarmed and say, "Let's go." He was supposed to run to our apartment and stop them from taking my mother to the hospital. But he just stood there, looking at me.

"Please, let's hurry. They're taking my mother."

"I can't help your mother, child. Did you tell anyone you were coming here?"

"No, I didn't." I felt proud. I was sure I had done my part well. I hadn't even told Eveli.

"You shouldn't have run off like that. They'll be worried. Go on home and do what the social worker tells you to do."

I couldn't believe my ears. This was the man Mama trusted, the man we were counting on. He didn't even seem to care. Mama's enemies were taking her, and he said we should just let it happen.

"Please, you've got to come. I promised I'd get you."

"There's nothing I can do."

"But she's counting on you. You're the only one we have."

"Go on home now, child."

I hated him. How could he have promised to help and not even lift a finger? We had been betrayed. I went home only because I could think of nothing else to do. Mama's instructions didn't cover this. I wondered how Father Barnes knew there was a social worker at our apartment anyway. Had he known about this ahead of time? Was he in on it, too?

I walked up the stairs slowly. I had failed and been failed. Eveli was in the living room with a young woman I had never seen before.

"Where on earth have you been?" Eveli demanded. "Why did you run off like that?"

"Where's Mama?" I demanded. "Where is she?"

"Your mother is very sick and had to be taken to the hospital." The young woman answered in a hesitant voice. She seemed too young to be a social worker. She probably didn't know what she was doing.

"But where is she? I didn't get to say good-bye. Can't you take us to her?" I knew she couldn't, but I wanted to demand it anyway. Someone ought to squirm for the wrongs done to me and Mama. The social worker was my only target.

Her voice quivered as she explained about "the special kind of hospital where children aren't allowed to visit." She went on about Mama needing a long rest but how she might like a letter. Did I know how to write a letter? Here, she had some stationary and would show me how to write a letter if I wanted.

I felt insulted. Of course I knew how to write a letter! This was the adult who was supposed to be in charge of us, and she didn't even know that our mother had already been to the "special hospital" twice, that our father had taken us to visit her there and that we had already written dozens of letters.

"I don't want to write a letter. I want to see her," I wailed. When I saw the social worker look flustered, I kept it up.

"I'll be taking you to a foster home in Delavan. I think you'll like it. There are babies there, too. Maybe you'll have fun with them." She tried to sound cheerful.

Foster home? Delavan? Babies? Mama never talked about what would happen to Eveli and me after her enemies took her, about what we were supposed to do. "But why can't we stay here? This is our home. I don't want to go anywhere else."

"There's no one to take care of you here. You can't stay here alone."

"Daddy can take care of us. He's just away on business. He'll be home soon."

"We're trying to contact him, but we haven't been able to reach him. Meantime, you'll have to stay in the foster home."

"Why can't we stay in Lake Geneva? All our friends are here, and we have swimming lessons three times a week." I missed half the classes anyway, but I had to protest. How dare she think she could take us away from our home, back to Delavan where there wasn't even a place to swim.

"When are your swimming lessons?"

Eveli explained. She sounded so grown up I felt proud, but I wanted her to help me fight. The social worker agreed to pick us up three times a week for our lessons. It felt like an important victory. Then I thought of Smoky.

"We can't leave. We have to take care of our mother cat and her kittens." The social worker looked dismayed. I led her to the back bedroom and showed her Goldie, Boots, and Cinders.

I felt proud showing off my kittens. She picked Goldie up. "Oh, how darling." I could tell she meant it by the way she looked at his little face. He meowed. I softened toward her.

"We'll find a good home for them, don't worry."

"Can't they come with us?" My heart was breaking.

"I'm sorry." She looked like she really was. "Not to the foster home. I'll have to find something else." She went out to use our phone while Eveli started packing. I wanted to spend every minute I could with my kittens. I prayed the social worker would say she couldn't find a place, and so she would have to let us stay here after all. I couldn't bear to think of giving them away.

"All taken care of. They're going to a farm. They'll be happy there." We put them in a cardboard box, and I held them on my lap all the way to the farm. When I found out Smoky and the kittens were going to live in the barn, I felt betrayed again. "But they might get stepped on by a cow. They're so little."

"They'll be okay." The social worker was trying to comfort me. "There are lots of cats in the barn."

Mean cats probably. My cats aren't used to fending for themselves. They're used to being petted and fed. My heart sank as we drove away. I cried by myself in the back seat, wondering if I would see them again.

On the far edge of Delavan, we drove down a treeless street of small boxy houses and parked in front of one. We entered the house through a sun room where the air smelled of urine and sour milk. Four babies with runny noses strapped in infant seats sat in a row. They were in day care, to be picked up by their mothers every afternoon. We were in foster care and would spend the night.

Our foster mother, Mrs. Jensen, a fat woman in a loose cotton house dress, looked us over suspiciously as though expecting to find something wrong. She showed us our room and the bathroom. "Two squares of paper, that's all any child needs, so don't use more than that." Then she fixed me with a cold stare. "I hear you're a runaway. Since you can't be trusted, neither of you have permission to step one foot out of the yard."

I was stunned. She didn't even ask where I had gone or why I came back so soon. If I was going to run, wouldn't I have stayed out all day? It was so unfair, and even more unfair for Eveli to be punished for what I did.

Eveli put our clothes into dresser drawers while I sat on the bed. "I'm sorry I got you into trouble. It isn't fair." I was sure she would be mad at me. I deserved it. Because of me, she was being treated like a two-year-old.

"Forget it, Kiddo. She'll calm down in a few days. Then I'll talk to her. So let's be good and show her we can be trusted, okay? Daddy should be back soon."

The days at Mrs. Jensen's felt unbearably long. Mrs. Jensen kept trying to get us to "play" with the babies, something we resisted because we knew she couldn't make us. We saw it as her attempt to exploit us into babysitting for no pay. Hardest of all was her barely concealed contempt when we talked about Daddy coming to get us. She was sure he had abandoned us. She almost came right out and told us we had best get used to the idea. The thought of living permanently in the foster home with its daily humiliations filled me with despair.

It seemed an eternity before Daddy called. When he said he was on his way to see us, I was overjoyed. Suddenly, I couldn't stand another minute at Mrs. Jensen's. We waited for him on the front steps, relieved Eveli would make it to her friend's birthday party the next day.

As soon as we saw Daddy's old car coming down the street, we ran to meet him. Now Mrs. Jensen would see how wrong she was. I wanted to hop right into the car, but Daddy said we had to wait. "I can't take you home just yet."

"But we've been waiting so long."

"I know. I'm sorry, but it's not so simple. I'm not allowed."

I couldn't believe what I was hearing. Wait longer after all this time? Why? It didn't seem fair. I threw myself down on the grass in tears.

"Get up for heaven's sakes," Eveli chided. She nodded toward the house, where Mrs. Jensen peered through the curtain.

"Ya, ya, I have to wait for the judge to say I can take you."

"The judge? But why?"

"The judge gave Mama custody, so when she went to the hospital, the county automatically got custody. And the judge is the only one who can change it."

"Did you call him? What did he say?"

"The judge is out of town. We'll have to wait 'til he's back."

So we were still stuck at Mrs. Jensen's. Eveli would have to miss her party. Something seemed very wrong. It was proof Mama was right. Someone *was* plotting against us.

12

Shopping

◆

1971

My childhood dream of rescuing Mama, on hold for more than twenty years, now bloomed forth and took me over. I had a car, I had money, and Mama had consented to let me drive her away from the hospital. Just like a kid, I was excited to be included on Mama's adventure.

I went down the hall, passing the nurse's station without saying a word just as Mama had instructed. I was intent on proving myself by following her instructions to the letter. I had to hold myself back from running as I walked to my car. Then I drove up to the entrance and waited. Within a few minutes, Mama appeared in the doorway, a clear plastic bag bulging with white lace cradled in her arms, a small smile of satisfaction on her lips. She seemed as excited as I was as she climbed into the front seat, and we drove away from the hospital grounds together.

It seemed too easy, this once impossible dream of childhood. I half expected someone to stop us, to say, "You aren't authorized to take your mother off grounds."

Mama looked at me with admiration as I drove onto the highway.

"You're smart to know how to drive." I loved her praise but felt embarrassed.

"It's not so hard. I'm sure you could have done it, too, if someone taught you."

"No, no, Biby, I couldn't. It was too hard for me."

Driving had scared me also. I avoided learning until I was twenty. Only when I had a private instructor with a second set of brakes did I dare get behind the wheel. I didn't trust myself with something as powerful as a car. I was sure I would make a terrible mistake like swerving over the center line and crashing head-on into an oncoming car. The first time I put my foot on the gas and felt the car lurch forward, I panicked. What if I slipped and pushed all the way down?

What if I couldn't find the brakes? I wondered why I was so different from my friends, who seemed to slide behind the wheel without a second thought. It took years before I could relax behind the wheel.

"You could have learned. It just takes practice."

"I wanted to when we lived in Oconomowoc, when you were a baby, but Daddy didn't want me to."

I was surprised to hear Mama once had the desire to drive. I could easily picture Daddy's reaction. Eveli had tried to persuade Daddy to let her drive, but he got agitated every time she brought it up. Then he would justify himself by explaining that he depended on his car for business, and if the car got damaged, he'd lose valuable time, and we might not have money for rent. Mama would have given up in the face of this kind of resistance, just like she gave up so many of her desires—for a job and for her own house. If only Daddy could have seen how important those things were.

For lunch, Mama chose the Chocolate Shop, the place that served the banana splits I craved as a teenager. The menu still had a full page of sundaes, but during graduate school, I had switched to cigarettes and coffee and no longer was tempted by gooey treats.

"I think I'll have a ham and Swiss on rye and a cup of coffee."

"Oh, Biby, don't eat that junk." Mama sounded horrified. "That will make you sick. Have a strawberry sundae."

Could this be Mama? My health-conscious mother who served fresh vegetables at every meal and warned us not to eat too many rich sweets? She never approved of meat, especially pork, but we ate plenty of cheese and bread.

"I don't want any sweet stuff. Just a sandwich."

"No, Biby, please, you mustn't eat it. It's poison. Please have the sundae."

Her voice took on a piercing, desperate edge. Panic rose in my chest. I didn't want to upset her, not on our first outing. "It's just one meal," I told myself. "What difference does it make what you eat? Eat the ice cream. Make her happy."

But a deeper part of me objected. "I can't eat ice cream every time she wants me to. She'll have to learn to accept me as I am."

But if I held my ground, I risked a scene. I pictured Mama standing up and crying, "No, Biby, please don't eat that poison, I'm begging you." I imagined everyone in the restaurant staring at me, blaming me as Mama walked out. I pictured myself running after her, begging, "Please Mama, come back. I'll eat whatever you want."

So I gave in and ordered the sundae. As we dipped our spoons into identical mounds of whipped cream, ice cream, and red syrupy sauce, Mama smiled. "See, Biby, isn't this better? Listen to me. I know what's good for you."

After lunch, as we browsed through one dress shop after another, I was glad I had chosen the ice cream. Mama looked happy, and that, I told myself, was my goal. Her eyes gleamed as she fingered the merchandise.

"Isn't this a nice blouse?" She held it up for me to inspect.

"Would you like it? Or do you want to keep looking?" I remembered how Daddy tried to restrain her: "Paula must you spend so much? Is it really necessary?" Now I had the money, and I wanted her to feel good. Mama looked at me hesitantly.

"You can buy it for me?"

"Sure, I can." I felt almost giddy.

"Are you sure you have enough money, dear?"

"It's okay, I've got my credit card." I held it up.

"Oh, like a charge card?" That settled it; we bought the blouse.

After the dress shops, reluctant to end the pleasure of shopping, we lingered in Kresge's, the variety store. I felt at home, just like in the five-and-dime back in Delavan, when I looked at paper dolls and Mama tried lipsticks. Now, as then, I fell into a trance. Together in a magical place full of bargains, we could surrender to rows of glittering stuff that promised to change our lives. I didn't want to leave.

13

On Our Own

❖

1948

After I had grown up, Daddy told me about his struggle to get us out of the foster home. "They thought I'd abandon you, can you imagine?" He shook his head in disbelief. "My own children."

The county seemed confused as to what to do with him, especially when he insisted he could take care of us with no female relatives to help. They hadn't even expected him to return to claim us. They wouldn't trust us to his care until he produced character witnesses who vouched he was a responsible father.

Abandon us! I tried to imagine it. As a psychologist, I worked with girls whose mothers had been found unfit and whose fathers had abandoned them. In them, I saw the life I might have had—stuck in a foster home, feeling unworthy, looking for love, pregnant at fifteen, running away, winding up in an institution—just like Mama.

Much later in my life I marveled at how well Daddy coped with the challenge of raising us on his own. I wondered if he drew strength from remembering his own childhood. Finding himself alone with two daughters, surely he thought about his own mother, widowed in her thirties and left with four children. Daddy, at age ten, was the oldest. He often told us stories of her struggles to keep her family together, to feed and educate them. For a woman on her own in Switzerland at the turn of the century, this was no easy task.

As his own life took on a similar shape, surely he must have felt a deeper appreciation of her, just as I felt for him as later I lived out my own variation of this recurring family script.

Eveli and I endured one more weekend at Mrs. Jensen's, certain we would be home as soon as Daddy talked to the judge. Each time the phone rang, I came running. "Not every call is about you," Mrs. Jensen snapped. She sounded gleeful to still have us in her power. I threw myself down on my bed, wondering if we would ever go home.

When Daddy came back for us sometime the next week, he said we would be going to camp for the rest of the summer. I would have preferred to go home, but at least we were getting away from Mrs. Jensen. She seemed crestfallen as we put our bags in Daddy's car. When she said good-bye, her face softened suddenly and turned sad.

I kneeled on the back seat, watching her house disappear as we drove away. "Is she really sad? If she cared, you'd think she'd have treated us nicer."

"Sure she's sad. We're the easiest foster kids she'll ever have," Eveli retorted. "She's sad thinking about all the money she could have saved on you, never eating any of her precious bologna." Laughing, I told Daddy how I wouldn't eat any bologna at lunch, because Mama wouldn't have wanted me to. Instead, I ate lettuce and butter sandwiches. I thought this should have entitled me to an extra cookie for dessert, but Mrs. Jensen had snapped, "One cookie apiece, that's all you get."

Daddy agreed we had been treated terribly, which somehow made me feel better.

Three weeks later, when Daddy returned to pick us up from camp, I still feared he would have to bring us back to Mrs. Jensen's.

"Yah, that judge didn't want to admit he'd made a mistake." I leaned over the front seat, my head between Eveli and Daddy, not wanting to miss a word. "I told him at the divorce it was crazy to give Paula custody. Anyone could see she wasn't stable. She had only been out of Mendota a few weeks. But, ach, I didn't have a lawyer."

This sounded like one of Daddy's long explanations, and I feared bad news. "Do we have to go back to Mrs. Jensen's?"

"Don't worry, Biby," Daddy laughed. "Rev. Hoffman spoke to the judge for me. Father Barnes, too."

I was confused. I didn't think we could count on Father Barnes, not after he let Mama down. And Rev. Hoffman hadn't been any better. But Daddy seemed to think they were friends after all.

"On school days, you girls are going to eat lunch and dinner over at the Hoffman's. They'll keep an eye on you while I'm out of town." The parsonage was only half a block from our apartment. "After Christmas, I'll be home every day. And if we're lucky, Mama will be home soon."

In today's world the plan sounds outrageous: two girls, ten and fourteen, left alone during the week, eating meals at a neighbor's, getting themselves to school and doing their homework without an adult standing over them. But it sounded wonderful to us.

Whenever we told people our mother wasn't living at home, they always took on a sad look, as if they were thinking, "You poor things." Actually, we had more fun with Daddy than we ever had with Mama. He even baked cookies with me, something Mama would never do. She always shooed me out of the kitchen. The truth was, I only felt sad when I read Mama's letters. If she could come home *and* we could keep having fun with Daddy—that would be perfect. I prayed for that while I ached for Mama. Did I ache because I truly missed her or because I knew she missed us? It was hard to tell the difference between her unhappiness and my own.

After we had lived on our own a few weeks, Daddy said the county wanted to check on us. "Yah, they can't believe it's going so well." He chuckled. "Dr. de Werdt will visit next week."

Dr. de Werdt, who lived in a nearby town, had been Mama's psychologist for a few months in between Mama's hospitalizations. Mama used to keep me home from school on the days she went to see Dr. de Werdt. We would ride the bus together and have lunch in a restaurant after her appointment. Then we would go shopping and take the bus home. Mama never liked Dr. de Werdt, and she surely would have been upset to hear she was snooping around in our apartment. I didn't mind. I had always been fascinated by Dr. de Werdt—a psychologist who was a woman.

The night before the inspection, Eveli baked a chocolate cake and had me vacuum and dust the living room. In the morning, we made our beds and hung up our clothes. After school, we waited nervously. When we heard the knock, I stood behind Eveli as she opened the door.

"Hello, I'm Dr. de Werdt."

"We were expecting you. Would you like to sit down?" Eveli waved toward our small couch. I was glad she was in charge. "I'm making some tea. And I baked a chocolate cake. Would you care for some?"

"Why, thank you, yes." Dr. de Werdt sat down. I could tell she was surprised to be offered cake. I felt proud, thinking to myself, "See? We can take care of ourselves. You didn't think we could, but we can. A lot better than in your lousy foster home." Eveli knew what to say and do, but still, I could hear the little waver in her voice that meant she was nervous. Eveli disappeared into the kitchen while I watched Dr. de Werdt. I was wondering exactly how old she was, but knew I couldn't ask.

"Do you have any children?"

Dr. de Werdt looked startled. "No, I don't."

"Aren't you lonely without children to keep you company?" Now she smiled. I could tell she thought this was a funny question. I couldn't imagine a woman being happy without children. Why had Dr. de Werdt become a psychologist rather than a mother?

"No, I'm not lonely. I have a husband and my work. What about you? What grade are you in now?" I told her about fifth grade, still hoping I could get her to answer more of my questions. Then Eveli brought in the tea and cake. We watched as Dr. de Werdt held her plate daintily and took a bite of Eveli's cake.

"Oh, my, this is delicious. So moist."

"Uh, I'm taking Home Economics, and we, uh, just had a unit on cakes. It isn't very hard." Eveli stammered a little when she got nervous, but I didn't know why Dr. De Werdt's praise would make her nervous. "Umm, would you like to see the rest of the apartment?"

"Why, yes, thank you, I would." She set down her plate and followed Eveli.

"This is the kitchen. It's a little messy right now." Eveli laughed. "And the bedrooms are back here." I trailed along behind. Dr. de Werdt glanced around taking everything in. "This is where we sleep."

"And this is where our kittens were born, right on Eveli's bed." Eveli shrugged as if that weren't important.

"We don't have the kittens anymore," she explained.

"Yeah, we had to take them to a farm when we went to the foster home." I hoped Dr. de Werdt would realize the injustice of this and perhaps do something, but she didn't seem interested.

"Well, you girls really do a good job of keeping house, better than a lot of adults. You must have had good training." I beamed with pride, and Eveli looked uncomfortable. We followed Dr. de Werdt back to the living room. "Thanks for the tea and cake. I'll be going now. You're doing a wonderful job."

We waited quietly until we heard the downstairs door close. Then we squealed in triumph. We had showed them! We could take care of ourselves!

14

Rescuing Mama

◆

1971–72

After our successful, first trip off the grounds of Green County Hospital, Mama and I went out every visit. We always had lunch at the Chocolate Shop. I learned to eat before I came, so I could make her happy by eating ice cream. After lunch, we walked from one dress shop to another as well as the drug store and the variety store.

My plan to bring Mama out of her depression had worked. Since we had started going shopping, she was always eager to see me. She had overcome her shyness about spending my money. In fact, she spent more each time. At first, I was glad to buy things for her since she had been cheated of so much. But I began to worry about the drain on my limited finances. I knew I should set some limits, but I had no idea how. Daddy had trouble with this, too. He would trail behind Mama in every store.

"Paula, Paula, must you spend so much?"

"All necessary items," she would snap. "I must have them." Her voice had an edge. Later, she would complain to me about Daddy's penny-pinching attitude.

I didn't want her to think of me that way. I couldn't bear the thought of making her angry.

After our next lunch, I tried to broach the topic. "Umm, Mama, I can't keep spending so much …"

"Don't they give you enough money, dear?" She looked puzzled.

"Well, my job doesn't pay...." She cut me off.

"Don't tell me such nonsense. You're too young to have a job. You're in school."

Her words shocked me. What happened, I wondered, to the conversation we had had on my first visit, when she told me how smart I was to have a job and children, too? Had that been a gift she had given me only to suck me in, and now that she had me, she could forget? Or was it recorded in a lost part of her brain, the sane part that surfaced only under extreme emergencies?

But when I thought about it, I realized that the last time Mama had visited *me*—actually had seen me in my life—I had still been a kid. I had been attending a small college not far from Green County. On Thanksgiving, Daddy brought her to visit, and Eveli had come by bus from the university in Madison to join us. We had eaten dinner in the nicest restaurant the little town had to offer. After dinner, I showed my family my dorm room and then we toured the campus—a dozen red brick buildings around a small quadrangle. Fifteen years had passed since that Thanksgiving, but to Mama, I was still that teenager, sheltered in an ivy-covered dorm.

"I finished school. I earn my own money. No one gives it to me." But she walked away from me, preferring her own version.

By our next visit, I had made a plan. Before we left her room, I handed her an envelope holding a few bills, her allowance for the day.

"Why are you giving me this, Biby?"

"I thought you would like this better. You won't have to call me over each time you want to buy something."

"I don't mind, dear."

"That's all I can give you today. I don't have any more." She put the money in her purse quietly. It was so easy I wondered why I hadn't done it sooner.

After lunch, we proceeded to the shops. I kept my distance, letting her be independent. I watched as she took something to the cash register. She looked perfectly comfortable paying for her own purchases.

In the third shop, she sidled up to me. "I have something to show you. Over here." She guided me past several racks of clothing and then held a blouse under her chin. "Isn't this lovely?"

I agreed, sensing what was coming. "Be firm," I told myself. "This is to be expected. Hold your ground."

She whispered in my ear. "Could you could give me just a little bit more money this time? I don't have quite enough."

"You've got to budget. You can get it next time."

"It won't be here next time. Oh, please get it for me today."

"No, I can't give you any more," I stammered. "I don't have any more." I turned away, hoping to end it.

"Oh, please." She followed me. "Oh please, be so good as to give me just a little more." She was crying now. I couldn't stand it. But if I gave in, there would be another blouse and another. Where would it end? I would have to stop visiting.

"I just don't have the money."

"Can't you use your plastic card?" she begged.

I wished I had never shown her my credit card. I imagined saying no. She would keep wheedling and crying and finally make a scene. I would have to walk out. She would follow me, saying, "Please, Biby, it would mean so much if you could just get me this blouse. I promise I won't ask for another thing." I would have to get mean. "Stop it. I'm not buying it, and that's final." I imagined her looking shocked and hurt. "Biby, don't talk to me that way. Don't come here if you're going to treat me like that, Biby."

I took out my credit card, hoping the sales clerk would say, "Oh we don't take that card here," but she rang it up with no comment. Mama looked pleased, but I felt used. I blamed myself for being weak.

Outside, Mama clung to my arm. "Oh, you're so good to me, Biby. Thank you so much. I'm so happy to have the blouse." Her gratitude embarrassed me. It only meant I had failed.

Our visits continued unchanged, with me spending more money than I could afford. We never seemed to get back to having real conversations. She was no longer depressed but had no interest in my life. Nor had she asked about her grandchildren or asked to see their pictures. She acted as though she had never heard of them. When I picked up toddler overalls at J.C. Penney's, she looked alarmed.

"Why are you looking at those, Biby? They're for boys." Hearing the alarm in her voice, I put them down. A moment later, I felt a deep sting. To keep Mama happy, I had betrayed my own children. I pretended Brian and Evan didn't exist.

The week before Easter, Kresge's had some cute stuffed bunnies on sale, perfect for Easter baskets. I hesitated, remembering the overall incident. I turned away, then came back, slipped two bunnies into my cart, and covered them with my coat.

I planned to keep them out of Mama's sight, but just as I put them on the check-out counter, she appeared behind me.

"Why are you getting those, dear?"

I was tired of pretending. "For my children, Brian and Evan, for Easter." I held my breath.

"Don't say that, Biby. That's not true. You're getting them for you and Eveli, aren't you? Aren't you?" I avoided her eyes. She was whining, begging me to reassure her.

I sighed and nodded. "Yes, for Eveli and me." Once again, I had betrayed my sons.

Back in her room at the hospital, I sat while she put her purchases away. I reached into my purse, fingering the photo of Brian and Evan I carried with me. I gathered up my courage and thrust the photo in front of her face.

She smiled blankly. "Why are you showing me this?"

"These are my children, Brian and Evan."

"No, Biby, don't say such things!" She grabbed her comb off the dresser and disappeared into the bathroom. She turned the light off and stood in the dark yanking at her hair in frenzied strokes. "Don't tell me such lies. I'm not old enough to be a grandmother."

I went numb. Why had I taken such a foolish risk? Who knew how long she would stay mad? She paced across the room, still combing her hair and chanting over and over, "Don't tell me those lies." I didn't move a muscle, wanting desperately to leave but afraid to go. I waited while she spent herself crying, swearing, blaming, accusing.

When she had calmed down, I said good-bye, not knowing if she would ever consent to another visit. I chided myself all the way home for being so foolish.

It didn't matter that I was a grown woman and a trained psychologist. I was still terrified of my mother's anger. Just like a little girl.

15

Easter Eggs

◆

1972

After growing up, I realized that the times Mama was in the hospital were not the hardest times in my childhood but the happiest. It was a shocking revelation, a complete reversal of the credo I had lived by.

When Mama was home, holidays were never happy. They were filled with tension, with pressure to make things perfect. Mama loved holidays, or at least the preparations leading up to the holiday—the baking and decorating—but we rarely got through an actual holiday meal without her erupting in tears and rage, casting a pall over our spirits.

Despite this, I never would have chosen to spend a holiday away from Mama. When we did, I was surprised at how easily other people had fun. The winter I lived with my godparents, Daddy, Eveli, and the family Eveli stayed with, all came for New Year's Eve. Besides Eveli and me, there was Erica, who was Eveli's age. After supper, we three girls played a new card game called *Pit*. We rang a little bell and shouted "Pit!" when we had a winning hand. I thought it was the best game ever invented and wanted nothing more than to play, but I was worried about the grown-ups in the next room. They didn't seem to be having as much fun as we were, so I felt compelled to invite them to join us. Laughing, they declined, but I was uneasy. I wasn't used to grown-ups entertaining themselves. I was sure I had let them down. As midnight approached, I gave up worrying and copied the older kids. We ran up and down the stairs, banging pots and pans, whooping and hollering. From the front room, the grown-ups called out a gentle warning to pipe down. They didn't even get up. They didn't care what we were doing; they were too busy talking and laughing. Exhilaration swept through me as I yelled at the top of my lungs, "Happy New Year!"

Then there was my sixth-grade year, the year Daddy, Eveli, and I were often invited downstairs to our neighbors and friends, the Bachmans. We had stopped eating at the parsonage when Mrs. Hoffman felt sick during her second pregnancy. Daddy then moved us to a new apartment where every night Mrs. Bachman sent up our supper on a tray covered with a towel. She also kept an eye on us the days Daddy was gone.

On New Year's Eve, we went downstairs to the Bachman's apartment where the grownups sipped wine and chatted, while Eveli and I listened to records with Gretchen, their daughter. Gretchen was in high school, a year behind Eveli, but she accepted me as an equal, not a little sister. Gretchen was glamorous and beautiful, and I adored her. Sometimes I sat on the back steps just listening to her play the piano, wishing I could play as beautifully.

Only later did I understand what was so magical about those nights: they were normal. For the first time in my life, I wasn't responsible for anyone else's happiness.

We didn't *feel* normal though, not without Mama. I always wished she could be enjoying these good times with us.

When Brian and Evan were born, I pledged to give them the life I had yearned for as a child, a life filled with happy times—trips to the zoo, to the beach, picnics in the backyard—all of us together, especially on holidays.

I thought it was what Ken wanted too, but no matter how hard I tried, I couldn't make it happen. He had been so enthusiastic about having a family, but now that we did, he was spending more and more time at work. I knew he loved Brian and Evan as much as I did, so I didn't understand how he could spend an entire beautiful Sunday at the law library. Sometimes I pressured him until he consented to go somewhere with us. Then he would act distracted and irritable, and I would feel hurt. I complained that he seemed to resent spending time with us. Then we'd fight.

Fighting didn't come naturally to me. I was used to trying to please, especially the people I loved. But if he got angry first, it made it easier for me to yell back. We would egg each other on until one of us withdrew. Then we'd brood silently. Sometimes it took a couple of days before we made up. When he complained about not feeling loved, I couldn't stand it; I gave in. But nothing changed. We fought about the same things over and over, with more bitterness each time.

I told myself to make allowances while he was in law school. "You want him to do well, don't you? Be supportive. It's only three years." But he had graduated now, and he still worked weekends. I had waited and waited. I was getting impatient.

Now that Brian and Evan were three, I wanted to start family traditions, like coloring eggs together. The day before Easter, as Ken left for the law library, I called out, "Remember to come home in time to color eggs with us."

"What time?" He sounded put upon. I knew he didn't want to. I didn't care.

"Around 4:00. We'll wait for you."

After lunch, Brian and Evan took their nap while I hard-boiled the eggs. When they got up, they wanted to dye the eggs. I told them we were waiting for Daddy and sent them out to play. I watched the clock. And waited. Finally, I called Brian and Evan in, and we colored the eggs.

When Ken came home, I wouldn't look at him. "What's the matter now?"

"Where were you?" I hissed.

"I told you—I had a lot to do."

"But you were supposed to come home. We were waiting for you."

"Is that what this is about? Easter eggs?"

"I wanted us to do it together." I couldn't hold back anymore. Tears started.

Ken was dumbfounded. "How can coloring eggs matter that much?"

I couldn't explain that I had waited all my life for someone I loved to come home for a holiday. Now I had someone I could count on, or thought I did. I didn't want Brian and Evan to know that terrible ache. I wanted them to have their mother and father there together, coloring eggs and wrapping presents and going to fireworks. It had to be together. It was no good just me alone. But I didn't have the words to explain, because I didn't understand it myself.

When I cried, it wasn't just for Brian and Evan, but for my own lost self, that neglected part of me that got left behind in childhood. Without realizing, I had made it Ken's job to give that child what she missed.

"This has got to be about more than those eggs." Ken sounded exasperated. "You must be angry at your Mom."

"Leave her out of this. It's you I'm angry with."

"But you're angry all the time."

"Haven't you been listening? If you would come home, I wouldn't be angry."

"But you're way too angry."

"You're never here when you say you're going to be."

"It's not true. I'm here a lot. I stay with them whenever you go down to see your Mother, don't I?"

"But I want to do fun things together. You don't seem to care."

"I'm sorry. I'm sorry, okay? I've got a lot on my mind. Look, it just seems like an over-reaction. It's got to be about more than those eggs."

"But that's what I'm angry about!" I screamed.

We weren't getting anywhere, so I went off by myself and cried. I cried the next day too, wondering if he could be right. But if I was angry at Mama, why didn't I feel it? All I felt for her was sorry. Why couldn't Ken understand what I needed and at least try?

16

Doing Onto Others

◆

1951–52

Of course Ken was right. I *was* angry with Mama. But I didn't dare feel it. Too dangerous. Only once had that forbidden emotion risen up in me, surprising me with its intensity. It happened a few days after Daddy died, when Mama called Eveli and me orphans. When she went on, criticizing our hair and our clothes, her self-centeredness suddenly became so clear. I had never been able to see it before that day.

During the years I was separated from Mama, I began to form a boundary. But it was a thin, untested thing, not muscled by years of adolescent fighting, and it dissolved the minute Mama said, "I'm sorry." I slipped right back into my child-self, erasing any capacity to stand up to her.

I wasn't ready yet to see the connection between Mama and my marriage—between Mama and all my relationships with boyfriends, husbands, girlfriends. So many relationships, all in search of love. A long, lonely labyrinth. Since grade school, I had been substituting boyfriends for my absent mother.

In the early grades, they were boyfriends in name only. In the sixth grade, I met my boyfriend secretly at the movies where we held hands in the dark. In the seventh grade, we went to boy-girl parties where we played spin the bottle and kissed in full view of others. In the eighth grade, shortly after Mama was sent back to Green County, I fell in love with Clark. He was tall and muscular, with one curl that dropped over his forehead. He was so good-looking I wondered why I had never noticed him in my previous searches for boyfriends.

Getting Clark to notice me proved difficult. I couldn't easily talk to him because my desk was several rows ahead of his. I took advantage of every opportunity to smile at him, but he didn't respond. One day, as I was retrieving a dropped pencil from the floor, I glanced behind and caught his eye. He had been looking at me. Just to make sure, I dropped my pencil again. Again, our eyes met, and I flashed him a smile.

After that, every day was charged with excitement. I looked for opportunities to be near him, although it was hard to think of anything to say.

My girlfriends teased me about Clark. I would blush but saw no reason to hide my feelings. Romance was our main topic of conversation. Walking to and from school, we discussed French kissing, who was going steady and who was likely to break up. I knew they would spread the word about my interest in Clark. Eventually, it would get back to him.

Soon, two grinning boys passed me a note saying Clark wanted to see me in the cloakroom after school. They tittered while they waited for my reply. I felt ripples of excitement as I said yes. I told my girlfriends not to wait for me.

It was too warm for a coat, so I felt self-conscious walking into the cloakroom. I hoped the teacher wouldn't ask what I was doing. I was only a little afraid Clark would ask me to stop bothering him. I was more afraid the two boys were pulling a joke. But Clark was waiting.

"Hi." He smiled. My heart leaped.

"Hi." I smiled back.

"I was wondering if I could walk you home."

My heart beat wildly. "You mean right now? Isn't it out of your way?"

"My brother took my paper route for me, so I can today."

I was thrilled that he had planned it, almost like a date. As we walked down the stairs, I tried to think of a way to start a conversation. Outside my girlfriends waited on the playground. When they saw us coming, they turned away giggling. I hoped they would leave us alone.

"Are they waiting for you?"

"Oh, we usually walk home together, but I don't have to today." They walked ahead now, turning only occasionally to peek at us.

Clark told me about his paper route, then about hunting squirrels with his brother.

"How can you shoot squirrels? They're so cute."

Clark laughed. "We miss most of them. But they're good to eat. Ever have any?"

"Never."

"I'll bring you one sometime."

I agreed to try eating squirrel, hoping this would cement our relationship.

"I can't walk you home tomorrow 'cause of my paper route, but I'll see you at school." I hoped he would say something about meeting at the movies, but he was too polite to rush things.

At home, I sprawled out on the living room floor with Fritzi, my fuzzy calico cat. He was a homebody and a cuddler, not a hunter like Michal. With the radio playing, I stroked Fritzi and gazed out the window at the woods, daydreaming, not about orphans, but about my own romantic future.

Sometimes I wondered why I had always been more interested in boyfriends than my girlfriends were. And why had I started so early? Even in kindergarten, I was looking the boys over, searching for a boyfriend. I wasn't copying Eveli. She never gave boys much thought until she started high school.

It was only when I was older that I understood it was Mama who taught me to dream about romance—the all-consuming kind that promises everything but leaves you empty as a broken pumpkin. Only after therapy did I realize that this was my only way of being a person: by hooking onto someone else, first Mama, then a boyfriend—joined at the hip, or at the psyche.

Soon, Clark and I were going steady. He was my anchor, my center. I no longer worried who I would go to the movies with or dance with at the next party. Knowing we would be together every weekend made me secure and happy.

We held hands as he walked me home. Then we stood hidden in the trees in front of my house, talking about the day and planning our next one. We didn't have much to say. Mostly we exchanged long drawn-out kisses and gave each other hickeys while saying good-bye over and over.

Romancing with Clark in the pine trees felt easy and natural. I was merely following Mama's blueprint for love: lots of physical affection and no disagreements. That way we could feel one with each other and that is the feeling I craved with Clark. All I had to do was keep most of my real self hidden.

Only once when the weather turned nice in the spring did I invite Clark into my private world—my special willow trees on the lakeshore path. I felt excited as I led the way; he followed, carrying the sandwiches and fruit I packed for our lunch. I was sure he'd find the path as wonderful and intriguing as I did. But Clark looked uneasy. "Are you sure we're supposed to be here?" he asked, gazing at the fancy summer homes bordering the path.

"Don't worry," I laughed. "I come here all the time. It's a public path."

Clark looked puzzled. "All the time? Why?"

I didn't answer. I was sure he'd understand when he saw the way the willows grew out from the shore, inviting us to crawl out on their broad trunks and dangle our feet in the water. But even sitting nestled in this safest of places, he continued to act uncomfortable. He just wanted to eat and leave. I was crestfallen. I didn't know how to react to this rupture of our feeling of oneness. I had no words to explain what the willows meant to me, or why I wanted him to understand. I only knew I couldn't risk sharing any more secrets with him.

I was disappointed, but it was what I was used to. Even Eveli didn't understand why I liked the willows so much. In every other way, Clark was a great boyfriend. He was always on time, kept his promises, and never looked at other girls. I could count on him.

Clark was, perhaps, the only stability in my life that year. With Mama back at Green County Hospital and Eveli going to the university in the fall, my life felt on the verge of upheaval. I didn't want to think about it, but Daddy and Eveli were constantly discussing what they would do about me.

"Why can't I just stay in the apartment? I'll be okay."

"Don't be silly. You're just turning fourteen. You can't live alone."

"Yah, Biby, Eveli's right. You're too young."

"Maybe Mama will be home by then." Daddy and Eveli looked at each other as if they knew something I didn't.

"Maybe, Biby, but we can't count on it. I talked to Grace Hoffman. They have plenty of room, and she could use help with the girls."

"You mean *live* there?" I had only good memories of past times at the Hoffman's when Eveli and I ate our meals with them, the last time Mama was in the hospital. I had never been around people who had as much fun as they did. Phil used to come up behind Grace as she stood at the stove, run his finger up her arm and ask, "When's lunch, Poot?" She would tap him on his hand with her spoon and push him away, saying "Just hold your horses a minute." Then she'd do a little boogie step and sing, "Rock-a my soul in the bosom of Abraham, oh, rock-a my soul."

Still, I didn't want to live there. Losing my home and being separated from Eveli filled me with dread. I wished desperately to go to Madison with her, but she would be in a dorm and wanted nothing to do with me.

"Let's go and talk with Mrs. Hoffman about it." Daddy ignored my reluctance and pressed ahead. "She invited us over to take a look at the room you would have."

At the parsonage, Grace greeted us in her usual cheery way, then led Daddy and me upstairs to see my prospective room. "I would love having your help," Grace said smiling over her shoulder at me. "You're so good with the kids." I frequently babysat her children, Julie, six, and Marcie, two. "And we've certainly got plenty of room." She led us into the room at the top of the stairs. "I thought you might like this one." Sunlight poured through three large windows forming a bay. "Of course, it needs a little fixing up." She dug her finger nail into the wallpaper. "There must be a dozen layers here. We'll get this stuff off and put up something fresh and pretty." She smiled at me as though a newly decorated room would compensate for losing my home and my family.

I appreciated her trying so hard and didn't know how to say I didn't care. I only cared about bringing my cat, Fritzi. I finally found the courage to ask. "He's no trouble. He's perfectly housebroken, and if he ever did have an accident or get sick, I'd clean it up right away."

Grace looked perplexed. "Well, I don't see why we can't have a cat. But I'll have to check with Phil. He's not particularly fond of them."

As we stood in the foyer saying good-bye, Grace squeezed me around the shoulders. "This is going to be fun. It's going to be just like your own home."

I was puzzled by Grace's enthusiasm. Why would she want me so much? It made me feel guilty for not feeling the same way. She was eager to get started on my room and wanted to recruit Clark to help.

"That Clark is such a nice boy, and so cute." She drew out the last two words and gave me a sly look.

Once school was out, Clark worked with Grace, steaming and scraping layers of old paper off the walls. I sat on the porch swing, reading to Julie and Marcie, feeling guilty for having the easiest job. I wondered why Clark would want to work so hard when he wasn't even getting paid. By mid-afternoon, they would stop work, and Clark and I would go swimming to cool off. Then he'd walk me home, and we'd stand hidden in the trees, kissing and hugging.

With each day of work, Grace got more excited. The walls were almost clean, and she looked forward to putting up new wallpaper. She took me to the paint store where we sat side by side on stools, poring over the sample books. She kept asking which one I liked best. I had no idea. I had no experience choosing anything for myself. The huge variety of patterns and colors confused me. Grace seemed disappointed, and I felt embarrassed by my ineptness. Her efforts to please me threw me off balance. I was used to pleasing Mama, not being given the freedom to please myself. To get the agony over with, I settled on a pale pink apple blossom pattern.

As Grace hung the paper, something she had never done before, I took care of the girls. When I heard stomping and swearing, I ran upstairs. Grace held up a brush dripping with paste, paste smeared over her clothes, face and hands. "If you ever hear me talk about wallpapering again, remind me not to." She laughed, but I worried she would be fed up with me before I even moved in.

When she finished, the room looked beautiful. Grace seemed pleased, although she kept repeating that she would never paper another room. Each time she said it, I winced inside. I hadn't meant to upset her.

She helped me hang Mama's white organdy curtains in the bay window, and Daddy moved in my furniture. With Mama's white shag rugs on the floor, it was the most beautiful room I ever had, all my own. Best of all, Fritzi was there with me, at least for now. Grace had said we could try it. Lying on my bed stroking Fritzi and gazing out my bay window, I felt a huge ache in my heart.

Living with Grace might have been the beginning of learning to trust, learning to talk, learning to get close to a normal adult woman. But I related to Grace in the only way I knew how—the same way I had learned to get along with Mama. I concentrated on trying to read her moods, trying to please, and above all, keeping my real self hidden.

On my first day of high school, I felt scared trying to find my way through the unfamiliar corridors. After school, I didn't feel like going downtown for cokes with the other girls. I came home and dropped onto my bed, wondering what to do with myself. Why was everything suddenly so hard? I missed Eveli. It never crossed my mind to turn to Grace.

I longed to see Eveli and wished she would answer my letters. I didn't understand why nothing, not even school, made me happy anymore. I tried to please Grace but wasn't sure how. She seemed to want something from me, but I didn't know what. Whatever it was, I couldn't or wouldn't give it.

I usually retreated upstairs unless I had a reason to be downstairs. I felt out of place in the living room. Sometimes Grace knocked. She would come in, sit on the edge of my bed and ask me how I was doing. When I'd say I was fine she kept asking questions, trying to start a conversation. I resented her intrusions. I wasn't used to someone prying into my thoughts. Mama never expected me to talk.

But Grace kept trying. "I know what we can do." She set the casserole on the stovetop. "Let's you and me go to the movies. What do you say?"

"But it's a school night."

"Oh, so what. It'll be girls' night out. We'll sit in the balcony and put our feet up and eat popcorn. It'll be fun."

After supper, we walked to the theater while Phil put the kids to bed. I looked to Grace for cues about how to act. She was laughing, wanting us to have fun. At the movies, I relaxed. This was something I knew how to do. Sitting in the dark and losing myself in someone else's story was easy.

Walking home, Grace was bubbly. "Don't you just love Cary Grant? He's so romantic, he sweeps me off my feet." She poked me in the arm and we laughed.

I loved it when she made me laugh. I wanted to have more fun with her but wasn't sure how. Even though Grace was cheerful most of the time, I was wary. I kept waiting for something else to break through. Yet even the day the casserole slipped out of her fingers and crashed to the floor, she managed to laugh as she heated soup for our supper.

Only occasionally, a darkness, a real anger, flickered behind her bright happiness. I tip-toed, wondering when that darkness would explode at me. I owed Grace something. Sooner or later there would be a reckoning.

Grace frequently complained that too much was expected of her: typing the church bulletin, singing in the choir, attending Lady's Aide, and participating in every church and community function. And all for no pay.

I sympathized. It seemed unfair. I wanted her to stand up for herself. "What would happen if you didn't do it?" She didn't answer. She gave me a look, the one that meant, "Don't talk so smart."

Sometime during that winter, a women's club event she was responsible for weighed on her heavily. We all felt her tension mount as the day crept closer. She snapped at Phil when he asked how it was coming. On the big day, Grace was blacker than I had ever seen her. I longed for the next day to come quickly so her bad mood would be over. She explained why she was nervous, but I still didn't understand. We sat down to a hurried supper, Grace's hair still in curlers, her dark eyes flashing. Phil tried to humor her. But even he fell silent when she said it was nothing to joke about. She was really angry. I looked at her face and withered inside. I wanted desperately to make Grace feel better. I opened my mouth, but nothing came out.

Her eyes bore through me. "Well, what is it?"

I froze, like a rabbit caught in headlights, my hand suspended in mid-air.

"Go ahead say it. What is it with you?"

I stammered. Still nothing came out. Phil looked at me sympathetically but could do nothing to rescue me. I wanted to melt away, to be invisible. I knew I wouldn't be released until I said the right thing, did the right thing. Grace stood up from the table in disgust. "If you want another cookie, just say it. Just say, 'Please may I have another cookie.' Is that so hard?" I tried to make myself say something. My lips moved without sound. The long moment passed. Grace stomped off to get dressed. Finally, I was alone in the kitchen. Filled with shame, I turned to the dinner dishes, relieved to have something I knew how to do. I moved quietly, fearful of making any sound and attracting more criticism.

Looking back, I wonder why I didn't run from the table in tears, saying, yelling, "I didn't do anything wrong, so get off my back!" Because I couldn't. I didn't know how. I had no experience standing up for myself; my job had always been to hold Mama together.

I wouldn't have dreamed of complaining. If I had problems with Grace, I was sure they were my fault. I poured my feelings into the piano. It seemed to be the only way I could release what was inside. When I was twelve, after hearing our downstairs neighbor, Gretchen, play the piano, I begged for lessons. We couldn't afford a piano or even fit one into our apartment, so Daddy got permission for me to practice at church. Grace had a piano in her living room, but Phil didn't want me to play if he was working in his study. And after dinner, Grace watched television in the living room. I didn't mind walking over to the church. I liked the privacy.

I chose the best piano in the church, the one in front, next to the altar. I imagined people sitting in the pews listening. Sometimes I would sneak up to the organ and play a few chords just for the thrill of hearing the deep, powerful sounds.

Usually, I had the church to myself. But sometimes the janitor was cleaning or women were working in the kitchen. Phil came in and out as well checking on things or getting books from the library.

He would pass behind me and sometimes stop for a minute. I kept playing, expecting him to say something like, "Nice going." He never did, I supposed because he didn't want to interrupt. When he began standing behind me, I thought it meant my playing impressed him. I was flattered but wondered why he leaned over so far. He seemed to be trying to see the music, but I knew he couldn't read notes. I got used to it and kept playing.

When one day he rested his hands on my shoulders, I thought it was his way of saying he was proud of me. He stood that way for a long time before sliding his hands toward my breasts. I didn't believe he was really intending to touch me that way—not him, the minister, right in the sanctuary. When his hands reached their target, my fingers froze in mid-air. I stared ahead and prayed silently for him to stop.

It seemed to last an eternity. Then, as he walked away quickly without a word, I resumed playing, as though nothing had happened.

I walked back to the parsonage, dreading supper, wondering what would happen when our eyes met. Maybe I should pretend to be sick and stay in my room. But then Grace would come up and ask me what was wrong. I wouldn't know what to say.

I felt nervous as I went into the kitchen. I was relieved to find only Grace and the kids. Maybe Phil had a dinner meeting, and I wouldn't have to face him after all, at least not today, the day it happened. But as we sat down he came in, joking and laughing as usual. He lowered his head to say the blessing; then looked me straight in the eye, acting as though nothing had happened.

He must have known I wouldn't say anything. I was too ashamed.

The next time I heard him enter the church, I tensed up, wondering if it was going to happen again. A few minutes later, I exhaled as I heard him leave. Perhaps it had just been a weak moment, a slip he'd never repeat.

But, of course, he did. I could never predict when. Each time he came in, I prayed he would leave me alone. I couldn't understand how a man of God could do this over and over in the place he preached every Sunday. He had to feel guilty. Perhaps he was fighting within himself, praying for strength but giving in to temptation.

What did it mean that he felt he could do it to me without explanation or apology? Was it something about me?

I couldn't bring myself to tell Daddy what Phil was doing. If he complained to the church trustees, no one would believe him. People loved Phil too much. I didn't even want to believe it myself. They would say I shouldn't have been at church in the first place. It would end up being my fault, and I would have brought disgrace to Daddy.

Eveli was the only person I could talk to. When she came for a weekend, we stayed up late discussing all the exciting things she had done at college with her new intellectual friends from New York City, like seeing foreign movies at the student union.

"American movies are crap. So juvenile. Look at how American movies deal with sex. They won't even show a married couple in bed together. Isn't that ridiculous? Foreign movies are more honest."

I hadn't given the matter much thought. No one had ever really explained sex to me. I found out about sexual intercourse only when a friend and I looked it up in the encyclopedia at the library. It sounded so repulsive, as well as physically impossible, that I couldn't imagine why anyone would want to do it. I had discovered the pleasures of my own body secretly under the sheets at night. I didn't see the need for anything more.

I didn't even have an accurate conception of male anatomy. Daddy was so old-fashioned, the only time I had seen him out of a business suit was at the beach.

My idea of how boys looked down there was based on a single experience when I was five. After making a deal with a neighborhood boy, I lifted my dress, pulled down my underpants, and proudly displayed myself. But he yanked his pants down and back up so fast that all I saw was a blur of wrinkled pink flesh, like a big wart growing on his lower belly. It was so ugly I felt sorry for him and forgave him for not allowing me a better look.

I couldn't imagine discussing sex with an adult. My periods started while Mama was in the hospital. Eveli taught me what to do, so I felt no need to talk about it with Mama when she came home. The subject of sex, and men and boys, frightened and disgusted her.

"Americans are so backward when it comes to sex," Eveli went on. "Especially in small towns. So bound by convention and hypocrisy." Eveli sounded so smart, I felt proud. "I've reached the conclusion there's nothing wrong with free love."

"Free love? What's that?"

"You don't have to be married. You can have sex with anybody you want, whenever you decide to." She started to get that impatient tone, the one that made me feel stupid. "The double standard. That's what I'm talking about. All these rules. They've restricted women's freedom. Men were never restricted. That's what I mean about the hypocrisy. Free love is really about equality for women."

Once she put it this way, I agreed. Anything that smacked of second-class status for girls made me mad.

"I've switched churches, too. I couldn't stand the dogma." In Madison, she had tried the Unitarian church and had found like-minded people. Very intellectual. This appealed to me too, since lately I had been asking Phil questions he couldn't answer. Why would God keep innocent children, who had been born in non-Christian countries through no fault of their own, from going to heaven? Wouldn't God judge how well they had done with the opportunities they had? Phil always tried to get away from me when I asked this. The answer seemed so obvious: God would forgive. I kept after Phil, because I was sure if we kept talking, he would finally agree with me. Maybe Eveli was right about our church. It was just too rigid and dogmatic.

"I got tired of being expected to believe things that didn't make sense," Eveli went on, "like heaven and hell, and life after death. It's contradicted scientifically. Metaphorically, okay. But I'm not going to take it literally. It's something they made up for people in the middle ages."

Her words stunned me. I tried to push them away, but they had already grabbed hold. No heaven? No life after death? I rolled the idea around until it no longer seemed strange. Life seemed to stretch eternally before me anyway. Maybe I didn't need more than a lifetime. I plunged in, like diving into cold water. In a second, the worst was over. It no longer seemed so bad—to live with no hereafter. I would just have to make every minute count. Above all, I wanted to believe what Eveli believed.

Finally, I got the courage to tell her what Phil was doing. Eveli turned red. "That creep. He used to do it to me, too."

"He did?" I was shocked. "Why didn't you tell me?"

"You were too young. Jesus, you'd think he'd leave you alone. You're only fourteen."

"How can he do it right there in the church where he preaches?"

"That's what I mean. So hypocritical. All that holy talk and look what he's doing. It's disgusting."

"What should I do?"

"I don't know, Kiddo. Not much you can do except find another place to practice."

"I can't give up the piano. I love it too much."

"Leave if you hear him coming."

"Wouldn't that be too obvious? Besides I might never get to practice."

Such is the power of denial. If I just pretended it was never going to happen again, I could somehow maintain my innocence. But if I acknowledged the possibility of what was about to happen—if I stopped playing when Phil walked up behind me and ran from the church—there would be a moment when our eyes would meet, a moment of shame and humiliation. I might not be able to sit down at the table with him ever again.

I wished Eveli and I could keep talking, but she had to go back to college, and I probably wouldn't see her again until Christmas. After she left, I felt more homesick than ever. I clung to Fritzi like a security blanket. He was all I had left. Grace thought Fritzi was a nice cat, but Phil complained. He didn't like looking up from his newspaper to find Fritzi staring. I suspected Fritzi's stares made him feel guilty. I tried to keep Fritzi in my room, but if he was shut in, he would meow and be a pest.

Then Grace told me Phil was sneezing—due to cat hair.

"But I haven't heard him sneeze."

Grace just looked at me. "Well, Phil's unhappy about it, and if it keeps up, Fritzi will have to go."

My heart sank. A few days later, Grace told me to find another home for Fritzi. I cried as I told Daddy, hoping he would have a solution. He suggested we take him to a farm he knew of. I felt numb as we drove there, not quite believing I would have to part with Fritzi.

I was horrified to learn Fritzi wouldn't even be allowed in the house; he would be in the barn with the other cats. When I asked the farmer what he fed the cats, he laughed. "Oh, they catch mice, and at milking time, we squirt a little their way." Fritzi had never caught a mouse in his life. I put him down in the straw and ran out of the barn.

Daddy, seeing the tears streaming down my face, started the car quickly. A sick feeling spread through me as we drove away. Daddy assured me Fritzi would be okay, and I would feel better the next day. But that night, alone in my room, the sick feeling grew worse. I could think of nothing but Fritzi—how he had counted on me, and how I had abandoned him. I pictured him, cold and hungry, pitifully mewing in the barn, waiting for me.

By Monday, I was desperate. I found Clark at his locker before first hour. I didn't even care when I burst into tears in the crowded hallway. Clark, understanding as always, promised we would find Fritzi a better home. Perhaps his grandmother would take him. The sick feeling started to drain away. I knew Clark would do his best.

The next day when Clark reported that his grandmother would gladly take Fritzi, the sick feeling drained away, replaced with a rush of excitement. I wanted to rush right out to the farm and rescue Fritzi, but I had to wait four long days until Daddy could drive us back to the farm.

On Saturday, I was happy and scared. I only hoped Fritzi was still alive. When we pulled into the farm yard, I ran to the barn, yelling, "I've come back for my cat. Where is he?"

The farmer smiled, looking amused. "Your cat? He's around. I think I saw him just the other day." I hoped I wasn't too late.

"Fritzi, Fritzi, come Fritzi." My heart pounded as I called him. I heard a meow and saw Fritzi trotting toward me. He sounded indignant, as though saying, "It's about time. Where have you been?" I scooped him up and buried my face in his fur as he purred loudly. "Fritzi, Fritzi, I'm so glad you're safe. I promise never to leave you in such a bad place again. I've found a nice home for you."

Clark's grandmother invited me to visit whenever I wanted. I waited a couple of days, so Fritzi could adjust to his new home. Then after school, I walked the long way to her house. Fritzi lay on a rug in the sun, flicking his tail. I squatted to pet him.

"He's a nice cat," Clark's grandmother said as she smiled and scratched Fritzi's head. He stretched to meet her hand. I could see Fritzi felt at home. "You come back to see us whenever you want." I thanked her, but I knew I wouldn't. Fritzi was content; he didn't need me anymore.

Clark had saved Fritzi for me. He really cared, which was more than I could say about anyone else. What if Fritzi had died? I shuddered imagining it.

I felt so grateful to Clark that I couldn't understand why I had started thinking about breaking up. The idea seemed to come out of nowhere. It didn't even feel like my own idea; it was some foreign thing that had wormed its way into my brain while I slept. I pushed it away, but it returned again and again to torture me.

I longed for the secure feeling I used to have, of knowing Clark and I belonged together, of knowing we would never hurt each other. But the old feeling was gone.

The idea of giving up Clark shocked me even more than giving up my belief in heaven; it was as shocking as the idea of jumping off a tall building and flying through the air. Scary but exhilarating.

I could think of no reason for breaking up. Clark was always sweet and understanding, never mean or angry, even when I deserved it, like the Homecoming dance.

It was our first big high school dance. We were meeting another couple for dinner at a fancy restaurant. Naturally, I wanted to look glamorous.

I had planned each step—washing my hair, shaving my legs—the way I had seen Eveli do it. I hoisted my leg to the side of the tub, lathered it with soap, then swiped it clean with my new razor, just like Eveli. The soap came off easily, and my leg felt silky smooth. I was thrilled. It didn't even hurt. I was on my second leg before I noticed the bright red flowing down my ankle, coloring the bath water. I got out of the tub, astonished at how much blood flowed out of such tiny nicks without a bit of pain. I pressed wads of toilet paper on the invisible wounds. Then I started working on my hair.

I planned to wear it in loose flowing waves around my shoulders. I had washed it earlier, and it had dried in a tangled mass. When I brushed it, there were cracks of electricity. My hair was flying in every direction. I peeled off the toilet paper from my wounds. They bled again, so I wadded them back up.

"How are you doing in there?" It was Grace. "Clark should be here any minute."

Already? Panic rose in my chest. How was I supposed to stop my legs from bleeding? And what should I do with my hair?

"Can I help you?"

I was ashamed to let her see the mess I had made, but I opened the door. I felt humiliated as Grace's smile faded.

"Oh, dear." She tried to smooth my tangled hair, but it crackled with electricity. "What are you going to do with this?"

"It just won't behave."

"Here, let me try." Then she saw the blood on my legs. "I better get some band-aids. Oh, there's the door-bell. It must be Clark."

"What took you so long?" Clark asked as we hurried to the restaurant.

I felt silly and didn't know how to explain. I looked down at the ugly band-aids under my new stockings. "I couldn't get my hair to behave." Grace had finally pulled it into a bushy ponytail and tied it with a ribbon. I was sure it looked terrible; not like the glamorous hairdo I had envisioned.

"Nancy and Ed are probably frozen by now." Our friends waited for us on the corner in a biting wind. It was the first time I had ever heard a hint of irritation in his voice. I was afraid I had ruined the evening for us all. I felt ashamed, but no one acted mad, and Clark said no more about it. Soon we were all having fun.

That's the way Clark was—steady, loyal, kind—somebody I could count on. Besides, he was so good looking. He was everything I ever wanted in a boyfriend. I never tired of kissing him. I didn't understand my need to break free.

Then an article came out in the school paper. A stupid little social article. "Clark T's Biby G" the paper said, like I was a possession, like he owned me or something. That was it. I told Clark I had to break up.

He was bewildered and hurt. He didn't understand why I was so upset about something somebody else wrote.

We stood on the front porch of the parsonage. "So is this really what you want—to break up?" He had tears in his eyes.

It hurt to look at him, so I turned away. "Yes, I have to. I'm sorry."

"You have to? Who said?"

"No one. That thing in the paper. It made me mad."

"But I didn't even write that. I told you. I don't think of you like that." He sounded exasperated.

"I know, but this is something I have to do."

"But why? Is it some other guy? Just tell me."

"No, honest, it isn't that."

"I don't get it. What did I do? Did I hurt your feelings?"

"Oh, no, you never did—you've always been great." I was crying now, too. "I'm so sorry."

I ran into the house, straight to my room. I threw myself down on my bed and wept, wondering if I had the strength to go through with it. Could I stand to cause us both all this pain? Did I really have the right to make someone hurt that much, someone who had been so good to me? I could end his pain. All I had to do was say, "It was all a mistake. Please forgive me. Let's go together again." It would be over, just like that. I held that power.

I had no words, no concepts to explain my confusing behavior to myself or to Clark. I had no name for the unfamiliar, inchoate feelings that compelled me to act. I only understood I had to break out of the trap I had built with Clark. A trap in which I had to be the perfect girl-friend just as I was the perfect daughter—always sweet, wanting to please, with no ideas of my own. Mama's little rag doll.

Only later in my life, as I repeated this drama over and over, would I begin to understand. Out of a yearning to be loved and taken care of, I would recreate the cozy twosome I had known with Mama. It was my basic pattern for intimacy, my recipe for love. But to be loved, I had to give up my true self and mold myself to please. And when the price of love grew suffocating, a mysterious force rose up from somewhere inside and demanded I break free. It was like being held underwater, then pushing up to the surface for a gulp of life-giving air.

It really didn't have anything to do with Clark. It was all about my inner struggle to grow up, to give up being Mama's baby, to become my own person. Perhaps, if I had had the words, I could have explained myself to him. Perhaps, we could have found ways to give each other more freedom, to discover more about ourselves, even to fight and disagree and, ultimately, to grow.

I understood exactly what I was putting Clark through. I knew what it was like to lose what you loved most. I had lost Mama, my family, my home, Fritzi—everything most precious to me—without being able to do a thing about it.

I took no pleasure in doing to him what had been done to me. It hurt me, too. But I felt compelled, as though I had to prove I was strong enough to stand the pain, strong enough to survive on my own.

Grace was baffled. "But Clark is such a sweet boy. And so good looking, too. I don't see why you're breaking up." She kept talking about Clark—he was so polite, so hardworking, so cute—as though she hoped to change my mind. She reminded me how hard he had worked on my room. She had even cooked the squirrels he had given us.

I couldn't explain it to her, because I didn't understand it myself. I suspected there was something terribly wrong with me. Maybe under all my sweetness, I was truly cold and selfish.

Later that week, I was in my room doing homework when the doorbell rang. Grace came halfway up the stairs. "It's for you."

Clark stood in the doorway with a package.

"Hi. I'm not going to keep bothering you. Honest."

He looked so handsome, I longed for things to be the way they used to. I wanted to hug him and pretend we had been through a bad dream. But I held back.

"This was going to be your Christmas present. But since we broke up ..." His voice cracked, and he looked away. He thrust the package toward me. "Open it."

Inside was a fancy dresser set—comb, brush and mirror—enameled with a gold floral design. I felt so mixed up, I didn't know what to say. "It's beautiful." I stroked it lightly with my fingers then closed the box. "I shouldn't keep it, though."

"Don't you like it?"

"Sure I do. But ..."

"I want you to have it."

I felt guilty for wanting it. I hoped he would insist.

"It's already paid for, and I don't want to give it to anyone else. I bought it for you."

I could barely speak through my tears. "Thank you. It's really beautiful." He stepped off the porch.

"Well, see you around."

I ran upstairs to my room, cradling the box in my arms. I knew I should have given it back; I should, at least, have made that sacrifice. But I wanted to keep it—as a reminder of how much he loved me.

17

Homesickness

◆

1953–54

In the spring, Grace told me they were moving to another town. Phil was taking a larger church and they would be leaving Lake Geneva in the fall. Their new house wouldn't have room for me. I didn't want to move to a new town, but I felt hurt nevertheless.

Eveli suggested I apply to the early entrance program at the university in Madison. "You won't learn much in high school anyway." The idea of living close to Eveli thrilled me, but Daddy said I was too young. He found a small college that also had an early entrance program. He drove me there for the entrance exam on a hot day in August. Going to college early seemed like an impossible dream. I tried hard not to want it too much, so it wouldn't hurt when I didn't make it. When the letter arrived announcing I had been accepted with a full scholarship, I read it over and over to make sure there was no mistake. It was the most exciting thing that had ever happened to me. I had no regrets about leaving Lake Geneva. I was sure that whatever lay ahead would be much better.

But the morning of departure, when I actually said good-bye to Grace and Phil, I burst into tears. I cried all the way to Shimer College, confused by my feelings. What could I be crying about? There was no reason to be sad about leaving Lake Geneva. There was nothing left for me there.

Daddy parked in the driveway near my dorm, already crowded with cars unloading other students. I stifled my tears as we carried my belongings up three flights of stairs. I didn't want to look like a crybaby on my first day of college. But when I walked out to the car to say a final good-bye, I could hold back no longer. Daddy assured me I would feel better as soon as he left, and I started making friends. My heart breaking, I watched him drive away. I didn't think it was possible to get over sadness so deep, a sadness that I had not prepared myself for. I had imagined the day I went to college would be the happiest day of my life.

I turned and walked slowly through the dorm, the ache spreading through my body as I passed rooms where girls chattered and laughed. How could they be so confident, so cheerful?

I went through the motions of putting my underwear into a dresser drawer, hoping to keep my tears back, at least until I was alone. I longed to run after Daddy and cry out, "Wait, please take me home, please, please." But even if I could call him back, it would do no good. I had no home to go back to.

My roommate, Wendy, two years older, was sympathetic. She didn't seem to mind being stuck with me even though I was sure I was a social handicap. I acted like a sniveling baby as other girls stopped in to introduce themselves. All of them were excited about meeting boys down in the lounge. I was scared talking with girls; I couldn't imagine trying to talk with boys.

Wendy didn't mind coaching me. She seemed to know everything. "We should go downstairs about fifteen minutes before dinner, so we can mingle."

"But I don't know anybody."

"That's the whole point. We want a good table."

"How will we know?"

"Just stick close to me. I'll steer us. Just smile and ask the boys questions."

We pushed into the crush of bodies in front of the dining room. I tried to copy Wendy, who was laughing and chatting, but all I could do was smile and nod. When the doors were thrown open, a wave of students swept toward the tables. I followed Wendy, taking the place she pointed out. We sat down, and just as she said, the boys did the talking and joking. I laughed and smiled a lot.

Back in the safety of our room, I felt relieved the ordeal was over. I wondered how I would manage to go through it every morning, noon and night for the whole year.

"See, that wasn't so hard. You were fine. Isn't that Steve Goldberg cute? I've got my eye on him. Jewish boyfriends—if you can get one, they're the best. They're smart and faithful."

"What do you mean 'Jewish'?"

"You know ... he's *Jewish*." Wendy looked puzzled.

"How do you know?"

"I can tell." She laughed. "It's obvious."

"How?"

"Just something you know. He's got a Jewish name for one thing. I had a Jewish boyfriend in high school."

"I don't think there were any Jewish kids in Lake Geneva."

"In Lake Geneva? Are you kidding? There are lots. From Chicago."

"Well, I didn't know them."

"How could you not know? Anyway, don't worry. I'll teach you. The easiest way is the name. Any name like Silverstein or Goldstein, that's Jewish. Go around the table, see if you can tell me who's Jewish and who isn't."

"Okay. Reuben Chapman. I guess he's not."

"No, definitely Jewish."

"How do you know?"

"Didn't you see that special food they brought for him? He's kosher and can't eat non-kosher food."

The more Wendy explained, the more fascinated I became. Here was a whole world I never knew existed. I was grateful for Wendy's willingness to teach me. Her lessons seemed more important than anything I would learn in class—how to tell who was Jewish, how to mingle and flirt and find a boyfriend, and how to dress. She pronounced my wardrobe a disaster.

"Didn't you notice hems are down this year? You can't wear skirts up around your knees. You need new ones. Let's see those plaid slacks." I put them on.

"Oh, my, you can't wear those. You're bulging out of them. You need something more flattering, something that shows off your waist and hides your hips and thighs."

Now, in addition to feeling ill at ease, I felt fat and unattractive. I hadn't noticed how much weight I had put on over the summer. No one had told me.

"I can't buy anything new. I don't have enough money."

"Well, you can't wear those old skirts, that's for sure. You'll just have to call your Dad."

"I can't. He worries too much."

"Don't be silly. Once he knows how badly you need them, he won't mind." Wendy offered to call for me. They decided he should send the money to Eveli. She would buy the skirts in Madison and send them.

When the package finally arrived, I rushed upstairs and ripped it open. Inside I found two fashionably long skirts. I tried them on under Wendy's critical gaze and looked in the mirror. They flattered my pudgy figure. Suddenly, I looked like a college girl, even a little sophisticated, I thought.

"There, that's more like it," said Wendy.

Naturally, I turned to Wendy for help with studies. School had always been easy for me, but now I was challenged. Since I never had to study before, I had no idea what to do. I was completely lost in science, so Wendy suggested I ask Steve Goldberg for help. It was part of her plan to find boyfriends for both of us. Soon,

I looked forward to getting help from various boys and the joking, teasing and flirting over dinner.

After studying, Wendy and I lay on our beds, playing records and talking late into the night. Though I still felt lonely, I held my tears until after classes in the late afternoon when I could be alone and sneak away from campus. I would cry as I walked through neighborhoods where children played in yards and in the warm light of kitchens, mothers cooked dinner.

In those lonely moments, I consoled myself with dreams of a boyfriend, a perfect one—cute, smart, and intellectual, from New York City, like the boys Eveli met in Madison. But no boy showed an interest in me during those first dreadful weeks. I panicked, fearing the pairing up process would become a game of musical chairs where I would be left standing when the music stopped. I was so desperate to avoid being alone that I grabbed the first boy who seemed nice.

Harry seemed baffled when I began sitting next to him at every meal. Wendy acted disappointed. "Are you sure you want to get involved with Harry? What exactly do you see in him?" I couldn't answer. He never had much to say and didn't mix with others. I didn't want Wendy to know I just wanted a boyfriend and was afraid I couldn't get a more interesting one. I would have preferred Steve, the smart, intellectual boy Wendy liked, but Harry, at least, was safe. He wouldn't expect lively conversations from me.

By the time Harry got the idea that I wanted to be his girlfriend, I was already bored. I dreaded a year of eating every meal with him. "You've got to mix," Wendy coached. "You won't get a decent boyfriend if you just hang around with Harry." I knew she was right. I dreaded telling Harry, but at least I had been through breaking up before. I knew the bad feelings wouldn't last forever.

I hoped Wendy would help me find a more suitable boyfriend. Every night we talked about sex and boys. Just like Eveli, Wendy believed in free love. "I intend to lose my virginity this year," she confided.

"Here? How?"

"Steve's going to sneak up to our room. Want to help?"

I was jealous but glad to be included in a small way.

Steve grinned at me through the side door of our dorm, the door that was kept locked at night. I grinned back and opened the door. I wanted to linger for a moment and share the excitement with him, but we needed to move quickly to escape detection. My job was to run up the stairs and wave Steve ahead if the coast was clear. If any girls happened to be on their way down, I would signal Steve to make a hasty retreat. He would hide in the cloakroom under the stairs until we could try again.

We made it quickly to the top of the stairs, where Wendy met us. They slipped inside our room, and Wendy closed the door.

I was disappointed to be left out. My part was over so quickly. Now I had to sit in the lounge and wait.

Wendy's face was flushed with excitement when she came to get me. "It was so romantic, we played *Bolero* the whole time."

"Weren't you nervous? That someone would walk in?"

"Oh, I had the door locked. I was planning to say I had a bad headache and didn't want to be disturbed."

Wendy's reports only made me more eager to find a boyfriend for my own romantic adventures. If I couldn't get an intellectual one, then I would have to take what I could find.

I paired up with Scott, not because I found him exciting, but because he pursued me and made me feel good. He was tall and popular, a conventional boy, not the type who would impress Eveli or Wendy. But he was fun to be with and, as his girlfriend, I had a place in his social group. I didn't have to figure out interesting things to say; all I had to do was laugh and smile. It was easy. Mama's little rag doll.

I wanted to lose my virginity just like Eveli and Wendy. That, rather than true love, motivated me to whisper the idea to Scott.

He was reluctant. Night after night we lingered kissing in the cloakroom under the stairs. "Let's take a blanket and go out on the golf course," I would say.

"Don't be silly."

"We could go all the way."

"We can't. You'll get pregnant." He looked pained.

"We'll wait 'till right after my period. I can't get pregnant then."

"How can you be sure? Besides, it's not right. You shouldn't be talking about this all the time."

I couldn't understand what held him back. Perhaps because it was my idea? I knew the boy was supposed to suggest sex. My taking the lead might have thrown him off.

One night, Scott didn't want to neck, only talk. "This thing you keep talking about, the sex thing, the way you're on it all the time, it's not normal. So I talked to Jim."

"Jim? Why?" Jim was Scott's best friend, an older boy everyone respected.

"He agreed with me. You shouldn't be talking about this. He talked to his girlfriend. She said you have a problem. It's abnormal. They both think you should talk to the college counselor."

"That is so conventional! There's nothing wrong with talking about sex!" I laughed. Eveli had warned me that not everyone had a liberal attitude.

I was annoyed. Me, abnormal? Me, see a counselor? What about their repressed attitudes? Shouldn't *they* see a counselor? I was insulted. I had seen the students who waited outside Miss Rudikoff's office. I didn't want to be associated with them. Besides, I didn't see how talking could help anyone.

18

Miss Rudikoff

◆

1955

I spent the summer in Madison with Eveli. I loved being in Madison, meeting men at dances at the student union, sitting on the terrace and seeing the crowds of students from all over the world. I decided that when I got back to Shimer in the fall, I would have to break up with Scott. We had gotten along only because I didn't say much. I hardly ever expressed an opinion, so he had little idea how different we were. Mostly, I knew Eveli and her new husband, Leonard, would ridicule me if they ever met Scott. He was too conventional to impress them. More than anything, I ached for their approval. Leonard, a Ph.D. candidate in chemistry, had no respect for anyone except scientists. I needed to find a boyfriend destined to be a scientist, or a mathematician.

Scott was hurt, just like Clark. Long tearful sessions. He even serenaded me with his friends. They stood under my dorm window and sang "Let Me Call You Sweetheart." I felt guilty, but I had to go through with it. It would only get worse if I put it off.

After breaking up, I went out with a few different boys, hoping to find an intellectual one interested in science. But I had no luck. Mostly I dreamed of Madison. When, day after day, I fell into melancholy daydreams, unable to concentrate on my studies, I finally took Scott's suggestion and signed up for a half-hour session with Miss Rudikoff.

I waited in the hall next to a girl sobbing with her head in her lap. She wasn't even trying to hide her tears. I pitied her and felt glad I wasn't blubbering all over myself as I had my first weeks at Shimer. The pain now was harder to grab hold of. No more sobbing or burning aches in my chest. This pain had no name—only a feeling of discontent and dissatisfaction with myself.

Miss Rudikoff wasn't pretty. She wore matronly dresses over her short, stocky figure, and her hair was pulled back in an old-fashioned style. But her face was kind and accepting.

I sat in silence, watching her, wondering what I was supposed to do. Miss Rudikoff seemed to be in no hurry. She just sat calmly, and her calmness made me feel a little calmer, too. She didn't seem to expect anything. In fact, she acted as if we had all the time in the world.

Since she said nothing, I forced myself to start. I began with one of my easier complaints: I told her how disgusted I was with myself because I couldn't concentrate. "I go to the library after dinner and try, but my mind wanders, and I don't get anywhere. I tried to study all day Sunday, but I got hardly anything done."

I felt I was confessing a terrible sin, but Miss Rudikoff seemed unruffled. I expected her to say, "How do you expect to do well? If you don't work, you might lose your scholarship." Instead, she said daydreaming was a normal thing to do.

I left feeling lighter and signed up for another session. In the following weeks I voiced all my complaints—I didn't like the way I looked; I didn't like my hair; other girls seemed more sophisticated; they knew how to dress, how to act; I felt fat and awkward but could never stick to a diet. Each time I confessed yet another failing, I felt lighter. Miss Rudikoff continued to accept me, and I basked in her approval.

I didn't understand the process, but somehow I started concentrating, I let my hair grow long and lost a few pounds. I felt better than I had since eighth grade. I didn't want to stop seeing Miss Rudikoff, but I couldn't keep talking about my grades and my diet. There were things on my mind, but the idea of saying them out loud scared me. They were too big for words, and not even something anyone could do anything about, so why try? Like the feeling Mama's letters gave me, the sinking feeling when I saw her—I was too ashamed to put any of these feelings into words.

Then there were the things I thought about in bed. How I tried to think about something else, but how my hand always crept down between my legs. I held my body stiff, not yielding to my hand. Then the daydream, the one about a man forcing me to do things, how I tried to resist, but always I yielded, exploding in guilty pleasure. Then I would promise myself never to do it again. Why, why did I have this same dreadful daydream over and over? I knew there was something wrong with it.

I suspected the man in the daydream was Uncle Frank, Auntie's husband, the man who had initiated me into the world of sex. I felt ashamed to admit I actually dreamed about him, so I made him over into a stranger.

I had not seen Uncle Frank since I left Auntie's house when I was eight-years-old. Whenever Daddy suggested we visit them, I made an excuse. What he had done to me felt a lot worse than what Phil did to me in church. Uncle Frank tickled and teased me whenever he caught me alone, then whispered that he was going to pull down my pants and spank me. I ran away scared, uncertain whether he meant it. Then he would laugh and pretend he was just joking. His teasing was exciting even though I was afraid of him.

The teasing game went on for weeks, until a day when Auntie went out and left me alone with him. Within minutes, he sat me on his lap and put his hand inside my underpants. "This is our little game," he whispered. "Don't ever tell Auntie. It's our secret." He didn't have to warn me. I knew it was wrong. I was too ashamed to tell anyone.

I wondered if Auntie suspected something, because she hardly ever left me alone with him again. But once, when he was driving me somewhere, he pulled off the road and parked. I dreaded what was coming. I was horrified when he unzipped his pants and wanted me to play with him. The idea disgusted me so much that I looked away. He begged me over and over in his wheedling voice while I sat still as a stone, staring at the far horizon until he gave up and drove home.

First Uncle Frank, then Phil, the minister of our church. Why did these things happen to me? I knew it was wrong, and I didn't like it. So why go back to it in my mind, over and over? Why did I get pleasure from my fantasies when I detested what they did to me? I felt terribly ashamed.

I tried to imagine different ways of saying it to Miss Rudikoff, ways to make it sound less terrible. But even if I told her, what then? Could I ask her if something was wrong with me? I knew she wouldn't say so even if there was. It would be against her policy. Some small part of me thought I would feel better if I could just manage to get it out, to tell her this terrible secret, so terrible I had never told anyone. *Tell her, tell her, just tell her.*

I went into my next session resolved to tell her. I squirmed, trying to fish up the words I had rehearsed. I couldn't find them. I tried again. Miss Rudikoff was patient, saying encouraging things about how it's hard to talk sometimes. That's the truth, I thought. But I couldn't open my mouth. My mind was a swirl. I could think of nothing safe to say out loud. As the time ticked away, I got more nervous. I was sinking.

Each time I came close to opening my mouth, I would panic. Miss Rudikoff was good at silence. She sat calmly, occasionally saying little things. But I only felt more ashamed—of what I would say and, even more, that I couldn't say it. I left her office knowing I had failed. I couldn't sign up for another session and waste more of Miss Rudikoff's time.

19

Searching

✦

1955

I left Shimer in June, knowing I wouldn't return. I moved to Madison where Eveli and Leonard lived. I planned to transfer to the university in the fall. For the summer, I found a job waiting tables in a pizza parlor and rented a room close to their apartment. I would have preferred to live with them, but they had a baby now and had no space for me.

I still craved their approval. Even though I had completed two years of college, Leonard acted as though I didn't know a thing. He lectured me on what I should study when I started at the university in the fall. "You can't consider yourself educated unless you take physics, and you can't understand physics without calculus," he told me. I resolved to take them both.

Leonard had definite ideas about everything. In their house, there was a proper method for every task, no matter how small. Invariably, I used an improper method and was corrected, sometimes gently but more often with ridicule. I felt clumsy and self-conscious. Eveli was completely under his spell.

My only hope of earning their approval had to do with sex. As long as I was a virgin, they teased me. They thought it was high time I lost my virginity and joked together as they considered one boy after another as my potential partner. I savored their attention, grateful to be considered worthy to date their friends.

When I wasn't with Eveli and Leonard, I attended dances on campus—square dances, folk dances, and ballroom dances. I loved them all, and there were always plenty of men to dance with. I wasn't actually enrolled as a student yet, but I blended in and no one questioned my right to be in the student union. Some of the men were attractive, but the one who pursued me most vigorously didn't appeal to me. He seemed intelligent and wasn't bad looking. I just wasn't attracted to him. I didn't know how to say no gracefully, so when he kept asking for dances, I accepted, even though I preferred others. When he suggested a drink on the terrace, I didn't know how to get out of that, either, so I went along reluctantly. He wanted to walk me home, but I had an out, as I had ridden my bike.

At the next dance, I managed to avoid him most of the evening. Then he accosted me as I came out of the ladies room.

"Hi. How about going out with me tomorrow?" His eyes bore through me. He seemed angry. I supposed it was because I had avoided him. I felt on the spot.

"I can't. I have to work."

"Well, what night don't you work?"

"Oh, I'm never sure."

"You must get some nights off."

I laughed, trying to think of an excuse. "I usually have to babysit for my sister." It was a total lie. He was making me nervous.

"You manage to get to a lot of dances."

"Sure, but we don't need a date for that." I forced a smile. I had a sinking feeling I wasn't going to get away from him without hurting his feelings. He might make an awful scene, and people would think I was terrible. I would never be able to come back to another dance.

"Well, the next night you have off, it's a date." I nodded, grateful he was walking away. I was safe, at least for the time being.

I knew I ought to be able to say no, even if I didn't know why I didn't like him. Other girls were able to say no, I was sure. But they would know how to do it without making him mad. Why couldn't I?

I wished he would just take the hint. I didn't understand why he kept pursuing me when I made it so clear I didn't like him. I resolved to be stronger the next time I saw him. He found me sitting on the terrace a few days later.

"Looks like you're not working, so how about that date?"

Confronted with him in person, all the strength I'd mustered drained away. I didn't know how to turn him down gracefully. I was sure I would look foolish if I got up and ran. I was trapped, so I decided to make the best of it. Maybe I could even enjoy it. Even get over my initial dislike of him. There was something flattering in his persistence. He was buying dinner, and he really seemed to like me. Besides, no one else was pursuing me.

We walked to a restaurant and sipped wine while waiting for our spaghetti. I relaxed as he told me about himself. He was indeed from New York and majored in chemistry. The very things I thought I wanted in a boyfriend. Maybe I *could* get myself to like him. I had done it before, lots of times.

After dinner, when he steered me toward the wooded lakeshore path, I didn't even try to resist. When he pushed his body into mine, kissing me with his wet open mouth, I felt only slightly repulsed. "Let's go to my room, he whispered." I didn't protest.

He was offering what I thought I always wanted. A boy from New York City who invited me to his room. I didn't feel the way I thought I was going to feel, but at least I would be able to tell Eveli and Leonard, "I didn't need your help. I found my own man."

"Come on," he said.

I could think of no reason to object, so I agreed.

His hot, stuffy room smelled like old socks. I was glad when he turned out the light so I didn't have to look at the dirty underwear strewn over the floor. We lay down on his unmade bed. I stared at the ceiling, wondering what I was doing, but knowing it was too late to back out. It was over in a few minutes; just pain and no pleasure. I knew I would never go out with him again. He didn't object when I told him he needn't walk me home. I couldn't wait to get out of there. I didn't even want to tell Eveli.

20

Daniel

✦

1955–56

Before classes started in the fall, I moved into Grove's Co-op, one of the few racially-integrated houses on campus. Finally, I was living the life I had dreamed of. Singing folk songs after dinner. Hanging out with kids from New York City. Circulating petitions for political causes. Wearing peasant skirts and sandals and a long pony tail.

We ate our meals at the Green Lantern Eating Co-op in the basement of Grove's. The men vastly outnumbered the women, so I knew it would be the perfect place to meet a boyfriend. Some tables had no women at all. I sat next to Daniel, because I had met him on a rock climbing trip before classes started. He had acted cocky then, but now seemed warm and friendly. I liked his attention, but I wanted an older boyfriend. Daniel was my age, just seventeen, although he was already a sophomore.

I resolved to change tables to meet a wider variety of men, but somehow I never managed. I couldn't resist the pull back to the friendly group at Daniel's table. He teased me and called me "Gupes," his own special nickname for me. I no longer noticed his cockiness. It seemed just part of his New York way of talking.

I didn't intend to get involved with Daniel; it just happened. He was always organizing groups of people to do something fun—sliding down Bascom Hill on trays or going dancing or, as spring approached, canoeing or rock climbing. It was fun playing and laughing, and I loved the attention and teasing as our romance developed.

On weeknights, we studied together. Daniel, a pre-med student with a 4.0 grade point average, was appalled by my study habits. "Gupes, if you want good grades, you've got to study. You think I like chemistry?"

"Why take it if you hate it?"

"Got to for med school. If you get into a routine, it's not so bad. You want "A"s, Gupes? You do what I say, I'll guarantee them. French—it's basically memorization. You have to do it every day."

No one had ever taught me how to study. I was relieved to discover even someone as smart as Daniel had to work hard.

"Math—same thing. You do it every day."

"But I get stuck."

Get someone to show you. Ask Al. He's taken calculus." Al was an engineering student who sat at our table.

"I wish you were taking it."

"Don't have to, Gupes. Not required for med school."

I appreciated Daniel's help with studies, but he wanted to improve my looks as well as my grades. "You're cute, Gupes, but just a little pudgy. You'd really look great if you lost a few pounds."

"Don't you think I've tried?"

"It just takes will power, that's all."

"That's all? Why don't you try it?" I wanted to lose the ten pounds I'd gained since the semester started, but I didn't like Daniel telling me I should. Every meal, every snack, he monitored me. Defiantly, I asserted my right to eat what I wanted. When I ate "bad" foods, like ice cream or pie, I felt his reproachful eyes and felt guilty.

"Why don't you quit smoking if you've got so much will power?"

"I don't have to smoke. I just like to."

"Then why do it? It's not good for you, you know. What kind of example will that be for your patients?"

Unlike my past boyfriends, Daniel needed no coaxing into sex. Our only problem was a place. Daniel, in his logical way, reviewed our options. Men weren't allowed in the co-op, and Daniel had a roommate. We were afraid to go to a hotel. Even if we could pull it off, it would cost too much. As soon as the nights turned warm, we found a secluded patch of woods and spread out a blanket.

We were both nervous. Daniel concentrated on the condom while I worried about someone shining a light on us. It was over in a hurry.

"Did you come?" he asked.

"Come? I don't know."

"You'd know. Maybe next time." I felt cheated, but I didn't want to let on that I didn't know what I was doing. I wondered what was wrong with me.

When we parted for the summer, I quickly realized I would have to break up with Daniel. From the beginning I knew I wasn't really in love with him. I had pushed my true feelings aside because I was having too much fun. Our sex life was a downright disappointment. He wanted to do it all the time, but I wasn't getting any closer to having orgasms. Daniel thought I needed psychological help. He was convinced there was some awful secret in my past that got in the way. He didn't want to listen to my suggestions about how our lovemaking might be improved. Deep down, I thought I just didn't feel enough passion for him.

But breaking up again? First Clark, then Scott, now Daniel. What if Daniel was right? There *were* some bad secrets in my past. Did those experiences have something to do with my problem? Would I ever be able to *really* love someone and feel loved in return?

At the time, I thought my only bad secrets had to do with my Uncle Frank and Phil—the two men who had molested me. I had no awareness that Mama was the biggest bad secret of my past; that I was still struggling to break free of the patterns I had learned with her. I thought all I needed to do was find a boy I felt cherished by *and* felt passion for. I didn't yet understand that in order to feel real passion, I would have to take the risk of being more than a rag doll. I would have to stop hiding and dare to be more of myself—to express my opinions, my desires and the full range of my feelings.

When I returned to campus that September, I dreaded my reunion with Daniel. He came to the co-op to find me as soon as he got back to town. "Why didn't you write?" He'd written many times, but I only answered once. I didn't want to tell him about the boys I had dated over the summer.

"I kept meaning to. Besides, I decided we had to break up."

"Break up? Gupes, are you serious?"

I nodded. He looked shocked and hurt.

"But why? I thought we had an understanding."

"Come on, I didn't promise to write."

"I don't mean that. I thought we had an understanding about us." I felt nervous under Daniel's grilling. I didn't want to hurt him by saying I didn't feel enough passion for him, that I longed for my freedom.

The truth was I still didn't understand all of my real reasons. That I had surrendered too much. That I couldn't bring myself to say, "I'm not taking all the blame for our sexual problems. You've got a few things to learn, too."

I had played the same underdog role with Eveli and with Mama. It was safe—no one got mad because I never disagreed. It was comforting to have someone else make all the plans and decisions, just like having a parent. The trouble was I felt stifled. No one, not even Eveli or Mama, had ever controlled me as much as Daniel.

"I want to go out with different people."

"I quit smoking for you."

"That's great. Much healthier."

"But I did it for you. I thought you wanted me to." My hopes that Daniel would break up without a struggle were fading. He had always acted so cocky I thought perhaps he wasn't that attached to me. I wasn't prepared for the hurt look on his face, a look that reminded me of Clark and Scott.

"I know it hurts," I said. "But it won't last." I could hardly wait to come and go and do what I liked.

That night at dinner, I sat at a different table and tried to ignore the puzzled looks of our friends. Daniel stared in my direction. After the meal, he demanded we talk. "It's not getting any better. I think only about you. Why are you doing this? We were so happy together." I saw the tears in his eyes and heard the catch in his voice. "You're making me feel so bad."

I ached for him, just the way I ached for Clark, for Scott, for Mama. It was too late to do anything about the others, but I could make Daniel's pain stop. All I had to do was decide to be unselfish. Thinking about it made me feel like a heroine. But I didn't want to give in.

As word got around of our break-up, our friends turned on me as though I was a traitor. "What happened?" one asked.

"I just want to go out with other people. Is that so wrong?"

"But you and Daniel were so in love. And now he's so hurt." I had hoped my friends would understand, but they seemed to want us back together. I thought of dropping out of the co-op, but then where would I eat? Who would I be with? I didn't want to be that alone.

In the days that followed, it seemed everyone in the co-op was taking Daniel's side. He was the underdog now, and they rallied to his side. I began to doubt myself. Did I have the right to cause him so much hurt, to cause anyone that much hurt? I felt selfish. It took all my strength to resist the urge to give in.

The week following our break-up was long and hard. He approached me after lunch on Monday of the following week. "Gupes, Gupes, I can't study. I can't sleep. I can't go to class. I'll have to drop out of school." I felt the noose tighten around my neck. "Yesterday I walked all afternoon, thinking about camping and hiking, all the things I was going to show you." He broke into tears. "Gupes, please just take a walk with me, like we used to?"

"Don't cry. It's okay." I could stand it no longer. I knew I had the power to relieve his unhappiness. Isn't that what I had longed for all my life? To release someone from a terrible unhappiness?

"Does this mean we're back together?"

"Yes."

"Really?"

I nodded, feeling only relief. We walked, arms linked around each other's waists, the way we always had. To celebrate getting back together, Daniel wanted to walk to the other side of town to his favorite steak house. It took us five hours, and all the way, he described our future.

21

A Test

♦

1956–59

Daniel and I were together every day until Christmas break. Being separated from him for two weeks rekindled my desire to be free. Once again, on returning to campus, I tried to break up. But my resolve quickly withered, and once again I gave in to Daniel's pleas. I felt foolish after a second failure, and so resigned myself to sticking with Daniel, at least for the time being. Besides, there were lots of benefits to being with Daniel. He planned everything—friendships, activities, vacations. I didn't have to worry about a thing.

We never spent much time alone. If we were not in a group, we were in a threesome with a special friend, usually an older guy, someone Daniel looked up to. Someone I had a secret crush on. Our threesomes were cozy little families—a perfect way for Daniel and me to avoid growing up. We didn't have to have conversations and really get to know each other. We could just play at being intimate. We were like kids looking for parents, clinging to each other and scared to let go.

As graduation loomed, the thought of being on my own terrified me. I longed for a home of my own. I had not had a real home since eighth grade. But according to the rules of the university, women students couldn't live in their own apartments until they were twenty-three—unless they were married. Daniel spoke of "us" and "we" as though he assumed we would be together in the future, but he never mentioned marriage.

"When are we getting married?" I asked. I started my marriage campaign the summer before my senior year.

"Gupes, we're not even twenty-one yet."

"But we've been going together since I was a freshman."

"You're not Jewish. How would you feel about never having a Christmas tree in the house?"

"You never go to temple. You look down on anyone who takes religion seriously, and now you're saying you care about a pagan custom like a tree in the house? Isn't that a little hypocritical?"

"My parents would be really upset."

"Why is it okay to go with me for three years but not marry me?"

"Look, I don't want to talk about it anymore. We're too young."

I was enraged. If he never planned to marry me, he should have told me. He was the one who never wanted to break up. And to bring up not being Jewish after all these years—what a joke! I started pressuring him at every opportunity. When we would pass a jewelry store, I would grab his arm and drag him to the window. "Let's look at these wedding rings."

"Oh, no, not this again," he'd groan.

"Oh, look at that one. Which one do you like?" But he was already walking away.

"Why do you want to get married, Gupes? How would that help us?" He meant our sex life. He would pout and complain when I refused, while his constant pressure for sex oppressed me. I still wasn't having orgasms. At the time, this was called "frigid," most likely due to "penis envy"—labels I resented but couldn't counter. "Why don't you go see someone? You've had this problem for three years."

I fell silent. I still hadn't told Daniel I had orgasms by myself. According to the psychoanalytic thinking of the day, this meant I was sexually immature, too attached to my clitoris.

"I don't see how a psychiatrist would help."

"Why not try? You've got to do something."

I hated him then, the way he made it my fault, as though I was some freak that was supposed to get fixed up to keep him happy. He just wanted his way. But what if he was right? What if I never wanted sex with anyone? What if I could never really love anyone?

"Look, if you don't want to marry me, why don't you just let me go? I told you I wanted to go out with other people, remember?" Daniel looked pale.

I kept up the pressure any chance I got. Whenever we saw a baby, I would say, "Look isn't he darling? Wouldn't it be fun to have one?"

Actually babies scared me, even repulsed me. I wasn't sure what kind of a mother I would make. But if Daniel knew my true feelings, he would use it against me, so I couldn't tell him. Even though babies scared me, I knew that eventually I would have children.

"I thought you wanted a career, Gupes. I don't want kids. But if I did, I wouldn't want them raised by a babysitter."

"Well, I'd stay home for awhile, just when they're little." In fact, the problem worried me. I couldn't picture how I would work everything out.

"I wouldn't actually have a baby until after grad school. But I want to get married. I'm tired of living in the co-op. And if I can't have a baby, I want a cat."

"My parents wouldn't let me."

"Are you going to let your parents run your life? They didn't like you giving up medical school, remember? But they came around." The year before, when I had persuaded Daniel to take calculus so he could help me with physics, he discovered he was a whiz at math. With my encouragement, he decided he would rather be a math professor than a doctor.

We got married in the middle of my senior year. Daniel, by then a grad student, had a teaching assistantship. With our scholarships, we could make it on our own. The day of our wedding, Daniel looked grim and pale, almost green, as though attending a funeral. His parents refused to come. After our brief ceremony in the co-op, Daddy took us and our friends out to dinner.

When we moved into our apartment, all I wanted to do was nest, but I needed to finish school. After starting a major in dance, then switching to a major in math, I had decided to become a psychologist. I would finish my undergraduate degree in math but start grad school in psychology in the fall. I didn't decide on psychology until my senior year, so I had several basic classes to complete. All through my undergraduate years, I had avoided social science, because Eveli and Leonard considered it "pseudo-science." But I didn't care about their approval anymore. I had tried to become a mathematician and failed. I had to work very hard in my math classes just to get by. I knew I would make a good psychologist. Even before I took my first psychology class, my decision felt right.

In my first year of grad school, I took a course on psychological assessment, my first taste of real clinical training. Finally, something I could actually use with patients. After learning how to administer intelligence tests, we took up the Rorschach, the mysterious inkblot test. Daniel and his friends poked fun at it. What a person saw in a blob of ink was good only for laughs over beer. I lacked confidence to argue back, so I laughed, too. Besides, maybe they were right.

Our professor, just out of grad school himself, told us he would be giving each of us the Rorschach, so we would understand the patient's experience. I was tempted to read ahead to find out what kind of responses would make me look good. But I resolved not to. It was a chance to get some real answers.

Dr. Weatherly greeted me formally, modeling appropriate professional behavior.

I sat down. "There are no right or wrong answers. Just tell me what you see." He laid the first card on the table.

The design was perfectly symmetrical, shades of black and gray, exactly what you would expect if you dabbed ink on paper, folded it and then opened it up. It looked just like a butterfly or a moth.

"Looks like a moth." I laughed. I was remembering jokes from the previous night: *Doctor: "You seem to be seeing a lot of butterflies." Patient: "You're the one showing the pictures."* I thought I better add something to make me sound a little smarter, so I went on. "Well, it also looks like a vertebra—an X-ray of a vertebra—these white spaces here and here in the bone." I pointed, feeling more pleased with myself. Dr. Weatherly wrote on his pad without smiling or frowning. I wondered what he was thinking.

He handed me the next card. I gasped. "Oh, it's red, like blood." I stared at the card. "I thought they would all be black, like ink, you know ..." I was embarrassed. I kept staring at the design but could make nothing of it. Dr. Weatherly stared at his pad and stopwatch. The seconds ticked away, and the blot still looked shapeless. I had to come up with something—anything. "I guess you could say it represents birth. This opening here and the blood."

The third card, with a more definite shape, was easier. "Two figures facing each other. Stirring something in this pot here. And these red things are butterflies."

"Anything else?" I wondered if I should add the rest of what I saw. I studied Dr. Weatherly and argued with myself: "Oh, come on he's a professional. You promised yourself you'd be honest, remember? Just use proper terminology."

"Well ...," I continued, feeling reluctant to say more, "well this does look like male genitalia here." Dr. Weatherly's eyes opened wide, but he re-composed himself quickly. He didn't seem like a prude, so I wondered why this startled him.

The cards continued. I decided to stay away from the sexual stuff no matter what. Many of the cards reminded me of drawings in my anatomy book. Towards the end, the cards got prettier. Pastel colors reminding me of fairies and circuses. Finally, it was over. I smiled and said, "See you in class," searching his face for clues. He pretended to be calm but looked shaken. I wondered what could have disturbed him. Mentioning sexual organs? *But doctor, you're the one showing the dirty pictures. Ha, ha.*

I hurried home and pulled out my textbook. Quickly, I flipped through the pages looking for answers. Color shock ... yes, when I saw that red ... a sign of emotional disturbance ... indicates fear of own emotions ... fear of losing control. Damn, I thought, I should have been smoother. Oh well, maybe it's true. So what. Seeing human figures is a sign of emotional health ... but I saw only three. Thank God, that was the minimum for normal. Pretty close, but I had signs of more severe disturbance: excessive numbers of body parts, anatomical references, especially frankly sexual ones. There it was in black and white. Evidence of schizophrenia. Could it be true? I didn't act crazy. I wasn't anything like Mama, at least not on the surface. Maybe it would only show up later.

Back in class, I watched Dr. Weatherly. He seemed to be watching me, too. Perhaps he was studying me for subtle signs of schizophrenia. Or, perhaps he wondered if I had deliberately tried to make myself look schizophrenic as a joke. He found excuses to talk to me, as if he wanted to get to know me. Was he curious about a schizophrenic passing for normal? Or was he just coming on to me? Wouldn't have been the first time a professor made a pass at me.

Finally, I confided what was worrying me to Daniel. "You schizophrenic?" He laughed. "You've got to be kidding. I told you that test was nonsense."

"It's not nonsense. It's true. I'm schizophrenic, just like Mama." I was close to tears.

"Come on, Gupes, don't get upset. Look, you're in grad school, you're a teaching assistant, and everyone likes you. How can you be schizophrenic?"

I hoped he was right. There was no solid research on the Rorschach anyway.

22

Unraveling

♦

1960–61

Married life was a letdown. I hoped having my own kitchen would make me content, even without romance, but Daniel's restlessness interfered with my domestic tranquility. After supper, I cleaned up while he stared into space, drumming his fingers on the table, his mouth turned into a pout. Either he was thinking about a math problem or brooding about our sex life. If he picked up a yellow pad and wrote equations, I felt relieved. Then I could study in peace. But if the math didn't go well, he would get disgusted and demand we go out—call friends, go to a movie, find a party—anything as long as it wasn't sitting at home with me.

"But I've got to study," I would protest.

"Oh, come on Gupes. You can study some other time. Please." He would keep pressuring until I gave in. Most of the time, I still played the role I learned so well with Mama. Keeping Daniel happy—that was what mattered, not my own needs and preferences.

The only time I seemed to be able to say no and stick with it was over sex. I had hoped that somehow, magically, our sexual problems would evaporate after marriage. But sleeping in the same bed every night only intensified our conflicts. Eventually, Daniel gave up asking. He skulked around looking hurt and angry. In his silence, I felt worse.

Our differences were so obvious, yet we were blind to them. I needed reliability and safety; Daniel needed excitement and adventure. He felt hemmed in and deadened by routine; I felt rejected by his adventure-seeking. Acknowledging these differences and talking about them would have required a maturity neither of us possessed. We were each caught up in our own private struggle to survive.

Before my second year of grad school, we found a spacious flat with hardwood floors and large windows. My hopes rose as Daniel got excited about fixing up our new home. Shopping together for second-hand furniture made me feel we were a real married couple.

But within weeks we were fighting over everything—how I failed to control the cats who were scratching our second-hand couch, how I spent money on frivolities not in our budget, and how I had failed to do anything about *my* sexual problem. I could never hold my own in these arguments, so he always won. Then the only way for me to preserve a measure of dignity was to resist doing whatever he had made me agree to.

During one of those fights, he blurted out that he had had an affair. He claimed his sexual frustration had driven him to it. I was shocked. It had happened when my old college roommate, Wendy, had visited us during the summer.

"Well, what did you expect? You were never interested." He seemed eager to tell me the details—how hot it was, how sweaty they were, and how sexy Wendy's long red hair looked spread out on the pillow.

I felt foolish. I was so naïve—I had never considered it a possibility.

"Look, I'm a normal male. I don't intend to go through life without sex. What did you expect, Gupes?"

As always, he was justified. His behavior was perfectly normal, and in any case, my fault. If I had been "normal" or bothered to get my problem fixed, he wouldn't have had to resort to this.

I walked out of our apartment not knowing what to think. I needed to be alone, so I headed for the student union and sat staring at the lake. I felt like an idiot, yet somehow strangely relieved, less like I owed him something. But I was still mad. He had done what I had wanted to do for years, but at least I always tried to break up first. He had done it deceitfully and right under my nose. If he wanted other women, why, why wouldn't he break up when I wanted? But now we were married. He had me in his pocket, and he could do what he wanted. Finally, I was entitled to leave him, but I was too scared. If I had the courage, that's what I would have done—just walked right out. But where would I go? How would I manage on my own? I blamed myself for my own cowardice.

Instead, I went inside the student union and bought a pack of cigarettes, wondering if I would actually smoke one. I had lectured my friends about the evils of smoking for years, but the smell of tobacco had always intrigued me. It reminded me of the Turkish cigarettes hidden in the glove compartment of Daddy's car.

"Smoke one for me, please, Daddy, please," … I used to beg.

"No, no, those are for on the road for when I'm lonely." Daddy always refused.

I lit one up, feeling very daring and proud of myself. I drew the smoke in and felt dizzy and light-headed. I did have courage after all. If not to divorce, at least to smoke.

I walked home with the cigarettes in my purse. Daniel was waiting. "Look, Gupes, I don't want a divorce. I didn't think you'd care. I've been thinking … why not have an open marriage? We'll have affairs with whoever we want. No reason we can't go on doing things together just like always."

I took my cigarettes out.

"Where'd you get those?"

"Bought 'em." I lit one and blew the smoke towards him. It was a cowardly way to assert myself, but the best I could manage at the time.

"You? You're smoking?" He stood up laughing. "You smoking, that's a good one!" He smiled. "Hey, give me one too."

We had prided ourselves on our freedom from convention, from religious dogma, from social rules. Our open marriage was just another way to flaunt society. As long as Daniel could pursue other women, he would leave me alone. Besides I could do the same. It was permission to act on my secret crushes. Deep down, I knew we didn't want the same thing. I was hoping an affair would give me the strength to break with Daniel once and for all.

Once we had agreed on the open marriage, Daniel talked of nothing else but women: those he found attractive, those he planned to pursue, what his chances of success were, and how I could help. I always co-operated but was impatient to have my own affair. No one was pursuing me. I flirted with men I found attractive, but I was married and everybody knew it.

I complained to Daniel that our bargain wasn't exactly fair. He laughed. "You could always have an affair with Roger."

"That lech? You've got to be kidding." Roger made no secret about his open marriage and his attraction to me. But I could tell his wife didn't like the idea. She wasn't having affairs. I wasn't interested in a roll in the hay with an overweight middle-aged guy with two kids and no intention of leaving his family.

I decided to pick my own—a professor in Daniel's department, a bachelor from New York City. One night, I knocked on his apartment door.

"Hi, I was on my way home from the library. Thought I'd stop up and say hello." He looked startled. "Aren't you going to invite me in?" I reveled in his surprise.

At the end of our amorous evening, I rushed home, eager to tell Daniel. He got a kick out of my story. I knew he would. We were pulling off our "open marriage" with a professor in his department, right under the noses of the other married straight-laced math professors.

Daniel wasn't satisfied, as I was, with just one partner. He seemed to want more adventure, more intensity. He came home from a weekend and rolled up his sleeves to show me the round red marks on his arm. "Cigarette burns, Gupes. Kay did it to me. Pain as foreplay." I shuddered.

When we agreed to open marriage, I thought I would be able to come home with evidence that there was nothing wrong with me—that I was finally having orgasms. I longed to say, "See, I was normal all along." But sex with the math professor went no better. It seemed thrilling at first, maybe from the sheer excitement of the forbidden. But after a few weeks, I felt let down.

When the professor said, "You seem to be looking at me as your next husband," I stopped seeing him. I went home feeling lonely and lost, but Daniel wasn't there. I had no idea where he was. I lay down on the floor and stared out the window. I knew I couldn't keep it up. Our marriage was a sham. Daniel was finishing his Ph.D. soon. If I stayed with him, I would have to transfer schools. He wasn't ready for children, and besides, if I was home alone with a baby while he was out having affairs, I would go crazy for sure. Just like Mama.

I felt adrift with no rudder, at the mercy of some powerful current. I tried to remember feeling independent and strong, before Daniel. I'd let myself grow so dependent on him. Any confidence I may have had in the past had seeped away. Could I ever get it back? I wondered if I felt bad enough to kill myself. My only hope was to find someone else to marry.

On the following Friday, when friends gathered at our apartment for beer and music, I looked the men over carefully, just as I had looked over my classmates in grade school, searching for my next boyfriend. I stopped at Ken, a friend of Daniel's. Ken! Of course! He had been here every week letting me know he had a crush on me. When I saw the opportunity, I sat on his lap. He didn't protest.

23

Ken

1961–62

Ken, like Daniel, was a math grad student from New York. Otherwise they were opposites. Ken was gentle and tender; Daniel, intense and driven. Daniel planned ahead, followed a budget, solved problems, and told me what to do; Ken never told me what to do. He was too disorganized himself, living day by day.

Ken gave me what I had always longed for—the feeling of being cherished. Our passion was intense. We couldn't bear to be apart. And as soon as we were reunited, we would fall into each other's arms. Slowly, patiently, he took me across the chasm I had longed to cross. Finally, I felt normal.

At first, Daniel was thrilled. He enjoyed showing off our unconventional marriage and insisted the three of us go out together. He loved pushing the grocery cart down the aisle together three abreast. He prided himself on being above jealousy.

But when I said I wanted a divorce, Daniel was startled. "Why? I don't care if you have an affair with Ken."

"But we want more—we want to get married." He looked shaken, just like the first time I tried to break up. "I didn't think you'd care at this point. You'll be free to do what you want."

"But Gupes, I thought we'd stay together, keep our life the way it is."

"But I want a real marriage."

"We'll have to split up everything we own. Did you think of that?"

When we met to divide our belongings, I was surprised at the anger that poured out of me, perhaps stored up for years. Or was the rage necessary to cut our ties to each other? We had clung to each other for so long, it was hard to let go, even though we made each other miserable.

Unlike Daniel, Ken found me just right the way I was. His adoration lifted me. He didn't need to be with friends every night, seeking excitement. Yet the more time we spent together, the more uneasy I felt.

I was scared by Ken's faith in me. He believed I was smart enough to finish my Ph.D. But how did he know for sure? Maybe I had fooled him. With Daniel, I could play at school; he didn't expect anything of me. And if I didn't succeed, I could count on him to take care of me. But Ken seemed to be counting on me. He couldn't manage money any better than I could.

Money wasn't the only thing worrying me. There was something deeper, something shapeless I couldn't put my finger on. Anxiety crept up on me slowly, rising up in my rare moments of solitude. My feelings confused me. Unlike Daniel, Ken never tried to control me. At first, I felt relieved to be free of constant direction. But without it, I was floating in a vacuum. If Ken didn't manage things, then I would have to—not just the budget, but the whole vague future. The thought of functioning as an adult and being responsible filled me with panic. Being with Daniel had been easy precisely because I didn't have to be a grown-up. All I had to do was fit into his plans and be taken care of. Just as with Mama, things went along better if I didn't come up with too many ideas of my own.

Ken sensed my pulling away. I cried when he asked me what was wrong. I was too afraid of hurting him. I couldn't tell him my anxieties about our future. That what I really wanted was to be taken care of. Instead, I talked about my guilt feelings. I thought my friends condemned me for divorcing Daniel. I was so sure they thought I was scum that I avoided everyone I knew.

Without belittling my feelings, Ken listened. I felt reassured, so I went on. "I'm afraid no one will like us, that we won't have any friends. And we won't have enough to talk about—like if we took a long car trip or something." When Daniel and I took car trips, he filled the car with other people, the way he filled our time with activities. All I had to do was join in on the laughter. I wasn't used to carrying on a real conversation. When Ken and I were alone, as we often were, I wondered how I was supposed to act. Keep talking? About what? If I couldn't think of anything, I would get more anxious, feel more pressured. Then I would hide deeper inside myself, unable to bring anything to the surface.

"I won't have anything to say, and you'll think I'm boring." It sounded so silly once I had said it. *"And stop loving me"* was the part I couldn't say.

I was too afraid, too confused to say it. Despite studying psychology, I didn't understand much about myself. I still failed to make the connection between my romantic difficulties and Mama; or for that matter, difficulties in basic social functioning and Mama. That being with Ken required me to be more of a whole person than being with either Mama or Daniel. That, just as with Grace back at the parsonage, something more was expected of me. That's what scared me.

Ken didn't laugh at my fears. First, he listed all our friends and the things we had done with them recently. Then we made a list of topics—things we could teach each other for instance. When we took the summer trip we were planning, we would have these things to talk about. I felt better with a plan.

There was more I held inside. I couldn't say the part about feeling guilty for not loving him as much as he loved me, that I didn't deserve to be adored the way he adored me. That he would think less of me if he really knew me—if he could see my emotional flaw—that I wasn't able to love anyone deeply.

We had fun on our trip. We only used our list once, but knowing we had it relaxed me. When we arrived back in Madison, we had four dollars to live on for a week. It was the kind of fix Daniel would never have allowed us to get into. I bought pancake mix and beans while Ken called friends and asked to be invited for dinner. We survived, but my fears didn't diminish.

I pushed my fears aside by spending more late nights with friends, escaping with alcohol and laughter. I pushed myself to keep up with my work, no time for healthy meals or sleep. I didn't care; I just wanted to stay busy to keep from thinking.

At the end of the semester, I was so run down that I wasn't surprised when I got sick. It turned out to be more serious than I thought: hepatitis. Ken nursed me with Jell-O and broth. Staying in bed all day was a relief. A sick person has no responsibilities.

When the vomiting finally stopped, and the doctor pronounced me well, I had lost several pounds. I felt weak and had no appetite—all I could get down was bananas and milk. I felt vulnerable and scared. Something inside felt changed. I wasn't sure why, but I could no longer imagine standing in front of a class. When the new semester started, I would have to start teaching again, or I would have no income. I lacked confidence to do even simple tasks, but without the excuse of sickness, I wasn't sure what was wrong with me. I decided to make myself walk to the bookstore to browse and buy supplies.

The coldness of the air surprised me. I hadn't been outside in three weeks. After walking a short ways, my legs felt shaky. The store seemed strange, almost foreign, like I had no right to be there. A clerk glanced at me as though he were about to ask if I needed help. The thought of having to answer terrified me. I imagined I would have to explain and justify my presence in the store. I tried to hide. I had to get out of the store before anyone asked me a question. I only hoped I could make it home.

I tried to run even though I felt weak and out of breath. With my last bit of strength, I climbed the stairs and flopped down on the bed. I felt too agitated to rest. My mind was racing. I had to get up and do something but didn't know what. After pacing back and forth I threw myself into a frenzy of cleaning. I was at the sink, tears streaming down my cheeks, washing dishes in the half dark room when a memory flashed through my mind: Mama washing dishes at the sink in a dark kitchen, tears streaming. *I was acting just like her.*

It had finally happened—I was repeating her life. This must be how the beginning of a breakdown feels, I thought. It had been this way for her, too. She divorced Daddy. Then she got scared and begged him to stay.

I made myself turn on the lights. They glared. I wanted to hide, just like Mama. I collapsed on the bed and stared out at the darkness. A voice inside me started scolding:

"This is what you get for marrying for security."

"I tried to break up, twice I tried," I answered back.

"Well, not hard enough. Admit it. You like being taken care of."

"No, no I resent it."

"Now you say you love Ken? You know it isn't real love. All you want is to be taken care of. And you don't think he can do it."

I could no longer hide from the truth. I knew the right thing—the mature thing—would have been to live by myself until I felt clearer. I knew I was supposed to be able to stand on my own. After all, I was twenty-three. But it felt impossible. I knew I couldn't survive alone.

The wild thought of returning to Daniel took over. He would be leaving soon, taking his first job as a professor. Maybe we could get back together and try to make it work. We could start over in a new place. Then he would take care of me. I wouldn't have to worry about teaching or paying bills.

When Ken came home, I was so withdrawn he knew right away something was wrong. I had to tell him what I had decided, but all I could do was cry. He pulled me to the couch and put his arm around me.

"Still worrying about people blaming you for the divorce?" I shook my head no. "Is it about us then?"

"I've got to have a few days to myself, just to think things over." I looked at the floor to avoid his eyes. I felt terrible letting him down.

"Are you thinking about going back to Daniel?" It sounded so awful that I couldn't bear to admit the truth.

"I've just got to be alone—to get clear."

"Promise me you won't do anything. Not without talking to me first." I tried to pretend I didn't hear the anguish in his voice.

I promise."

I was so exhausted. I collapsed on the bed and fell asleep as Ken got his things together. When I awoke the house was dark, and I was alone. In my confusion and fear I wondered out loud what I should do.

"So now what am I supposed to do?"

"Just lay here until you're sure of something."

"Is this the way Mama felt? Am I going crazy? I should talk to somebody, but who? Who would understand? How could I ever say out loud what I was thinking of doing? It was too awful."

All I could do for two days was lie in bed writhing, asking myself questions and trying to figure out what to do. Ken called to check on me, each time asking if he could come over and see me. "No, not yet" I would say each time he asked.

"How long is this going to go on? I'm going crazy."

"I have to see Daniel."

"See Daniel? Why?"

"I've got to talk to him. To be sure."

I called Daniel, and he agreed to come over. Then Ken called again.

"Are you going to sleep with him? Tell me you're not."

"I don't know. I've just got to see him, that's all there is to it."

When I opened the door, Daniel looked stiff—either scared or angry or both. But he often looked this way.

"So, what'd you want to talk about, Gupes?" I started to tell him everything that had been going through my mind. When I started crying, he reached out to comfort me. I didn't resist. In a few minutes, we were in bed.

It was no better than it ever had been. I felt no passion. How could I? My mind was going off in a dozen different directions. Was I really doing this? Why? Did I really want to go back to Daniel? Was he going to expect sex regularly now that I had offered myself to him so willingly? Will I just end up going through all this again?

I felt confused when Daniel stood up to get dressed. "I thought we were going to talk," I said.

"Face it, Gupes, it's no good. I'm leaving in less than a week."

"Was this just to even the score?"

"No, Gupes, but think whatever you want."

Daniel's rejection surprised me. I felt humiliated but strangely relieved. Suddenly everything seemed so clear. How could I have been so confused? I called Ken, knowing he was waiting. I promised myself I would make up for all the hurt I had caused him.

In a few days, Daniel left town while Ken and I started our life together. This time, I would make my marriage work. I would do whatever it took, even support us if necessary. In my heart, I promised to be the best wife I could be.

With the memory of acting like Mama fresh in my mind, I pledged to do what it took to keep myself sane—finish my Ph.D. and work at my career. I had experienced my worst fear. I knew now I could disintegrate as she had.

I had almost given up on grad school during the last year of my marriage to Daniel. I had stopped believing I could be a psychologist. How could I counsel others when I felt so lost myself? But Ken believed in me, and gradually, I learned to believe in myself. With each year of success, I felt more secure, until finally I had earned the reassuring title of *doctor*. Since *doctor* is the opposite of *patient*, I would never have to be a *patient*. Such is the logic of the unconscious mind.

24

Birthing

◆

1969

As long as I was in grad school, I could put off the question of having a baby. Once I finished my degree, it loomed again. The idea of becoming a mother scared me. Babies scared me. Even at the age of nine, I recoiled when I was given a baby doll for Christmas. There she lay in her box with her little layette and tiny plastic bottle. She came already named: "Georgina." I didn't want her, but I felt guilty rejecting her. Mama had picked her out for me, so I did my best to act happy. But after Christmas morning, I neglected poor little Georgina. I tried to create the feeling of love I thought I was supposed to have for her, but it wasn't there. When I picked her up, I wondered what I was supposed to do with her. After I changed her clothes she didn't interest me. Yet I felt an overwhelming responsibility for her. I was sure I was failing to give her the doll-life she deserved.

As a teen-ager, I took babysitting jobs but always with children who were at least two-years old. I enjoyed reading them stories and playing. I didn't even mind changing diapers. It was the tiny babies who scared me.

And yet I longed for children of my own. If only I could skip the scary part. I never reached out to hold a newborn the way other women did. I tried to keep my fear from becoming obvious. It was my most shameful secret: babies scared me so much they repulsed me—their red rawness, their transparent skin, their utter vulnerability.

Unlike Daniel, Ken often mentioned how much he looked forward to having a family. This was, indeed, one of the reasons I married him. Whenever Ken talked about having a baby, my panic grew. Finally, I confessed my shameful secret. Ken wouldn't hear my doubts. He was sure I would be a great mother, regardless of what I said. No matter what awful things I told him about myself, Ken always seemed to believe in me. I wanted to believe he was right.

When Ken started law school—he had lost interest in finishing his math degree—I felt secure enough in our future to try getting pregnant. I went into labor when Ken was halfway through law school. Between contractions, I remembered a movie we had seen about missionaries in Hawaii. The missionary's wife was struggling in childbirth when the native midwives said to the husband, "Your wife will die unless we crush the infant's skull." The missionary and his wife looked at each other in horror. They agreed to risk her life rather than kill the baby. I thought they were crazy. I was certain I would never make such a stupid choice.

My labor started six weeks early, not unusual with twins. There were lots of worried doctors and nurses running in and out, hooking me up to machines and monitors. When I realized I felt the same as the missionary's wife, I was shocked. *Me? Willing to die?* It couldn't be.

Suddenly I realized what was happening. *I was experiencing love.* I was capable of love—real love! I loved my unborn children enough to die for them. Finally, I had earned my right to be a member of the human race.

We brought Evan home first. Brian, still under five pounds, had to spend a few more days in the hospital. We laid Evan in his crib, his knees curled up under him, his little rump in the air. I lay on the bed, tired but too excited to sleep. When Evan cried a few minutes later, I felt liquid dribble out of my breast. I was amazed. Did some invisible cord still tie me to him? I hadn't anticipated being part of anything this big and mysterious. I found myself in an age-old drama over which I had little control and in which I played only a tiny part. My heart felt stretched wide open.

The swelling of love sustained me through the stressful days and nights. Since I had never cared for an infant or seen one cared for, I felt clumsy. Daily, I feared I would be deficient in some vital way, like those lab monkeys raised without mothers who let their infants starve.

I couldn't help but think of Mama and wonder how she had managed. Did she feel the same love and suffer the same fears? She must have, and Daddy, too. I felt closer to them both, as if I had crossed a river I had never known was there. Now I stood shoulder to shoulder with them.

25

Dreams and Daydreams

1972

Towards the end of grad school, I dreamed of Mama. She was chasing me up and down the scaffolding of a half-built house, scowling, threatening me with a long, black whip. I awoke frightened, puzzled over the dream. Why, when Mama had never lifted a finger against me, would I dream this?

Years later, I realized the scaffolding represented my adult self. I was building the self I wanted to become—sturdy and able to stand on my own. But Mama lived there too, threatening me with craziness. Before I could live peacefully in my house, I would have to tame her, whip and all.

But I would have scoffed at this interpretation at the time. I was sure I had banished Mama's power over me simply by refusing to see her. My unconscious dreaming mind was reminding me I was avoiding something important. In order to finish growing up, I would have to face her.

When I did, I slid right back into being a child. I had made no progress in being a grown-up in her presence. That I was taken for one in the rest of my life only made me feel like a phony. Underneath, I was still that desperate little girl, willing to go to great lengths to secure Mama's love. Visit after visit, I catered to her whims, yet she asked no more questions about my life. What I wanted felt so close yet so out of reach. She could act so normal. To me, her craziness appeared almost willful, something she deliberately used to avoid unpleasant realities. It was tempting to believe she could set it aside if she really wanted to; if she loved me enough.

I couldn't help but remember Daddy's refrain throughout my childhood: "Please Paula, be reasonable." He must have felt the same frustration, the same heartbreak.

When I was a teen-ager, Daddy and I spent hours talking about Mama. I was still hoping we could find a way to get her out of the hospital and bring her home.

"What if we owned our own house? Don't you think she'd be all right then?"

Daddy sighed. "It wouldn't work, Biby. I'm on the road all week. She'd be alone, and sooner or later, she'd get into trouble."

"She used to be all right. When we lived in Delavan."

"Yah, that's when she got into trouble in the first place."

"What trouble?"

"Yah, yah. It's kind of complicated, Biby." Daddy looked uncomfortable.

This was the part of the story that often turned vague. I had to beg for the details. Only when I was in my twenties did he explain how she had been sent to the hospital in the first place.

"It started earlier, on our trip south. Of course, I didn't realize it at the time. It was a scary time for us with the war starting and all. We didn't know if Hitler would attack Switzerland, and I didn't know if I'd be able to get shipments. My whole business depended on imports. That's why we decided to look for some textile suppliers here in this country. You girls were still little—three and seven."

"Traveling was hard on Mama. She worried about every little thing, like getting your clothes washed—you know how fussy she is. I tried to tell her, 'Paula, please relax—you're wearing yourself out.' But you know how stubborn she can be. We were in North Carolina eating at a restaurant. I was talking with the hostess, and Paula was very quiet. I didn't think anything of it until we got back to the tourist home. Then, out of nowhere, she accused me of going behind her back with this woman." He sighed, looked out the window and shook his head. "How could she think it? How could she say those terrible things? I don't know."

It pained me to see him suffer from rebukes made so many years ago. I couldn't remember this trip, but of course I had seen the photographs—Eveli and me in dresses sewn by Mama, feeding birds in a park or standing with an Indian chief. This was the first time I had heard the dark side of the trip. I could easily imagine Daddy, handsome and outgoing, flirting with the hostess. I had seen him charm my own friends. And Mama, sensitive as she was, would have felt rejected.

"I told her, 'How can you think that of me, Paula, that's crazy talk. When would I have the time?' I didn't take it seriously until she started that crazy business with the grocer in Delavan."

"What crazy business?"

Daddy looked embarrassed. "Oh, that grocer at the National Tea store she made trouble for."

"Nobody ever told me."

"She was lonely, you know, and she didn't see many people, so when he was friendly, she got the wrong idea. She wrote him notes on pink stationery suggesting all kinds of things. But he was engaged, and he asked her to stop. When she kept it up, he went to the police. Can you imagine how I felt, the police chief calling me and telling me my wife is throwing herself at a grocer? And at the same time, she's accusing me of having affairs. It didn't make any sense."

It was classic projection. Accusing Daddy of what she herself was doing.

"So what happened with the grocer?"

"The police chief told me I should control my wife. I pleaded with her—we even had some talks with Rev. Frieling—and we both warned her. But she wouldn't listen. The grocer got a court order, which she violated. That was all they needed to send her to Mendota."

"That's why? Because she wrote notes to a grocer?"

"She wouldn't stop. She wouldn't recognize that the man wanted to be left alone. A person has a right not to be bothered. In court, a doctor testified she was mentally ill."

"That's all there was to it?" I was shocked a person could get locked up for life for doing so little.

Years later, it still shocked me. It had been almost thirty years since she wrote those notes to the grocer. Even if Mama had crazy ideas, she still had a right to live her life. Lots of people had crazy ideas, and they weren't locked up. I still felt it fell to me to right this wrong. Now that treatment ideas for mental patients were finally changing, I could press my case to get Mama back into the community.

Despite my failure to put Mama on an allowance, my fantasies filled every idle moment, whether driving or waiting for an elevator. All I would have to do was get her on Social Security. I was sure she could take care of an apartment. She used to be so good at managing money. The more I thought about it, the more frustrated I got. In my head, I scolded myself: "Go down there and tell the social worker. You've got to stick up for her. Give her a chance. Look how little chance she's had to live her own life. Twenty years in that hell hole. Not able to go outside or take a walk downtown to go shopping by herself. She deserves a little happiness. If you don't help her, who will?"

Then I would imagine her in an apartment somewhere in Madison, maybe that complex for the elderly. I even drove by one to have a look. How happy she would be to have her own little place, how grateful. I would stop by with groceries. We'd have a snack before I went home.

That's when the daydream ran into trouble. When she would say, "You couldn't leave me a little more money, could you?"

"But I gave you your allowance. I can't give you any more."

"But I need some things. Please, couldn't you give me a little more?"

"I have to pay for my own groceries, too."

"No, you don't. You could eat with me. I could cook for you."

"I've got to get going." I'd give her five dollars, just to quiet her.

"You don't have to go yet, Biby. Stay for a while."

"But I have children."

"Don't tell me those lies." She'd cry and cling to me.

"I have to go." I would have to pull myself away and worry all night, wondering what she might do after I left.

The fantasy always ended in the same place—self blame. I was too weak or too selfish. I should be firm with her. Or I shouldn't care about money. One way or the other, it was up to me to make Mama's life better.

Late that summer, right after my thirty-fourth birthday, Mama's social worker informed me that Green County Hospital was closing. Wisconsin had joined the nationwide movement to de-institutionalize mental patients. Mama, along with others at Green County, would be moved to a less restrictive community setting.

"Would you like me to try to find a placement for your mother in Madison, closer to your home?"

Here it was. The perfect opportunity. Mama's social worker was on the phone. It was the right time to ask, "Do you think she's capable of living on her own? Could you help me set that up?" But now that I had my chance, I was too scared. I wanted to say, "Please don't leave me alone with her." Instead the adult in me answered. "That sounds good."

"We'll keep you posted."

I intended to call the social worker back and ask about Mama living in her own apartment, but I had other problems. After losing my teaching position, I had started a new job at the Dane County Mental Health Center. After a month, I still didn't feel part of the clinic. The fights at staff meetings didn't help. Then, there were angry memos and furtive conversations behind closed doors. Tension permeated the air. After two people were fired, I felt too anxious to concentrate. My thoughts were turning paranoid, more and more like Mama. Everything seemed to be crumbling. Everyday I felt more and more like an impostor.

Then, I got sick. The fever and headaches stopped after a week, but the diarrhea continued. I kept losing weight. Finally, my doctor prescribed morphine.

Morphine? I feared I'd turn into an addict.

He assured me I wouldn't. The morphine controlled the diarrhea, but I felt weak and defeated. I begged him to sign a form saying I needed a medical leave. I wanted to stay home and collect disability insurance. I wanted to be taken care of.

"It's just a virus," he said. "You'll be fine."

"No, no I won't," I wanted to say. "I'm falling apart. Please help me. I can't do it anymore. I tried, but it's too hard."

Sometimes I thought of calling a therapist, but I was sure therapy couldn't help me. A therapist couldn't change Mama. All a therapist would say was that I should concentrate on my own life and stop worrying about Mama.

I remembered the time I had been sick with hepatitis, when I stood at the sink in the dark, crying. Just like Mama. Since then, I had been on guard. Forcing myself to act strong. Now I was finally unraveling, like a sweater with a loose thread. You pull on it, and the whole thing comes apart. I couldn't hold it together anymore. I was thirty-four, Mama's age when she started coming apart.

Every morning I felt exhausted but stumbled ahead anyway. I had to work to pay the bills. My mind in a jumble, I hurried Brian and Evan through breakfast. After dropping them off at nursery school, I was often late.

One morning, later than usual, I pulled into the parking ramp and felt the sudden darkness surround me. I hated the ramp. The smelly, stale air, the massive concrete, like a prison. Worse was my anxiety about finding a spot on the first floor. My terror mounted as I drove up one, two, three levels. Still nothing, and I was already late. My heart beat faster as I crawled up to the next level, higher than I had ever gone before. Up still farther, I drove out onto the top, saw the open sky and felt a giddy rush.

The yawning space pulled me toward it. I felt a sudden impulse to press the gas pedal down, to surge through that guard rail. The power of it. The freedom of sailing though space, like letting go of a huge breath. What if I did it? What if I couldn't stop myself?

"Look down," I told myself. "Keep your eyes on the ground, that spot right in front of the car. Don't look at the sky. Think of Brian and Evan. Go slow. Slow and steady. You can do it. Just get down. You never have to come up here again, I promise, just get down."

My heart pounded as I pulled into a two-hour meter on the ground level. I would get a ticket. So what.

It was almost impossible to concentrate at work. My mind went in dozens of directions: Mama, the hospital closing, fighting with Ken, the parking ramp. I didn't really want to die, but the image of the open sky, seductively offering relief, stayed with me.

Driving home, I usually lulled myself with daydreams, and that day I needed a happy one. I pictured Mama set up in her own cute little apartment in that complex for the elderly. We would go to garage sales and find bargains to fix it up. I would bring her home for Thanksgiving, and she would cook red cabbage. I would tell her how it turned blue when Eveli and I tried to make it. We didn't know what we did wrong. We would laugh. Then we would bake Christmas cookies, and she would let Brian and Evan decorate them. After she was on an allowance, what could go wrong? She was too old for romantic adventures. She could get sick of course, even cancer. Suddenly, I pictured Mama semi-conscious on white sheets, moaning in pain.

"Please help me, Biby, please, please." She writhes under the sheets. I have nothing to give her for the unbearable pain. I'm helpless to alleviate her suffering. I can barely stand to be with her. I don't know what to do. Then I think of something. Have I the courage? Yes, I think bravely. I'll do it for her sake. Let them throw me in prison. I plunge the needle deeply into her arm and watch her face relax. At last, her suffering is over. I feel complete relief.

Suddenly, I realized I've had this daydream before, perhaps several times. Why? And why did I find this morbid fantasy so comforting?

The answer hit me hard: *I'm murdering Mama.* It's me—not cancer—killing her in this daydream. The depth of my rage startled me. It was like cleaning a closet over and over, going through the same old tired junk, and suddenly uncovering a human skull.

I used my best clinical skills to calm myself: "You're not really going to murder her, it's just a fantasy, a way of telling yourself that you're angry."

"Yes, yes, exactly," I answer. "I'm not really going to do it. I just couldn't admit I was angry. I was trying so hard not to be selfish." Relief poured through me, just to know I wasn't going to do anything terrible to myself or anyone else.

I called the social worker at Green County Hospital and told her to place my mother anywhere but in Madison, anywhere but close to me. I told her I would have to stop visiting for a while. She didn't ask why. After that, the urge to drive off the top of the parking ramp and the daydreams about cancer stopped.

26

Awakening

✦

1973

When I married Ken, I was determined never to go through another divorce. I had such high hopes for Ken and me—supporting each other's careers, sharing child care and household work. I thought I had everything figured out. I tried so hard, yet it wasn't working. My life felt like it was crumbling in my hands.

I knew we should see a therapist. I would have recommended it for anyone else, but I didn't believe it could help us. After years of struggle, I was worn out. I couldn't find the will to work at our marriage any more. I had no more love in my heart, only anger. I only wanted to blame Ken.

I still hadn't admitted my fears of therapy. I was afraid of being found crazy like Mama. I was ashamed of having a mentally ill mother and was afraid that needing therapy made me more like her.

When Ken told me he couldn't stand my anger, my coldness, my treating him like a non-person, I knew it was true. I had acted like that. He said he needed to move out for awhile. The tension between us had become unbearable.

We sat in our living room and cried, wondering how it could have gotten this bad, how we would tell Brian and Evan. We couldn't imagine divorce. Too painful. This was just a separation—so we could recover. We would still see each other. Maybe we could talk things out if we weren't aggravating each other every day.

Sad as it was, the thought of living alone was a relief. Once Ken had made the painful break and moved out, once I had waved good-bye to Brian and Evan for the weekend and cried myself to sleep, I discovered how much I needed rest, a quiet house with no one demanding anything of me. While Brian and Evan spent time with Ken, I actually had time to clean, to organize, to think. If I could get the house under control, maybe my mind would clear, too.

Ken came over once a week, so we could spend time as a family. We didn't fight as long as we avoided difficult topics. We treated each other gingerly, careful to keep away from the black morass we had struggled out of. We were afraid of getting back together, but the thought of divorce tore our hearts.

I hadn't visited Mama for months, not since the parking ramp incident. I had finally given up on my job at the mental health center and joined a private practice group. I felt relieved when the social worker at Green County called to tell me Mama had been transferred to Welbourne Hall in Watertown, a town about an hour's drive from Madison. She didn't ask when I had last visited. I didn't want to bring it up; it was too hard to explain.

In early December, Mama's new social worker called. "Your mother feels lonely. She's been asking for you. Can you visit?"

She didn't ask how I was doing, or if I wanted to visit, or what it was like to grow up with Mama. She acted like I was put on earth to take care of Mama.

I wanted to tell her I couldn't visit because Mama asked for more and more money and wouldn't look at pictures of my children. But then she would think I was a real baby. I pictured her rolling her eyes, thinking, "What a whiner." Then she would say, "Well, she's mentally ill. You have to make certain allowances. You can't expect her to act normally, now can you? You ought to know that. Aren't you a psychologist? Can't you find it in your heart to help your poor mother? You're the only one she's got."

And I would want to say: "I've already made too many allowances. No, I can't come. It's too hard on me. I tried—I tried really hard. I'm sorry." But if I said it, I would feel terrible.

"Yes, I suppose I can come before Christmas."

I called Ken. He was the only one I could talk to. After all, he bore some responsibility for the mess I was in. He was the one who had encouraged me to visit her in the first place.

"I could go with you." He said it so calmly that I was sure he didn't realize how radical the idea was. It would never have occurred to me to ask him.

"What about Brian and Evan?"

"We can get a sitter. Or take them along. Let them meet their grandmother."

Take Brian and Evan? To see Mama? Was he crazy? But there was something thrilling about the idea, something rebellious.

"She would be really upset. I don't know if we should."

"Why not? They're four, and they've never met her."

"You're right. I've danced around her long enough."

On Saturday morning, Ken and I zipped Brian and Evan into their snowsuits. "We're going to visit your grandmother," I said, trying to sound cheerful.

Brian looked confused. "But she's in New York."

"This is your other grandmother, one you've never met." I felt sad, realizing they thought they had only one grandmother. In the car, I explained that this grandmother had been sick and that was why they had never met her. I was beginning to wonder if the visit was a good idea after all.

We drove to Watertown, a small city an hour east of Madison and found Welbourne Hall, the former community hospital, at the edge of the business district. I marched down the wide marble hall surrounded by Ken, Brian and Evan—my own personal army—ready for a fight. I was ready for Mama to shout, "Don't tell me you're married. Don't make me out to be a grandmother. I'm not that old."

Just let her. I was ready to yell back, "Yes, I'm married. Yes, these are my children. And if you don't want to see them, then you can't see me, either."

We found Mama's room on the first floor, just past the dayroom where patients slumped on vinyl chairs, gazing at a blaring television. They looked just like the Green County patients, except this group included both men and women. The front doors were unlocked, and patients could walk downtown whenever they chose.

Mama's door was open a crack. I knocked lightly and peeked in. Sitting by the window, she looked up and smiled. "Biby, is that you?"

I opened the door wide, and all four of us walked in. I expected her to tell me to get Ken and the boys out. I planned to say, "They stay or I go." I was ready to turn around and walk right out of Welbourne Hall.

But Mama watched quietly. She smiled sweetly at Ken and reached out a limp hand. "Pleased to meet you," she said. She shook his hand as if she had been expecting him. She peered at Brian and Evan, who hid behind Ken, and even managed a shy smile at them.

"This is Ken, my husband. And Brian and Evan." I pushed them toward her. "My boys." The moment had none of the sweetness I had once dreamed of. Nevertheless, I felt a sense of triumph. She acknowledged Brian and Evan. Now she turned her attention to Ken. Brian and Evan scrambled to hide on the other side of the bed while she pulled one of the two chairs toward Ken.

"Please sit down," she said graciously. I sat on the other chair while she perched on the edge of her bed.

"I am so poor, such a poor lonely girl. I have no one. I am so homesick, please take me out of here. I am so unhappy." Her eyes swept from Ken to me. "Please take me home with you. I have no one else."

Her performance amazed me. So did my lack of tears. I was strangely unmoved.

"I'll be good. I'm miserable without my mother, father and brother. Please take pity."

For once, her performance wasn't working on me. I felt like a neutral observer behind a glass wall, seeing her not as my mother but seeing her clearly for the first time. She didn't really care about me or my children. She was only interested in manipulating me, to get me to take care of her. All these years, I thought she loved me. How stupid I was to mistake possessiveness for love! I felt a wave of disgust. I had been so desperate to prove I was a "good daughter," I had failed to notice she was not a "good mother." It suddenly seemed pathetic.

Our family had been so isolated that I had rarely been with Mama in the company of anyone outside the family, other than a waitress or a sales clerk. It was the first time I had ever been in the same room with Mama and my husband. Something about this gave me new eyes. I looked from one to the other, realizing how I had acted the same part with both of them: the perfect wife, the perfect daughter. Wife or daughter it boiled down to the same thing: I had to perform perfectly as if my life depended on it. Any ripple in their mood put me on edge. It felt dangerous if either showed unhappiness. I deluded myself into believing that if I was very good and took care of them, then eventually they would take care of me. I kept hoping and waiting for her to be the mother I needed, for him to be the husband I needed, but I could never count on either of them. Both were wrapped up in their own projects. Mama had written the secretary of state about Hitler's secret whereabouts while Ken, since he had graduated from law school, worked long hours protecting young men from the draft and helping the tenants' union keep people from eviction. They were worthy causes, but I wanted him to spend time at home with me and the boys, coloring Easter eggs. They both were on their own march to Washington, D.C., looking for glory. In that moment, I hated them. I decided to divorce them both.

27

A Mother Bird

◆

1974

After my revelation, I felt serene, almost detached. I could see clearly, just as I had on a backpacking trip I had taken in my undergraduate days. At the top of the mountain, the whole trail was visible: where we had come up and where we would go down. But back down in the valley, I felt closed in by the trees. It didn't look as it had from above. I stumbled, wondering if we had lost our way, until I thought I would drop from exhaustion.

I waited a couple of months before filing for divorce, just to be sure, even though I felt confident I had to go through with it. After all, we had been living separately for months, and Ken had already started a new relationship. I had already accepted that. How much harder could divorce be?

But Ken was furious. "I thought we'd decide together."

"Nothing's getting better. And you're already involved with someone else."

Once we started the divorce, our earlier promises to stay friends dissolved. We were at war. Everything felt unfair. I had tried so hard, and he didn't appreciate it. I wanted him to admit he had let me down, to say he was sorry, that I deserved better, that the whole thing was his fault.

One day, when Ken came over to pick up the boys, we started bickering. Suddenly, I erupted. I heard venom pour out of my mouth. My body trembled. I understood how people committed murder. I sounded just like Mama. I was thirty-five, very close to the age she had been when she went crazy.

The next morning, panic set in. I awoke with a sense of dread, my body already stiff with anxiety. How would I get through the day, let alone the rest of my life? I imagined myself divorced, unattached to anyone. I felt without substance, as if I didn't quite exist. I pictured myself floating in my own world, a recluse, unrelated to anyone—free to go crazy, maybe even to lose Brian and

Evan. It was too frightening to imagine. As long as I was fighting with Ken, I was real. I had someone to blame.

I was turning into Mama. I had started a divorce I couldn't finish. I felt as though I was in one of those dreams, running as hard as I could but getting nowhere. I was scared to death of cutting my last tie. Maybe I wanted to be stuck. I tried to argue with myself. "Look at it rationally, you've got a career. You can support yourself. You've got friends. You're not going to end up like Mama."

But a childish voice deep inside whimpered, "It doesn't matter what you say. I'm too scared." I couldn't quiet that little voice because I refused to listen to it. I didn't want to admit I could be that needy.

I didn't yet understand that the cord tying me to Ken also tied me to Mama. He had always been a stand-in for her. As long as I was attached to him, I could avoid facing my emotionally crippled state. I was still his other half, Mama's other half, not able to stand alone and feel real. I couldn't move forward or back. I couldn't live with Ken or without him. I was stuck.

I felt so desperate I finally knew I had to go to therapy. I called Ken. "What about seeing Carl Whitaker with me?"

"Sure, I'll go," he said. I was surprised. We had not agreed on anything since starting the divorce.

"It wouldn't be to work on our marriage. Just some help getting unstuck."

"Yeah, I think it's a good idea."

I didn't have to explain my choice of Dr. Whitaker. We had talked about him often. In grad school, when I read his first book, I laughed out loud. "Listen to this!" I called out to Ken. "This guy is doing therapy with a schizophrenic, and he falls asleep in the middle of the session. Then he wakes up and says, 'I dreamed I had breasts, and I was suckling you.' Can you imagine?" We laughed, wondering if Dr. Whitaker was brilliant or crazy.

After Dr. Whitaker joined the faculty of the local psychiatry department, I heard more stories about him: he insisted that every patient bring the whole family, even parents from distant cities. He thought there was no such thing as divorce; he didn't believe married people could ever get rid of each other.

Over the years, I had often thought of him when I thought about seeing a therapist. Lots of other therapists in town saw Dr. Whitaker. He was known as the "therapist's therapist." But I was too scared. Mama would refuse to come. I didn't want to stay married. I was sure one of us would go crazy if we did. Only when things could not possibly get worse did I feel desperate enough to call Dr. Whitaker.

He answered his own phone, which shocked me. I was prepared only to talk to a receptionist. "Umm, I was wondering about an appointment for myself and my husband?" I stumbled. "It's not really marriage therapy we want. We're in the middle of a divorce and having a hard time. Will you see us?"

I was prepared to hear him say no or give a long list of conditions. "Sounds like you need some brief crisis counseling to get you unstuck."

"Yes, I guess so." I was lying. My therapy would need to last forever. But the friendliness of his voice relieved me. He didn't sound like the uncaring Zen Master I had imagined.

I waited for Ken in front of Dr. Whitaker's office, wondering if the step we were about to take would help or make things worse. I still didn't trust therapy.

When I saw Ken get out of his car, I was relieved. I had been afraid he would forget or be late. "Thanks for doing this," I said as he approached. I felt a little sheepish. First, I had insisted on divorce, then suggested joint therapy. My actions may have looked confusing, but they only reflected the confusion I felt. Before calling him, I was having the same dream over and over:

I'm in the back seat of a car. The car is moving, but no one is in the driver's seat. The car speeds up. I reach over and try to grab the steering wheel. I can't reach the brakes.

We climbed the stairs to the fourth floor rather than take the tiny, rickety elevator. There was no waiting room, so we leaned against the wall, caught our breath and wondered if we were in the right place. "Do you think this is crazy?" I asked Ken. "I can't imagine how he could help us."

"We probably should have done it years ago," Ken answered. I picked up a torn magazine from a pile on the floor and tried to forget why we had come. The minutes felt like hours. Just as I decided we had made a mistake on our appointment time, the door opened and a large family filed out. I studied their faces, wondering what had happened in their session.

Dr. Whitaker shook our hands and welcomed us in. He was only a little taller than I was, gray haired, with a comfortable amount of padding. There was something warm about him, yet I wouldn't let down my guard. His eyes were too penetrating.

His office was large and unpretentiously furnished—two old couches, chairs, a desk, a table with coffee and tea. We sat on chairs in a small triangle. I was relieved there was no co-therapist, one of Dr. Whitaker's usual conditions. Talking to one therapist was hard enough.

Dr. Whitaker asked about Ken's family and then mine while scribbling notes on a yellow pad. He expressed interest and warmth. He didn't say we had to bring our mothers. I told him how I had exploded in rage at Ken, how our five-year-old sons ran to stand between us, and how Brian had put his hands on his hips and demanded, "Who's fighting here?"

Dr. Whitaker chuckled. "Well, there are orgasms and there are orgasms." His easy acceptance of my frightening emotions calmed me. Did he really think it was okay to get that angry? Then I worried he meant Ken and I should work on getting back together.

Before leaving, we scheduled another session for the following week. I felt better but didn't know why. There was nothing I could put my finger on, but I looked forward to coming back.

Ken and I met weekly with Dr. Whitaker, whom we soon called Carl. We rambled without direction or plan. I longed for Carl to explain what we were doing, and why it would help. I wanted him to tell me what I needed to do. But he let us talk about whatever we wanted. Though I knew better, I wished he would side with me and tell Ken how he had failed me.

Therapy sessions were not easier because I happened to be a psychotherapist. As a therapist, I was comfortable in a therapy session. Unlike patients, therapists can hide behind a mask; they're not required to admit fears and vulnerabilities. As a patient, I was too embarrassed to show my fury, despair, and pain. I hoped to get through this with dignity. But real therapy can't be done wearing a mask.

After a few weeks, Carl told us that since we weren't doing brief crisis intervention anymore, he would need a co-therapist. This was exactly what I had dreaded. I hated the idea of some psychiatric resident, no older or more experienced than I, sitting on his high horse making pronouncements about my mental health. I resented the intrusion into our safe little triangle but knew it was futile to resist. It was one of Carl's requirements. He believed he needed a partner to keep from becoming another family member, just another person bound by family dynamics, unable to challenge the family's unspoken rules. And I didn't want to quit. I couldn't imagine pushing off in my own little boat again out onto my lonely sea of anxiety. Our weekly session was all that held me together.

When our co-therapist, Don, a psychiatric resident, joined us, I tried to be polite. My prickly resentment came through anyway. I brooded after the session, playing over and over what Don had said, and why it couldn't possibly be right, the knowing way he had joked with Carl as though we were guinea pigs in some experiment. Then, Carl telling me in that offhand way that I had to go into my anxiety, not run from it, as if that should be easy. What right did they have to tell me what to do? I decided I had to tell them I wasn't taking orders from either of them. That night I dreamed:

> Robbers sneer in my window at me. I call the police, but the robbers listen in. They've already robbed my neighbors, putting their stuff in a van. It's a systematic plan to empty every house on the street. I try to call the police again, but my phone is dead. I run to my other neighbor's house but the robbers are already there. They pretend to be there for a party, so I pretend also. Brian and Evan are asleep back home. I hope to keep the gangsters' attention so they won't discover my sons. Everyone goes upstairs for a sex orgy, and I follow, not wanting to attract attention. Everyone takes off their clothes and paints their bodies. I pretend to enjoy it until I'm too repulsed. Then I push my way to the stairs. A man with a nylon stocking over his head blocks my way. With a burst of strength, I push out into the street. I run until I see a state patrol car. "Quick, come and help me. There are gangsters on my street." The police pull off their masks and leer at me. They're gangsters in disguise.

I woke in a panic. At our next session, I blurted out the whole thing.

"You're the good mother bird," Carl said. "Running from the nest to draw the robbers away from your babies. Making the crazy guys follow you."

"The crazy guys?"

"Yeah, those robbers—they're your craziness, your mother's craziness coming down through the generations to you. You're running from it, hoping it won't find your boys."

I wept. After this, I was ready to do whatever Carl asked. He had found goodness in my most shameful flaw. He affirmed me as a mother, the part of myself I doubted most. I was the good mother bird.

28

Growing Up

✦

1974

Carl wanted us to bring Brian and Evan to our next session. "Are you sure?" I asked. "They're awfully active. They'll probably make a mess." I dreaded bringing them as much as I dreaded bringing Mama. Therapy would no longer be just "talking." Now Carl would see me at my worst—in action as an inadequate mother.

But Carl had won my trust, so despite my fears, I brought Brian and Evan. By the time we got them up to Carl's office, I felt limp. I sat on the edge of the couch certain something terrible would happen. Carl and Don didn't seem worried. They ignored Ken and me, turning all their attention to Brian and Evan, now five years old. Within minutes Brian and Evan were jumping on Carl and Don, almost knocking them out of their chairs. Carl and Don were laughing and playing, looking as if they were having the time of their lives. I sat tensely, waiting for Carl or Don to say, "Can't you settle these kids down so we can get started?" Or worse yet: "These kids are seriously disturbed. They should be on medication." But Carl and Don seemed content spending the entire session playing while Ken and I watched. For once, I was grateful for Don's presence and his warmth toward my children.

Carl wanted Brian and Evan to be a regular part of our therapy group. I was amazed that within a few sessions they fit into our session in their five-year-old way, claiming attention for only a share of the hour. After a few minutes of rough-housing, they were content to sprawl on their bellies behind the couch, drawing tanks, planes, and gunboats. I no longer worried. Once I got them inside, I could relax; Carl would take charge.

That is until the day neither Ken nor Don could attend the session. As Brian, Evan, and I came in, Carl was leaning back in his chair opening his mail. I sat down on the couch while Brian and Evan tried to get Carl's attention. He let them rummage in the toy drawer but kept looking at his mail, not responding. I wondered when he would start the session, and what I should do. With half our group missing, we had no structure. Brian and Evan grabbed a couple of plastic pistols out of Carl's toy drawer and started fighting. Carl kept looking at his mail. I started to get uneasy. Brian and Evan were yelling now, jumping on the couch and running around. I wondered if Carl thought this was therapeutic or expected me to quiet them down. I still hoped Carl would take charge, but he didn't move. I told Brian and Evan to settle down. They ignored me. I tried again. My voice sounded feeble. I felt like a complete failure as a mother.

I had already realized that my problem saying no to Mama was identical to my problem with Brian and Evan. It came down to the same fear: something terrible would happen if I was too firm, too mean, if I caused them pain. Something precious would be severed, and I would be cut off forever, adrift and alone. No amount of money, no amount of mess to clean up later mattered, only preserving my connection with them.

"You're being too nice to them," said Carl from over his shoulder. He didn't look like he was about to take over.

"But I can't be mean to them, I just can't."

"You think what you're doing isn't mean?" Then he told me the story of the man who cut his dog's tail one inch at a time, because he wanted to spare his dog the pain of cutting it off all at once.

"What should I do?" I whimpered.

"Don't be afraid to show them your power." I wondered what he meant. I felt completely powerless even though I knew I wasn't supposed to.

"How would I do that?"

"Sit on them."

"Sit on them—you mean literally?"

"Yeah, sit on them. Let them feel your weight. You're bigger. It's cruel to pretend you're not."

"Sit on them on the floor?"

"Yeah."

I felt silly, but I tackled Evan, straddled him, and pinned his shoulders to the floor. I only did it because Carl said I should. Somehow, if he was there, it felt okay. I didn't think it would help. I went along so Carl would see the problem was impossible to solve. Evan squirmed, protesting in indignation. I was surprised how easily I could hold him down. I looked at Carl to find out what I should do next.

"Just stay there. Sit on him all hour if you need to, until he knows you're the boss." I was relieved. All I had to do was wait. Brian sat frozen on the couch, watching. Realizing he was scared, I felt a surprising surge of satisfaction. Then I felt Evan go limp underneath me. He had conceded. I was in charge.

"Remember you can sit on them whenever you need to," Carl said as we left.

At home my confidence grew. I waited for a chance to sit on one of them again but never had to. We all knew I could. The balance of power had shifted.

After four months of therapy, Ken and I completed our divorce. I worried Carl would end our therapy now that we were no longer married. Instead, he suggested we include Deirdre, Ken's new girlfriend. Ken and I both thought it was a good idea, since she was already part of our new family.

The first time Ken picked up Brian and Evan on Friday night to spend the weekend with him and Deirdre, I sat in the window and waved while they waved back. Then I cried for two hours, jealous of Deirdre, who would be spending the weekend with them. Over time, the good-byes got more bearable. I was grateful to Deirdre for caring about Brian and Evan. When she joined us in therapy, I fantasized that someday we would compare notes and agree that Ken caused any problems we once had.

By Christmas, my anger had melted. Ken and I were divorced. The three of us were friends. I wasn't alone. We had made a new family, one that lived in two houses. Between the three of us, we would raise Brian and Evan. I drove to their farmhouse for Christmas, believing a miracle had happened. Ken and I had gotten unstuck, yet were connected in a new and better way. We didn't have to be angry. We could be co-parents and friends. I was grateful Deirdre could accept me. I stood at the window of their guest bedroom, struck by the beauty of the frosted countryside lit by a full moon. I felt a surprising sense of peace.

29

Family Therapy

✦

1975

My anxiety reappeared abruptly after the holidays. I was frustrated. Why did I have to go through this again? When I complained to Carl, he told me to bring Mama to the next session, the very thing I had dreaded. But after my taste of peace and happiness, I would do anything Carl said was necessary to get better. I resolved to get Mama to Carl's office if I had to carry her.

Mama had no love of psychiatrists. They were her enemies. She held them responsible for locking her up. I was afraid if I called ahead, she might decide to be shopping when I arrived. Besides she never came to the phone anyway. A surprise attack would be best. I would drag her to the car if necessary. Carl told me to take Brian and Evan along for support.

When we pulled into the parking lot of Welbourne Hall, Mama was standing in the doorway. Uncanny! How did she know? Were we connected by some psychic thread?

I marched toward the door, Brian and Evan flanking me closely. As we reached the door, she retreated. By the time we were inside, she was moving swiftly down the hall. We ran after, trying to catch up. She went in her room and closed the door. We barged right in. She stood with her back to the window, staring at us.

"Who are they?" She pointed to Brian and Evan. "They aren't yours, are they?"

"Yes, they are. You met them last year, remember?" How dare she forget.

"Am I going somewhere? Are you taking me somewhere?"

How did she know? "Yes. I'm taking you to see my therapist."

I expected her to refuse. I was prepared to make the speech Carl had coached me to give: "My therapist needs you to help him help me to be happier." But I didn't have to say a word. She was already putting on her coat and hat.

"I'm frightened," she said. Suddenly, I felt sorry for her.

"It'll be okay. My doctor is very nice." She didn't answer but followed me. I could hardly believe she was coming so easily. Maybe it was my new sense of power. She must have heard the determination in my voice.

She settled in the front seat while Brian and Evan climbed into the back and started munching cookies. She paid them no attention. Evan leaned forward and whispered in my ear, "Ask your mother if she wants something to eat."

"They want to know if you'd like some cookies."

Mama shook her head, whispering in a barely audible voice, "no." She looked annoyed.

After this rebuff, Brian and Evan gave up on their strange grandmother. When their play and noisy chatter intruded into the front seat, Mama visibly tensed. She was annoyed by her grandchildren, not interested. She showed them no warmth or affection. Her reaction hurt but no longer devastated me. Rejection and disinterest—this was how I had expected the whole world to react to my children. Now I understood why. And why I was so grateful when anyone showed a positive interest.

We waited in Carl's office for Carl and Don. Mama sat silently while I busied myself gathering up copies of the papers laid in piles for Carl's seminar students. I buried myself in reading. I couldn't bear to sit next to Mama in silence. Brian and Evan took their usual spot behind the couch and started drawing. Finally, Carl and Don came in. Carl introduced himself and told Mama how glad he was that she could join us. I watched in amazement as she took his hand and replied, "I'm glad to meet you, too."

He explained he wanted her to help him help me. When she replied she would be glad to do what she could, I dissolved into tears.

Carl asked Brian what it was like being with his grandmother. He replied confidently, "That's not my grandmother. My grandmother lives in New York. That's my Mom's Mom."

I was sure Mama was relieved to hear that she was not really a grandmother. Carl asked her if I had as much energy as Brian and Evan at their age.

"Oh, no," she replied. "She was a good girl."

"She was good? Did she ever get angry?"

"Oh, no, she was always good. She always did what I said."

"Was she shy?"

"Oh, no, she always talked to people. She was a good girl."

"Well, I'm trying to help her to be not so good," he chuckled. "Do you see your daughter very often?"

"No, I don't see her so much, but I talk to her a lot."

"You do not!" I blurted. "You never talk to me." It was the only thing I said during the whole hour, and I was embarrassed to sound like a ten-year-old.

When Carl asked Mama about God and religion, she came alive. It was her favorite topic, even if her ideas were a little quirky. She seemed pleased with the questions and flattered by Carl's interest. I hadn't heard her talk this much in a long time.

I didn't know what to make of the experience. I only knew I had accomplished the impossible task and felt stronger for it. Carl had talked with Mama for the entire hour, but I could remember little of what had been said. I knew better than to expect Carl to help me make sense of the session.

On the elevator, Mama whispered anxiously to me, "Did I look all right?"

Was this all she cared about? "Yes," I sighed, "you looked very nice."

She leaned toward me and whispered once more, "I don't suppose you have any money?"

"Yes, I have some money."

"Could you spare me some?"

"Yes," I sighed in resignation. "I can spare you some."

30

Going Deeper

✦

1975

In the weeks that followed, I felt invigorated and more whole somehow. I couldn't recall anyone treating Mama with as much dignity as Carl had. I knew he wasn't being phony; he truly respected crazy people. He called schizophrenia "the disease of integrity." Slowly, my shame began to melt.

When my anxiety returned a few weeks later, I was caught off guard. Each time it returned, I was surprised. I never understood where it came from or what triggered it. I would wake in the morning with a terrifying sense of dread. The day ahead seemed unbearably long. I walked around like a zombie, unable to concentrate. I busied myself with mindless tasks because that was all I could manage. I felt too agitated to sit still. I was grateful when Brian and Evan were with me since then I didn't have to think about myself. I looked forward to work, because there I could switch into my competent adult self. Listening to a client made my own problems fade. By evening, I could relax a little, relieved to have made it through the day.

Carl told me anxiety gave me the opportunity to find my authentic self. All I had to do was go directly into it, not run away from it. He said it as though it was as easy as buying a newspaper. But I wasn't sure I wanted to give up my "false" self, the self I had constructed to survive. An "authentic self" sounded risky. After all, I was a crazy woman's daughter.

I began to feel in my bones that my anxiety must have been exactly what Mama had felt in her younger years. It must have been the force that drove her to pace and cry, to study books on mystical subjects, to write love letters to the grocer or try to tell the Secretary of State where Hitler hid in South America. I felt similarly driven, searching for happiness in fantasies or romantic affairs, looking for answers in books. She had been as alone and lost as I was—without parents or family to turn to. But being an immigrant in a strange country without a job or profession, it must have been even harder for her. My compassion for her was growing.

One weekend morning, waking with the usual dread and anxiety, I felt tired of running. I didn't want to spend another day battling it. It was a fight I never won, even though it took all my strength. With Brian and Evan at Ken's, I had the luxury of time and privacy. I felt brave, so I shouted out loud at my inner demon: "Who are you? What do you want from me?"

To my surprise, I sensed a clear answer: "You make me pursue you because you avoid me. I make you anxious so you'll pay attention. You're always so busy with lists of things to do. You're so proud when you get things done, when you can point to your accomplishments. You think you're good because you get your list done. I need to remind you I'm here, too."

"Who are you, and what do you want?"

"I'm the squalling infant that annoys you. You forget about me. NO! I won't let you. I am your neediness. I am your ugliness! I am your disappointments! I am what you try to hide, control, and do away with. You try to escape me by having affairs. Won't you ever learn? Take care of *me*. You think you can get rid of me with a new boyfriend. When will you learn?"

"What do you need?"

"Time and attention."

"Haven't you had enough?"

"No. You never give me anything voluntarily. You owe me. I'm due, way overdue."

"You scare me."

"You keep running from me. You act like I'll devour you."

"I *am* afraid you'll devour me."

"Get to know me. Maybe I won't be so scary then. Maybe I'll be useful."

"How?"

"I am your selfishness. You've always been afraid of me."

Hearing this, I felt surprisingly peaceful. Something was coming together inside me, something torn and very old.

"Come back little orphans of the marsh, come back to me. Now I know you and where you belong. I know your names. You are my shadows, you belong with me. I need you."

That night I dreamed:

> Carl and Don are at my house for a session, but we're constantly interrupted. Carl is in the kitchen wearing an apron, cooking for everyone. I'm worried the time will be up without any therapy. I should prevent the interruptions,

but I can't seem to manage it. My cleaning lady arrives with several friends and their children. I tell them I don't want them here. The basement floor is cracked and flooding. In the corner, a friend has a fever. I try to bring her water but am intercepted by a group of partiers. I dance with a small dark foreign man. In the next room, a woman is in labor. Carl delivers the baby and shows everyone. It looks so new and raw; it appears to have no skin. He holds the baby out for me to take, but I'm repulsed. I give it only a quick touch. The others are happy to hold the baby. I'm surprised no one else is frightened. I'm afraid I might hurt the baby, but no one else seems concerned. The baby looks fragile and unpredictable. I turn away while the baby is in Carl's arms. I'm relieved to leave it with him.

"That baby is your newborn schizophrenic self," Carl said in our next session.

My schizophrenic self! That fragile, transparent, tiny baby? So, deep down I was schizophrenic, just as the Rorschach revealed many years before, just as I had feared. For the first time, I dared ask out loud, "Carl, do you think I'm schizophrenic like my mother?"

"No, you're a pseudo-schiz. You're mother is the real schiz. You just copied her."

"What do you mean my schizophrenic self is trying to be born?" I wasn't sure if I wanted a "newborn schizophrenic self."

"That baby is your authentic self, the source of your creativity."

My heart sank. He really meant I had to care for that repulsive baby. No one else would.

I began to understand. Half of me had gone into hiding back in the marsh in Delavan—the half that wasn't sweet and good and kind, the half that could have fought back, that got mad when my rights were trampled, that could have shouted, "I want it! I have a right!" I never learned how to temper raw passion. I just pushed it underground, then covered it over by eating too much, smoking too much, wanting too much. Now I had to take on the work of accepting the rejected part of me, of making it part of me again.

"Carl, Carl, you old trickster. Pseudo-schiz! How did you ever come up with that? I don't think that one's in the diagnostic manual!"

Carl made my most shameful flaw acceptable, made it an asset, pointed out how I had been loyal to Mama all along, even when I refused to see her. Can a daughter be forgiven for turning her back on her own mother? I guess so. Carl put all my craziness under my control. My choice. My strategy to survive. A mask

I could put on and take off. But not my true core, which he saw and loved. I know he did.

When Carl asked me—told me—to bring Mama to therapy, I didn't understand how it could possibly help me. I thought he probably didn't have any idea how far gone she was. I only did it because he said I should. If he had told me to stand on one foot, I would have.

I knew Mama wouldn't change. I was surprised she came. She got in the car so meekly. That was empowering in itself. But in Carl's office, I dissolved into tears. It was embarrassing, but it felt surprisingly good to sit like a child while he handled the session. The thing that always stands out when I think back on that session is the respect and kindness he showed her. I could tell he truly respected her. Before that, I had never seen my mother treated as a person, with a right to dignity. Some deep ancient wound began to heal that day.

Carl is still with me all these years later, everyday when I'm in my office with my clients. There are moments when I distinctly feel his presence. Something he said or did comes back to me, and I feel his support. I know I can be more of myself because of knowing him. He helped me connect with the most potent source of healing—my raw, authentic, sometimes still frightening, core.

Sometimes I feel as though the healing I experienced with Carl flows through me to my clients. I picture a great web: I'm linked to him, and through me, he is linked to all my clients, and through them we're both linked to people neither of us will ever meet. Yet we're all connected.

31

Falling Apart

◆

1975

Each breakthrough in therapy exhilarated me. I felt so confident it seemed impossible that bad feelings could ever overtake me again.

But the good feelings never lasted. After talking with my anxiety and feeling better about my "schizophrenic self," I woke one night, feeling strangely empty. I stared at the dark ceiling and waited for my middle-of-the-night anxieties. They didn't come. I stumbled to the kitchen in slow motion and slumped into a chair. My arms felt like cement. The hum of the refrigerator was deafening. Why had I never noticed before? I scanned my insides for a feeling I could recognize. Nothing. Only numbness, like a limp balloon. I was beyond caring.

The next day, I lay on the couch and watched leaves rustle. Outside, the summer day was beautiful. I didn't care. I had no desire to do anything. I no longer cared what others thought. I was a stranger to myself.

I called Carl because I didn't know what else to do. "I feel so strange. I guess I must be depressed."

"Time to bring your mother again."

I agreed only because I trusted Carl. I wasn't even nervous as I drove to get her. I didn't care if she came or not.

By the time I reached Welbourne Hall, I felt so exhausted I could barely make it down the hall. I pushed open Mama's door and plopped down on her bed, not even bothering to act cheerful.

Mama stroked my face. "Are you sick, Bibili?" She sounded worried.

A rush of feelings. I longed to be taken care of just like a little girl. It felt dangerous, but I was too weak to resist.

"Bibili, do you want some juice?" Mama's face was inches from mine. I nodded. She spooned Tang into a glass and walked down the hall for water. When she returned and handed me the bright orange liquid, I drank, surprised at how comforted I felt as she hovered over me.

When we got to Carl's office, he asked Mama about her childhood. She told him everything—how her mother got sick with tuberculosis; how they didn't have a good doctor, but Mama was only thirteen and couldn't do anything; how she and her brother, Fritz, took the train every Sunday to visit her in the sanitarium.

I listened, glad Carl was in charge. I had heard it before, but never realized how Mama's childhood resembled mine. We were both emotional orphans.

Mama and Fritz were left in the care of a grandmother who made them kneel and pray while she told them about hell and Satan. Her mother finally came home but was too weak to get out of bed. Mama and Fritz watched as their father knelt by her bed and promised her he would never re-marry. She didn't want Mama and Fritz raised by a stepmother. But soon after she died, their grandmother died, too, and then their father married their mother's best friend, a beautiful woman with a daughter of her own. The new stepmother was an erratic, moody person who favored her own daughter and made Mama and Fritz feel like second-class citizens. Their father spent most nights in the tavern to avoid fighting with his new wife. Mama and Fritz pleaded, but their father refused to stand up for them. When Fritz left for engineering school, Mama was sent to live with a relative. Later, she worked as a housekeeper at a resort. When she left home, never to return, she was only fifteen, the age I had been when I left for Shimer College. When Mama married Daddy, she called her father to tell him she was leaving for America. He told her not to come home to say good-bye because he didn't want to upset his wife.

I offered a silent prayer of gratitude that Mama had married Daddy and not a man like her own father. Daddy had stuck by us and stood up for us. Is that why she picked him? Had she sensed this with her uncanny intuition?

Carl asked us to come again, and I was surprised when Mama agreed so easily. I didn't have the energy to worry whether she would change her mind.

When I picked her up the next time, I had Brian and Evan with me. It was a hot day, and they had taken off their shoes. I didn't think Mama paid them any attention, but as we were getting into the car, she pointed to their bare feet. "Shouldn't they be in shoes?" A tiny glimmer of hope. Maybe she did care about them.

At our session, Brian and Evan started a game of twisting a rope around all of us. We each had to hold onto the rope. I was surprised when Mama let Evan place the rope in her hands. She held it throughout the game, a tiny, nervous smile on her lips. She looked uncomfortable, but she had connected with us. Maybe we could still be a family.

Each session lifted my hopes, but afterwards my depression only deepened. Spending the whole day with Mama made me ache with longing. I would leave the session feeling buoyed. On the drive back to Welbourne Hall, I talked to Mama, trying my best to sound like Carl. But Mama never answered my questions. She only smiled secretively as I sank into a well of loneliness. I wanted so much more.

Between sessions, I tried to figure out what was happening to me, but my thoughts and feelings were so jumbled. Oh, no I never felt abandoned—not me; I could take care of myself. Mama was the one in the hospital, not me. Mama was the one we had to worry about. But the shreds of denial were slipping. I did feel abandoned. She abandoned me, once, twice and more, over and over. Just because I didn't feel it that day in Delavan when she went to the hospital didn't mean the feeling wasn't there.

I remember that day clear as a bell. Mama had been happy, and I was expecting something good. But when I came home, Daddy looked worried. He told me I would be living out in the country with Auntie and Uncle Frank. This must have been the exciting thing that was supposed to happen that day, the thing I had felt in my bones. Daddy acted like he expected me to be upset. But I wasn't. I wondered what was wrong with me.

I don't know when or how the real feeling of abandonment—of not being lovable enough to stay with—set in. All that dreaming about orphans, and bringing home lost cats, and acting like Mama's little therapist, were ways of avoiding the pain. It's still down there, like a debt coming due. A pain so powerful I couldn't face it when I was little.

Until now, my childhood was just a story. I had separated myself from it, so I didn't feel anything when I told it. I was surprised, even embarrassed, by other's reactions. Smugly, I thought they were overreacting. But now I had to experience the depth of my own pain. Could I ever cry enough?

I looked at myself through a new prism and saw variations of only one theme—abandonment. My early obsession with boyfriends. What does it mean when a five-year-old thinks she needs a boyfriend? That she can't count on love at home? I was good at acting in love. Someone to send valentines to, dream about, and make me feel special. Then came the creeping doubts, feeling stifled by the burden of being the perfectly loving girlfriend, deciding I didn't really like him after all.

Breaking up was the hard part. It was my own private test. Was I strong enough to stand the pain? I had to prove I could stand on my own, had to prove it over and over. None of it had anything to do with love. It was only a game, like playing doctor when Mommy goes to the hospital.

Was I even capable of love? Or was I too needy, too infantile? Would I ever be capable of real adult love? My loneliness felt keener than ever. Except for Brian and Evan, I was alone in the world. I felt raw and vulnerable to every slight, no matter how small or unintended. When I came to a therapy session expecting to find our usual group and learned that neither Ken, Deirdre, nor Don would be coming, I cried through the whole session. It was just Carl and me. "I can't count on anyone," I said through my tears. "I feel so abandoned."

I was acting like a whimpering child and didn't care. I looked at Carl, waiting for words of magic to make my pain stop. But he only looked at me helplessly. After an unbearably long silence, he said, "You have to learn to tolerate the comings and goings of your mother." I knew what he meant. When people left, I needed to trust they would return. I needed to trust I could survive in their absence, that I could tolerate the terrible sinking feeling I had when Carl closed his eyes for a mid-session nap. I sobbed, believing the pain would never, ever stop.

32

Healing

✦

1975

When it works, therapy is a miracle. Nothing changes, yet everything looks different, like a light going on in a dark room. All the obstacles that caused bumps and bruises remain, but with light, the room is livable, even friendly.

By August, I felt a sense of peace. The empty places inside me had filled in. The cloudy membrane separating me from the world had lifted. People seemed friendlier; I only needed to open myself up and connect.

I took Brian and Evan and our dog, Cinnamon, camping. I felt nourished by the soft sand dunes, the endless expanse of sky and water. I watched my sons run to meet the waves, and I felt grateful for the beauty around us. I followed them slowly into the surf, feeling the water caress each inch of my skin. Being in the water awakened memories of swimming in Lake Geneva—senses alert, so keenly alive, some mysterious connection to the lake. *I've come back to you, great mother of my childhood. You were always there; a presence I could count on. I feel your silky embrace and know I'm home.*

In early September, I drove over to pick Mama up for our scheduled session. Brian and Evan were back in school, in first grade now, so I was alone. Feeling happy and centered, I realized I wouldn't need to bring her many more times. My goal had been accomplished. I felt sad to think our sessions would end. I liked listening to Carl and Mama talk.

I knocked, then pushed open the door of Mama's room, expecting to find her getting ready. She sat with her arms folded.

"Don't you need to get ready?"

"I'm not going to see that doctor of yours anymore!"

"But we have an appointment." I was unprepared for this. Things had been going so well.

"He's brainwashing you. You used to be such a nice girlie."

"He is not. He's helping me more than you ever did."

"I know better than him. I'm your mother."

"You're the one who brainwashed me! He's helped me to be happy. You just left me. You only thought about yourself." I felt amazed to hear what I had just said. Could this be me, fighting with Mama? I wasn't even scared. I no longer cared if she didn't like what I said. I was free! "You aren't being fair. I was counting on you to come. It's the least you can do for me. You're always letting me down."

"You can't boss me, Biby. No one can boss me."

"I know I can't boss you. And you can't boss me either."

"We don't have to go to that doctor. We could walk downtown for lunch."

"I don't have time for lunch. I have an appointment with Dr. Whitaker." I wasn't about to give up my appointment to placate her.

"Don't go there. It's not good for you. Please don't go. I'm never going again. It's not good for me. I have to listen to myself. Every time I haven't, it's been a mistake. I never should have married. I never should have had children. I never should have listened to those people telling me what to do."

"How can you say that to *me*? You even said it when I was eight-years-old! How could you tell a child she never should have been born? That you'd have been better off without her? Don't you realize how that made me feel?"

Mama looked startled, as though she had never considered how her words would sound to me. "You don't need me anymore."

"That's right! I'm not a little girl anymore."

"You used to be so good. You were such a good girl when you came to see me down there at Green County. You've changed. You aren't nice." She began to cry.

"That's right," I relished my turn to hurt her. "I'm not a little girl who does what you want. It was killing me to pretend I was still a little girl. That's why I stopped coming."

"It was not killing you!"

"Yes, it was."

"I was a good mother to you." She spoke through tears. "I worked hard. I cooked good meals. I baked cakes and pies and cookies. I carried out the ashes from that old coal furnace. I knitted your clothes. Look, I knit this sweater and hat when I was at Green County. Do you like it? I could knit you one." She was pleading. Despite feeling pity for her, I pushed away the impulse to rescue her, to assuage her pain by slipping back into my old role.

"I don't need a hat. I don't need a sweater. I didn't need those fancy clothes you made for me when I was a kid. I wore them to make you feel good. I wanted to look like the other kids. You made me into a little fashion plate. All I needed was for you to love me and for you and Daddy to love each other. You didn't love him. That hurt me very much."

"I did love him, but he wasn't good for me. He didn't stick up for me. He left me locked up like a criminal."

I knew it was true. She felt betrayed by Daddy. He did his best, but he hadn't been able to save her. There was too much against him. My strength dissolved. I sat down on her bed and cried over the tragedy of our family.

Mama sat down next to me. "Biby, Biby, you used to be such a good girlie, a nice girlie." It was her sugary baby talk voice. She stroked my face.

"Don't touch me." I jumped off the bed. "Don't you *touch* me." Now that I had blurted the words out, I liked their sound. They rang in the air like bells pealing victory. I had dared say no to Mama.

I no longer had anything to lose, so I said what I wanted. "Do you miss Daddy? Do you think about the last time you saw him?" I had never been brave enough to ask before.

"He's not dead. He just left us. He left you. He doesn't want to see you."

"He's been dead for six years."

"You tell me lies. You've been brainwashed by that doctor. You need me to watch out for you. I have people watching out for you that you don't even know about. They're secret agents. I only have love for you. I hope you have it better than I did. I'm glad you didn't make the same mistake I made."

"But I did. I got married and had two children. Now I'm divorced."

"You have children? You're divorced?"

"Yes, I'm divorced. My two children, Brian and Evan, they were with us this summer each time we went to Dr. Whitaker's. Don't you remember? You're their grandmother."

"No, no, Biby don't say that. Don't make me look older than I am. I'm too young to be a grandmother."

"You *are* their grandmother. Why can't you accept that? Why can't you enjoy them? They're wonderful little boys. You don't act like you love them or me. You don't accept my children. You won't answer letters. You won't come to the phone."

She didn't answer, so I left. I walked to the car still exhilarated. I had fought with Mama, and for the first time in my life, I had said exactly what I felt. Finally, I was grown up. I was free.

I drove to Madison imagining how I would tell Carl about my fight with Mama. Then I started imagining Mama's reactions after I left. That's when my exhilaration turned into anxiety. I had shocked Mama. She was old and fragile, probably not strong enough to survive such a shock. Since I was born, we had been joined at the heart. I kept her alive by being her good girl. Suddenly I had said, "Don't touch me." It was like I had seized a knife and cut us apart. Now she lay on the floor bleeding. I had committed the ultimate selfishness: I chose myself.

I was sure the social worker at Welbourne would call that night to tell me that Mama was dead of a heart attack.

33

Reckoning

✦

1975–76

Back home, I waited. Each time the phone rang, I prepared to hear that Mama was dead. But the call never came. Weeks passed, each day proving she could exist without me. Would I ever see her again?

In the spring, I took Brian and Evan to Milwaukee to visit museums. As we passed Watertown, I considered dropping in to see Mama. I ignored the impulse. Why be that foolish?

But on our way home, the idea returned with greater vigor. My hopes started spinning from strands fine as spider's silk. She got in the car with us, didn't she? And she noticed their bare feet. She must care. Maybe I should have stopped taking her to Carl sooner. It was probably too much to expect. I could have taken her to lunch instead, with Brian and Evan, like it was a natural thing to do. Maybe if we just showed up, we could pick up where we left off. The car turned itself toward Watertown.

I told Brian and Evan we were visiting their grandmother as we pulled into the parking lot. At the front door, three patients guarded the entry like sentinels. They greeted us as we passed through the foyer and into the lounge where several patients puffed cigarettes in front of a blaring television.

Mama's room was just beyond the lounge. I knocked on her door. "Mama, it's me. Are you there?" She cracked the door, barely enough to show her face.

"Biby? Is it you?" She glanced down quickly and saw Brian and Evan standing next to me. "Who are they? They're not yours, are they?"

"Yes, they're mine. Brian and Evan, don't you remember?"

"Don't bring them here." She slammed the door in our faces. I was stunned.

"We just want to see you for a few minutes. Open the door."

"Not with them. Come back without them."

I stared at the door. I wasn't prepared to be shut out like this. I had to get in there and demand an explanation. I hustled Brian and Evan into a small lounge and told them to wait.

"How long?" They eyed two almost comatose patients dosing in the chairs across the small room.

"Just a few minutes. I'll be next door, in Mama's room."

I charged back into her room. "Why did you slam the door? They're just little boys. Why can't you accept them?"

"Don't come to see me unless you're alone." She walked to her mirror, brushing her hair with long, angry strokes.

"But we had nice times this summer, didn't we? We went out to lunch, remember? You were okay with them then."

"I never should have gone to that doctor with you, never."

"But it helped me so much. I never thanked you."

"No, Biby, it didn't help. It was no good for me."

"But we could go out to lunch with Brian and Evan like we did this summer, couldn't we?"

She snorted. "You just want to get me into the car so you can drive me back to that doctor."

"No, I promise. No doctor. I don't have an appointment. We're driving home from Milwaukee. I took Brian and Evan ..."

She cut me off. "Don't tell me about them. And don't bring them here again. Come back alone."

Her words still stung as I gathered up Brian and Evan and took them to lunch. While they consumed milkshakes and cheeseburgers, I replayed the scene over and over. This was the worst thing, by far, that she had ever done to me—slamming the door in my children's faces. They were the best part of me. Could I ever forgive her?

I felt swallowed up in a wave of pain, and I still had to drive home. I hustled Brian and Evan back to the car and pulled out of the parking lot. As I pulled up to a stop sign, I glanced to my right. There she was, standing on the curb—Mama, in her white coat and pants, her long white hair hanging loose around her shoulders, clutching her white pocketbook tightly to her chest. Her eyes stared straight ahead. She slowly made her way across the street, crossing in front of our car, without looking our way.

"Isn't that her, Mom? Is that your Mom?"

"Why does she look like that, Mom? Why does she look so funny?"

"Why didn't she want to see us? Is she our grandmother?"

"I didn't like those people. They were creepy. Let's not go there again." Brian and Evan leaned forward from the back seat, vying for my attention.

But I had no answers. Tears streamed down my face. Mama was only a few feet away, but it seemed like a thousand miles. Her life, limited as it was, continued without us. She didn't need us. We didn't enhance her life in any way. I watched until she disappeared down the street. She looked like a ghost figure, out of place in this town, in this country, on this earth.

I drove home in a daze. Why would she reject her own grandchildren? I wasn't asking for much. All she had to do was sit at the table with us. Didn't she care enough about me to do that?

For days after, she stayed on my mind. Whenever I had a free moment, my thoughts went to her. Did she know how much she had hurt me? Was it a choice or an automatic defensive reaction? Could she even make choices?

Questions with no answers. The only answers I would get were those I invented. She would never explain, I knew that. She seemed to be driven by forces she didn't control or understand. She had no relationships, no intimacy, no companionship. She didn't talk to anyone or read or watch T.V. Shopping seemed to be her only activity. Why visit her if I couldn't talk about myself or my children, if I couldn't bring her to my house for Thanksgiving or a birthday? What would our relationship be about? Images of silent lunches and afternoons rummaging for bargains in K-mart came to mind. Loneliness overwhelmed me.

Longing for answers, I thought of the letters she had written so long ago, letters sent to me by Chaplain Love when he retired from Mendota State Hospital. When he called, I recognized his name immediately, though I had never met him. Mama had spoken of him often. He was one of the few people she ever trusted.

"I have some things of your mother's. I thought you should have them." His phone call had surprised me. It came during the time I had, for the second time, decided I had to stop seeing Mama.

"I don't want anything of hers. I do better when I don't see her."

"I'm sorry to hear that. But these letters belong to you. You might want them some day." When the large manila envelope arrived, I put it away without opening it.

Now I rummaged in a basement cupboard, desperately hoping I had not thrown that envelope out. When I found it, my heart sped up. Eagerly I opened it and inside found several sheets of pink stationary covered with Mama's delicate penmanship:

> I never wanted to live in Delavan, Wisconsin, but I do not regret coming to the United States. I studied English for four years at the Handelschule in Zurich before I ever met Mr. Hans Gubler. When I met Mr. Gubler, I thought he was the right man for me, because he acted like a gentleman, and he lived in America. There were many men interested in me, but I wasn't interested in them. I did not want to be a Swiss Hausfrau. I thought Hans was the one, but now I know I was wrong.... I never believed in divorces, but finally I might be forced to get one.
>
> I now know I must always listen only to myself, not to what others tell me I should do. Whenever I have gone against my own sense of what is right, I have lived to regret it. I was not meant to be a wife and mother. I am nothing more than a servant. I cook and clean and shop and wash and iron and mend all day, every day with never so much as a thank you. Not a penny of my own to show for it....
>
> When I first saw Lee Baxter, I felt there was a special understanding between us. He smiled at me in a very special way, not the way a grocer would ordinarily smile at a customer unless he meant something special. I didn't understand it at the time. I have never made a habit of chasing after men the way some women do. All I did was smile. I didn't know if I should believe the impression I was getting....
>
> I swear before God and the Holy Ghost, I don't know how I am getting these strange impressions. I get them in my sleep. I would prefer not having them. If they are not real, I would have to doubt myself. I have received other impressions, too, almost too strange to believe....
>
> With the help of Mr. Baxter's new invention, they started working on me. In May 1943, I suddenly noticed that I was told to stop crying and do as I was told. I did not know who was talking to me.... I became aware of all kinds of facts. I was told to send letters to Mr. Baxter.
>
> When Mr. Baxter came back from the army in 1946, naturally I wanted to talk to him. He acted as if he didn't know me. But it seemed to me he told me, "You are not finished yet. You have to do a few things yet, and it will be tough." He was right. The things I had to do brought me to Mendota State Hospital.

This is the third time that I am locked up. The charges against me are that I made trouble for Mr. Lee Baxter in his place of business. My intentions were never to make trouble. I wanted to help him, but being spontaneous, I probably chose the wrong way. I don't believe he called the police. That is what the judge tried to tell me, but I do not believe it. I think a store should be responsible for what happens to a customer in that store. I certainly have suffered a lot on account of what happened to me in Mr. Baxter's grocery store on May 31. I have never been safe from police hold-ups since. As a rule, I do not mix up with other people's affairs, but because I was in love with Mr. Baxter, I did. I don't think I have been treated fairly. I have done nothing wrong, absolutely nothing, and I am locked up like a criminal. I miss my home and my children terribly, so terribly. I have had my freedom taken away without so much as a trial. Is this justice in your United States of America?"

I have the impression I have really been married to Mr. Lee Baxter since June 21, 1946. Nobody asked me whether I wanted to marry him. I would not want anyone else, since I certainly love him. I am extremely sorry to have imposed on him by writing. I wish he would have had the courage and backbone to inform me instead of leading me on. Why didn't he return the letters to me and tell me himself, if he didn't care for them?

It has been five years now that I have been receiving communications from unknown sources. I have no proof how much truth there is in this. I can only say: I believe. In this time in which we are living, it has been almost 2000 years since the birth of Christ. It has been told to me that the time is here for the second coming. I know this is possible because we have immortal souls. Truthfully, I was told of being the prospective mother and Lee Baxter the selected father. We have both lived a chaste life, and this is necessary. I believe Lee to be my legally wedded husband ...

There it was in her own words—proof of her craziness. For years, I had harbored the hope that she really wasn't schizophrenic. I used to think of her as an oppressed housewife with a sensitive, artistic temperament. Neglected, unappreciated, isolated—who wouldn't get frustrated? And maybe a little strange. So what if she read astrology magazines? Lots of people did. So what if she had a crush on the grocer? Didn't lots of women indulge in fantasy and flirtation? After years of being locked up in institutions, of course she had gotten even more strange, more afraid. I had hoped I could get her over her fears. Instead they had gotten more entrenched. And now here was evidence of her disturbed thinking. She had been crazy all along—"strange impressions;" voices telling her what to do; the "prospective mother" of the second coming of Christ.

"Okay, okay you're crazy. I get it. What does being chosen for the next virgin birth have to do with us? You're still my mother. You're still my sons' grandmother, whether you like it or not. I don't care if you're crazy. You can believe whatever you want. All that matters is that you're nice to my children."

She didn't even have to give up her delusions. I didn't care what she believed. All she had to do was push them aside for a few hours every month and be interested in my children and me. She had done it once, for one brief visit. She talked to me like a normal person and told me she was sorry she had been such a bad mother. She told me I was smart to have a job and children. That gave me false hope.

She came through for me once more when she got in the car with Brian and Evan and came with me to see Carl—a second miracle. But she couldn't sustain the effort anymore than the catatonics who get up and save people in a fire. She had performed the super-human feat twice: once to save herself, once to save me. That was the miracle. Then I assumed the miracle could go on and on, that I had a right to expect it. But she was imprisoned in her illness.

For days, whenever I thought of her, I cried. But no matter how much I cried, she wouldn't change. No matter how much I begged or bargained, or how much I spent on buying her things, I couldn't make her into the mother I wanted.

In the same manila envelope where I found Mama's letters, I also found letters I had written as a child, letters pretending we were just a normal mother and daughter, soon to be re-united:

Dear Mama,

I received your nice letter. Thank you very much. I will send some tooth powder tomorrow. I will also send some pink socks. Last week, Daddy and I went to the eye doctor in Kenosha because my glasses were broken. We went in all the stores for a bathing suit, but we couldn't find one I liked. But I bought a real nice skirt for only $5.00, and I saw those socks for you. I bought some red ones to wear with my white tennis shoes. I found a bathing suit in Geneva for only $6.00.

I'm going to Green Lake Church Camp a week from tomorrow. I hope I'll have as much fun as I did last year.

I hope you got the yarn for my sweater. I know it will be pretty. I wish you could come home very soon. We miss you very much. Fritzi is fine.

Love, Biby

My heart ached as I remembered the girl who wrote that letter, a girl who didn't dare let herself know what she longed for—a mother who could understand and comfort. That would have been too disloyal. Her mother wasn't capable of writing the letter she yearned for, a letter that might have said:

Dear Biby,

My dearest daughter. The sadness that has kept me away from you and Eveli and Daddy has finally lifted. I understand now what made me so angry. I don't want to feel that way anymore; I don't want to waste my whole life feeling bitter. And so I've decided to forgive the people who have wronged me. I want to enjoy the rest of my life and be there for the rest of your growing up.

I was driven mad with grief over all I've suffered and lost—first my mother, then my grandmother, then my father breaking his promise and marrying again. Then, I lost my home and even my father. He wouldn't even see me when I called to say good-bye. It broke my heart. I never saw him again. I hoped for a new life in this country. I had no idea how hard it would be. I had no one to help me, only a husband who didn't understand what I needed. I didn't know marriage would be so hard, that so much would fall on my shoulders. A lot is expected of women in this life and not much credit is given for it. But I will not let that stop me from enjoying the rest of my life. I want to help you find happiness, too. I hope to be home with you soon.

All my Love, Mama

This was my true task: to write myself letters, answer my own questions, and become the mother I had always longed for. Inside, I could feel that little girl, still lonely and hurting, still needing a mother.

I could picture that little girl sitting alone, eyeing me suspiciously. How cute she looks with long braids and rosy cheeks, how serious and how unhappy. I long to put my arms around her, to tell her everything will be all right. But she's stiff and stand-offish, as her mother taught her to be. She doesn't trust me. Well, why should she? I have to earn her trust.

"Hi," I venture. "Can we talk?"

She's suspicious. An adult interested in her? What for? Her tears burn to come out. The thought of trusting someone frightens her beyond words. This is not something she is supposed to do. Mama warned her. Daddy would say, "Be a nice girlie. Don't make trouble. Remember, people get upset hearing little girls have problems they can't fix."

To play it safe, she acts aloof, self-sufficient, and very grown-up. She performs well. She doesn't want to make me angry. She must be careful.

I know I'll have to prove my own trustworthiness to this recalcitrant, unforgiving, self-sufficient, tough, wounded child. She's had to act in certain ways. Will I ever convince her it's safe to let her guard down? Can I convince her that I, now adult and capable, will be there for her? I'll never again criticize her for her feelings, judge her neediness, ask her to discount her feelings or be false to herself for the sake of others. I'll have to become that reliable and loyal parent. She'll never be fooled by pretending.

I put my arms around her. She relaxes. "I'm glad you're here," she says.

I hold her tight and remind her of a good memory, one from Delavan. It is early spring; only the pussy willows are blooming. The trees and bushes are still brown and bare. Our family is taking a walk on the path along the marsh. Eveli and I are wearing matching blue sweaters Mama knit for us, with hoods and wooden toggle buttons and yellow butterflies embroidered on the front. We skip down the path as our parents walk slowly and steadily behind, Mama's arm tucked under Daddy's. He coughs, and she fusses with the scarf around his neck. He is getting over a cold, and she worries that the wind on his chest will make his cough worse. He basks under her attention.

I am filled with contentment.

34

Gifts

✦

1976

Letting go of my old expectations of Mama, though painful, gave me peace. With my old dreams evaporated, there was space for something new. I didn't know what was possible for Mama and me. I was afraid to hope.

As our family therapy with Carl and Don tapered off, I started going to therapy workshops in Milwaukee. It was exciting to get away for a weekend, meet new people and learn more about myself. I was also improving and deepening my skills as a therapist. My route took me past Watertown.

About three months after the disastrous attempted visit with Brian and Evan, I was on my way home from a workshop in Milwaukee. I felt a sudden impulse to visit Mama and at the last minute swerved off the freeway toward Watertown. I felt ready to face her, no matter what happened.

It was late on Sunday afternoon, an unusual time for a visit. The building seemed deserted: no sentinels, no one in the lounge. I pushed Mama's door open and peeked in. When I found it empty, I guessed she was down in the dining room. I ignored her old rule against being seen together in Welbourne Hall and headed downstairs.

The clatter of silverware and murmur of voices coming from the dining room reminded me of my college dorm days. An aide stood at the doorway. "Oh, you're here to see Paula, aren't you?"

"Yes, is she here?" How did she know who I was when Mama had tried so hard to hide our connection?

"Over there." Mama sat alone facing the wall.

"Is it okay if I sit with her?"

"Certainly."

As I approached the table, Mama looked up and motioned me to sit down. I was relieved to be welcomed. She smiled at me, then whispered, "Are you alone?"

"Yes, I'm alone."

"Good. Do you want some coffee? I can get you something to eat."

"I can get it. You eat your dinner." I walked through the cafeteria line, picking out cold cuts, cheese, and potato salad. As I set my tray down on the table, Mama puckered up her face in disgust.

"Biby, you're not going to eat that are you?" She pointed to the ham. "Please don't eat it, Biby, it will make you sick." The same old dilemma. Do I become her rag doll again? Or do I risk ruining the visit? If I gave in, eventually I would have to stop visiting to save myself.

"Do you eat supper this early every day or just on Sundays?" I hoped to distract her.

"Every day. We eat every day the same." She answered in a flat voice, looking out the window as she spoke. Then she stood up. I feared she was angry and would leave me sitting by myself, perhaps refusing to speak to me again. "Do you want some more coffee?" she asked, reaching for my cup.

"That'd be great." I quickly finished the ham while she was gone. I watched her move slowly back across the room with the two full cups of coffee. She looked so frail and vulnerable I couldn't help but be touched.

We sat silently sipping our coffee. Then she wrapped up some bread in a napkin. "Is that for a snack later?"

"To feed the birds," she whispered. "I feed them in the back."

"Oh, I like to feed the birds, too." A moment of connection. I felt lighter knowing she took an interest in something outside of herself.

We walked out of the dining room together. "Don't you want to take the elevator?"

"No, no. It's not safe." She motioned toward the stairs. I followed, surprised she let us be seen together. When a man asked if I was her daughter, she ignored him. Then she whispered, "They're all so nosy here. Pretend you don't hear them."

Back in her room, I settled on the chair by the window. I gazed out at the evening light, enjoying my newfound ease in being with Mama. She began showing off her latest purchases. She held up one item at a time, telling me where she bought it and how much it cost: white polyester pants followed by a jacket with lace sleeves and a lace shell.

As she put her things away, I said, "I don't need you to come with me to see Dr. Whitaker anymore. I'm feeling a lot better. Dr. Whitaker would like to see you, though, because he enjoys talking with you." Carl had asked me to tell her this.

"I don't need to see him. He's probably too busy counseling students. They need to see him. I don't need to see him."

She was full of surprises. I had never told her Dr. Whitaker worked at the university. How could she figure that out but be so unreasonable about things that mattered?

"Did you get his letter? He told me he wrote you." She refused to answer even when I repeated the question twice more, so I changed the subject. "We should go out to lunch now that you have such nice new clothes. We could go over to Madison and see the flower gardens."

"You have good ideas." She laughed, not about to be pinned down. Evidently, she still didn't trust me enough to get into a car with me. Then she held up two slim bracelets she had recently purchased.

Memories of Delavan flooded me: Swiss polka music on the radio, Mama waltzing around the kitchen, a mixing bowl on her arm, her bracelets tinkling like tiny bells, her lips puckered up in a whistle. Mama smiling at me and winking.

"Those remind me of the bracelets you wore when I was little, the silver ones. Whatever happened to those?"

"Oh, those." Her voice fell flat. She seemed disappointed I was more interested in her old bracelets than her new ones. "I have them somewhere." She lifted a stack of cardboard boxes, pulled out the bottom one and rummaged inside. In a minute, she held up two tarnished and slightly dented silver bracelets. I reached for them. A magical piece of childhood lay in my hand. I inspected them closely: one had a braid-like design, the other, little square flowers. In a couple of places, the design had been rubbed smooth and was barely visible.

"Weren't there three bracelets?" I hoped the third was still in the box.

"Yah, yah, I had three, but a lady down there, she liked them, and so I gave her one. It was the prettiest one. I never should have given it away." She reverted to whining.

"Yes, yes you were right to give it to her." I was pleased to know she had been kind and generous to someone else. I slipped the two bracelets on my wrist. "Where did you get these?"

"At Bradley's department store in Delavan." I had always imagined they came from Switzerland, perhaps a gift from her mother or grandmother for some special occasion.

"You like them?" She acted surprised that I liked something so old and worn. "You can keep them." I jumped up to hug her. She hugged me back, making wordless sounds of emotion.

"I am good to you. I was a good mother to you, wasn't I?"

"Yes, yes, you were," I answered through my tears. I held my arm out to admire the bracelets.

"They're real sterling." She sounded proud.

My cheap wrist watch detracted from the antique charm of the bracelets. I took it off, remembering the beautiful Swiss watches my father had given me. The first I had dropped in the lake, the second one was stolen, and the third I managed to keep for several years before one of my two-year-old twins dropped it in the toilet. I was sad, realizing it was the last watch I would ever receive from my father. After that, I managed fine without one. But before I brought my mother to see Carl, I bought myself a twelve-dollar Timex. I was worried I would lose my sense of time around Mama and didn't want to be late for our appointment.

"I don't like the way this watch looks with these bracelets. Did you wear a watch on the same wrist?"

"I never had a watch," she replied wistfully.

"You never had a watch?" As I said it, I realized I had always known this. I had assumed she didn't want a watch, but perhaps it was one of those items she couldn't buy for herself.

"Would you like one?"

"Yes. I have to go out in the hall to look at the clock when I want to know what time it is."

I didn't know she even cared about the time. I thought she wouldn't want my cheap Timex since it didn't look very feminine with its black leather band. "Would you like this one?"

She squinted at it. "Yes, I can read it, five minutes after six. You'll need it though, Biby. You keep it."

"I don't need it. I have another at home," I lied.

"Do I need to wind it?" She sounded hesitant. "Should I wind it every day?"

Once more, I was taken aback that she didn't know something so basic. Watches evidently were part of the mechanical world, the masculine world she didn't feel privy to. Then I remembered that I had felt this way about my first watch also—uncertain, hesitant, afraid I would break it. I showed her how to set and wind it.

"You are a smart one!" She laughed.

"Yes, I've learned a lot!" I laughed with her.

"Oh, you were a smarty when you were little already."

35

Balancing

❖

1980

I rolled down my car window. It was going to be hot, and I wanted to feel the breeze and smell the hay. Once again, I was on my way to visit Mama. At a stop sign, I shook my wrist just to hear my bracelets chime. Even though I had been wearing them for many years, their music still had a magical effect on me.

After the gift of the bracelets, Mama and I reached a truce. I was able to visit her regularly again, taking her out for lunch and shopping. It sounded easy, the least a daughter could do for her mother. But it never felt easy. Almost always, I left feeling sad and drained. Most days, I had to force myself to go.

Every visit with Mama was the same, yet I never knew for sure what a day with her would hold. Near her, I was caught in a force field. I felt her steady, silent plea that I join her paranoid world. Every thought, every action was an effort. I fought to hang on to sanity while outwardly going along with her view of the world; one foot in her reality, one in my own.

Once, after an exhausting visit, I missed my turn for the interstate and found myself on the old highway. The road wound so tightly around fields and farmyards, I could almost touch the Holsteins. Back on the interstate, I missed the gentle faces of the cows, the friendly wave of farmers, the small boys casting lines from the abandoned railroad bridge. After that, I always took the two-lane. It felt less lonely.

On the old road, connected to the green and growing world, I felt happier. I checked the progress of the corn, now tall and lush, recalling how in November it waved paper dry in the wind. I had to ask my new and third husband, Bob, who had grown up on a dairy farm, why, when it was so late in the season, it still hadn't been cut. The corn cobs were still good, he explained, no matter when they were harvested.

I met Bob just weeks after my truce with Mama, at one of the therapy workshops in Milwaukee. As we gathered on the opening night of the workshop, I noticed him at once. I quickly warned myself not to start building hopes. I had started believing I could survive—even be happy—alone. He's probably married anyway, I thought. If not, he must have a girlfriend.

The next morning, Bob volunteered to start. The purpose of the workshop was to get in touch with our needs and to experiment with being open and honest in expressing them to others. Most of us were therapists. Bob related his story to Joseph, the workshop leader. Yes, Bob was married, but his wife had left him, and he was preparing for divorce. Joseph helped him realize that by being "too nice," he had failed to express his own needs in the marriage. This weekend, Joseph suggested, he could experiment with being "not so nice." He was to go around the room and say "not so nice things" to each of us. Bob's eyes darted over to me, back to Joseph, then back to me. I braced myself. I was sure he was getting set to fight with me, probably the fight he should have had with his wife. I was ready for him.

Bob started going around the circle person by person, struggling to carry out the exercise. He was uncomfortable with meanness. Joseph intervened. "Okay, let's change it. This time say what you want; be demanding. Stand up and say, 'I demand....'" Without hesitating, Bob turned to me. I stiffened, ready to defend myself.

"Biby, I'm attracted to you. I demand that you be attracted to me." I gasped. Laughter rippled through the group. Joseph jumped to his feet to urge Bob on.

"Tell her you demand she show she's attracted to you. This weekend." Everyone laughed again, including Bob. Then he turned back to me.

"And I demand you show me you're attracted to me." I knew he meant it. It wasn't just an exercise. He said it with too much passion.

I stood up. "How do you want me to show you?" I asked coyly.

"How about coming here." I walked to the center of the circle and stood inches away from him. We were exactly the right height for each other. I couldn't help noticing his wide shoulders and deep blue eyes. "And giving me a hug." I did.

That was our beginning. Romantic. Perfect. I could find nothing wrong with Bob, which made me uneasy. He was sensitive, reliable, self-sufficient, not moody or needy, no bad habits, not in debt. My kids loved him as soon as they met him, and they were much less tolerant than I. Still, I held my breath, waiting for a problem.

After we had been seeing each other a while, I brought him to see Carl. I had already explained Bob's background: he was a former priest, now in business but wanting to become a therapist.

Carl looked at Bob. "So you divorced the Virgin Mary. Having more fun with Mary Magdalene?" We all laughed, then chatted through the hour. Finally, in reply to my searching looks, Carl said, "Sorry, I forgot to bring my X-ray glasses." I was on my own.

Despite my fears, our relationship deepened. In two years, we decided to live together. The night before moving day, I lay awake, unable to sleep, overwhelmed with fear. "Stop it," I told myself. "There's nothing to be afraid of." The now-familiar voice of that little person inside responded:

"But I'm so scared. What if it doesn't work? I can't stand to have my heart broken once more. How do I know I can trust him?"

I embraced the scared little person inside.

"I couldn't stand it if he left."

"That would be hard. I know you would like me to say that won't happen. But I can't promise. We don't know what's going to happen. But no matter what, I'll never leave you."

"Promise?"

"I promise."

That was several years ago. Bob kept all his promises to me, and I worked at keeping mine to the eight-year-old. It wasn't always easy. It was tempting to forget about her and concentrate on pleasing Bob. It was a familiar struggle, the very same with every visit to Mama. I had learned, through my work with Carl, how important it was not to surrender my own needs and desires completely. Otherwise I would end up wanting to drive off the top of the parking ramp again. Carl had told me that every visit with my mother was an opportunity to practice being my true self with her. If I could be myself with her, he assured me, I could do it with everyone else. In fact, after Mama, it would be simple with anyone else. I thought of his words every time I walked into Welbourne Hall; putting them into practice was not as easy as it sounded.

By the time I got to Welbourne, it was almost noon. Mama's room was empty, so I headed to the cafeteria. I was surprised to find her sitting with another resident, a wispy red-haired woman. Mama, bent over a dish of green Jell-O, lifted her eyes in a small expression of greeting. I knew she wouldn't talk to me in front of another resident.

The red-haired woman, dozing and nodding in front of a full plate of chicken and vegetables, woke with a start. "Oh, hello! It's you! How are you?" She acted as though she had known me for years, though I had never met her. "I fell asleep this morning in the back. I go out there every day. But I can't be out in the sun. My doctor doesn't want me in the sun. Cancer, you know. Paula likes to go out there, too, don't you Paula?" Mama ignored her.

The woman's sugary tone evoked memories of potluck suppers in the church basement where women—well-intentioned and Christian—did their best to befriend Mama.

Mama always rebuffed them. Please, please just smile back, I thought. Make friends. The lady's being nice to you. Please be nice.

Undaunted, the red-haired woman turned to me. "You're here to take Paula out today? She's missed that. Haven't you Paula?"

Mama looked at her Jell-O.

"Oh, I'm so happy for you, Paula." She touched Mama's arm lightly. Mama shrank back from her touch. A terrified laugh, more animal-sounding than human, came from Mama's mouth. She almost ran from the table. I hurried to follow.

"You have a lovely day now. A perfectly lovely time," the red-haired lady called after us.

Upstairs, I watched Mama comb her long white hair. "She was friendly." I hoped Mama would agree.

Mama rolled her eyes. "You'd be surprised, Biby. She's lots of trouble." Mama laughed sarcastically. "She makes trouble behind my back."

"What kind of trouble?" Just as when I was a kid, I kept trying to get Mama to explain herself.

"She was in the pink sweater."

"Pink sweater?"

"Last time. Sitting in the front. We went by her."

"I didn't notice. What did she do?"

"She makes trouble behind my back." Then she whispered, "About my clothes."

"What about your clothes?"

She didn't answer, but I understood. Mama, certain others were jealous, feared she would be punished for looking better than those around her.

I should have been immune to Mama's paranoia, but it descended on me like thick fog, cutting me off from everyone else, from the world. I couldn't stand it. I felt like fleeing but submerged myself in a magazine instead. I was tired already.

After changing into her best white outfit, Mama adjusted the rhinestone headband that kept her long, bushy white hair in place. Store clerks in town had nicknamed her *"the bride."*

I tried to remember when Mama began wearing only white. She had always loved white—white lace blouses, white organdy curtains, white shag rugs—but she had loved color, too. She used to wear blue, pink, red, and even black and brown occasionally. I longed to ask, "Why do you refuse to wear anything but white?"

"Who told you to ask?" she would probably reply, implying her enemies had duped me into spying on her. She accused me of spying whenever I asked anything. I never got any explanations. Mama, like the rest of us, probably didn't know her real reasons for doing things, even if she had been willing to share. I was left to make sense of her on my own. Perhaps wearing white was her way of warding off the evil she felt threatened her from all sides, her way of saying, "I'm pure." Perhaps white, the color of death, was a protest, her way of signifying she considered herself only a phantom on her way to a better world. Or perhaps it signified she had elected herself to sainthood, a status earned through her long life of suffering.

After rubbing her face with a final coating of Oil of Olay, Mama picked up her purse. "Did you bring any money?" She leaned toward me as she asked in a whisper.

I nodded and handed her the bank envelope with her monthly allowance. Her inheritance from the sale of her father's house in Switzerland, about twenty thousand dollars, had finally come through. It had been held up for years by the Swiss Consulate in Chicago. When it came through, Green County immediately filed a claim for the cost of her years at the hospital. I was incensed. I thought they should be paying her for false imprisonment and twenty years of sorting laundry for no pay. So I called a lawyer. He was able to save only six thousand. But I put it into short term investments and withdrew some for her every month. And she never asked me to use my credit card.

Mama put up her hand to stop me as she peeked out the door. "Not yet, wait." She made a face. Someone was coming down the hall. Unless she protected me, she was sure I, too, would be hospitalized against my will. After checking again, she waved me forward.

"I'll go out the back way," she whispered. "Bring the car around. Don't let anyone see you." The same old, secret ritual. She hadn't changed. I was the one who had changed—no longer the eager child, hoping to please Mama. I went along with the game because it made the day go easier.

We drove down Main Street to the Welcome Inn where I parked in the back parking lot. From there, we could go in the service entrance and avoid the receptionist's cheery greetings. We could slip directly down to the dark, cave-like restaurant, the only one Mama would set foot in.

The waitress greeted us with a friendly smile. "Coffee for you ladies?" She filled our cups without waiting for our reply. We were regulars here. "Our soup today is French onion."

Mama rearranged her napkin and silverware and ordered the soup without looking up. Looking at Mama, the waitress continued. "Would you care for dessert?" She recited the pie list in her sweetest voice. Mama ordered lemon meringue without looking up.

The waitress, befuddled by Mama's subtle rebuff, turned to me. "I know she's got a bit of a sweet tooth." I laughed with her, wishing she would sit down and have lunch with us.

After the waitress left, thick silence hung over our table. I told myself I should start drawing Mama out, but I felt too tired. Across the room, people at a large table talked noisily and happily. They were the only other diners, so it was difficult not to stare, as though they were the show, and we the audience.

They were in high spirits. Children wandered in and hung on the backs of chairs, listening to the grown-ups tell stories. It wasn't hard to guess they were in town for a wedding. They were celebrating, and the mood was warm and festive.

Before I met Bob, this scene would have meant nothing to me. Only after becoming a part of his large family did I learn what family could mean. Before Bob, I had never spent a Sunday with relatives. In our first years together, when we drove away from those family events, I would be in tears. I had no idea why I felt so sad. Bob worried it was something he had done. I didn't understand it myself, so I couldn't explain.

Only gradually did I realize that, though I loved being part of his family, I still missed my own. Every gathering seemed to announce, "See? This is what it's like to grow up with grandparents, aunts, uncles, cousins. This is what it's like to be surrounded by people who love you. This is what it's like to be a child with other children while the grown-ups are in charge. See? This is what you missed."

My throat tightened as I watched the family across the room. I longed to join their circle.

To keep from crying, I turned back to Mama. She smiled. She wasn't paying any attention to them. An unspoken plea rose in my throat: Couldn't you talk to me? Couldn't you laugh and tell me something cute I did when I was a baby?

Sometimes I had succeeded in coaxing Mama into telling me some tidbit from her childhood or mine. Once, she shared old recipes while I jotted them down on the back of a place mat. After all these years, she still remembered how she made white bean and barley soup. Once, she let me drive her to Oconomowoc, the town where I was born, where she showed me the houses where we lived and the parks where I played as a toddler.

But I was too tired today. Besides, I might start crying.

"What do you need from the store today?"

Mama's face brightened. "Noxema, toothpaste, Ex-Lax, maybe some nylons, and look around a little bit, see what they have out new."

I braced myself for our familiar routine—the drug and department stores, followed by the grocery and bakery, ending with a silent snack in Mama's room.

36

A Foot Sore

❖

1981

"That sore on Paula's foot is worse. Be a shame if it turned into gangrene, and they had to cut it off." The sentinels at the front door of Welbourne Hall sang out their warnings like a Greek chorus. I knew they were right. On my last visit, I had brought some salve to treat the sore, but Mama accused me of trying to poison her. She wouldn't even take off her shoe to let me put it on. And when I mentioned a doctor, she got angry.

I had given up, yet images of the festering sore floated in my mind: Mama in a hospital, her foot swollen with gangrene, pleading, "Please, Biby, don't let them do it. Promise me." It was just like her teeth, only this time she would die unless I let them cut off her foot. But without her foot, without being able to walk downtown to shop, what life would she have? Shopping and browsing were her only pleasures. She would end up lying on her bed staring into space. How would I comfort her? She would turn into a black hole, sucking me in, begging me to relieve her suffering.

I wrote Eveli about Mama's foot sore. She hadn't seen Mama for a few years. I didn't want to make her feel guilty. I remembered that sickening drop in my stomach, the voice inside telling me I was a terrible person for not visiting my mother. I was certain Eveli felt the same way. I was grateful not to be stuck in those feelings anymore, not that I didn't slip back often enough to remind me how it felt. I wished I could help Eveli but knew she had to do it herself.

Back when I was seeing Carl, I mentioned to Eveli that I had brought Mama to therapy. "It was to help me really, not really for her...." I started to explain, but Eveli broke in.

"I should do that." Her voice sank. I knew she was reproaching herself. She couldn't hear the rest of my story.

"Why don't you come out, and we'll take her together?" She got excited and my hopes rose. Mama, Eveli, and me. Carl helping us come together. Lunch, shopping, laughing ... finally we could be friends. Finally, I could tell Eveli how I used to feel when Mama criticized her and praised me, why I had to be silent. I'd tell her how I wanted to defend her but was afraid, how I could never fight with Mama the way she did.

But two days before she was due to arrive, Eveli phoned to tell me she had decided not to come. She wasn't up to seeing more shrinks. Maybe another time.

"But I was counting on you." I could hardly get it out. I had built up my hopes. For me it was more than a simple visit. It meant bringing my family together again, the very thing I had longed for since I was twelve. Now I was abandoned all over again, and I blamed Eveli. I didn't have it in me to empathize with her, to understand that her experiences with shrinks had not been as positive as mine. All I could do was feel my own pain. I hung up and sobbed.

A year later, we planned another visit. This time, she promised she would come even though Mama had since refused to see Carl. It would be just Eveli and me. Just as well, I thought. We could talk more freely about what we had gone through growing up together. But a few days before her arrival, she told me she didn't want to see Carl.

I felt slapped. An unfamiliar energy surged up from my stomach and into my throat. The words flew out of my mouth. "If you won't go to my therapist with me, if you won't do this one thing for me—I told you how much this means to me—then don't come at all." My breath turned rapid and shallow. I could hardly believe what I had said. It seemed to happen by itself, though I knew there was a split second when I made a decision to let it out rather than force it back down.

Eveli was quiet for a couple of seconds. "You mean you don't want me to come, just because I won't see your shrink?"

"That's what I mean." I was shaking. "You promised last year, and you let me down. So if you're going to do it again, don't come."

Growing up, I treated Eveli the way I treated Mama. I was always striving to be in Eveli's good graces. If we differed, I was certain she was right, and I was wrong. I never could defend myself against her. Now I had done something radical—exploded at her. I wondered if she would ever speak to me again.

She called back a few days later. Since it meant so much to me, she could get through it, just for an hour. I was amazed and grateful.

We saw Carl the day after she arrived. The appointment felt stiff and uneventful. We never really talked about our childhood as I had hoped. I wanted Eveli to relax and realize how wonderful Carl was. But to her he was still a shrink, and what's more, my shrink.

After our session, I drove her over to see Mama. Eveli had never been to Welbourne Hall. I felt pleased to be the one taking her to see Mama's new private room. I was proud, too, of the progress I had made. I was stronger than the last time we had all been together, the day Mama called us orphans down at the old county hospital. In the intervening years, I had faced my fears and now could hold my own with Mama, an accomplishment I hoped Eveli would notice.

We spent the day having lunch and shopping with Mama. It was just like our childhood shopping trips for school clothes. Then, as now, Mama pleaded with Eveli to buy the outfit she picked out for her. Eveli used to resist but this time Eveli gave in, probably to please Mama. And Mama was pleased.

On our drive home, I expected Eveli to express relief and gratitude that Mama was out of the locked ward where we had last seen her. I hoped also to hear a few words of praise—how I had grown up, how proud she was of me for visiting Mama regularly.

"Jesus, that's a terrible place! How can you leave her there?"

"What do you mean, terrible? Did you forget Green County Hospital? Now *that* was a terrible place."

"All that smoke. Doesn't it bother you?"

"Just in the lounge."

"But you have to walk through it. And those people! Would you want to live with them?"

"They're the same she lived with for twenty years. Here, at least, she's got her own room. She can come and go. Have you forgotten how bad Green County was?"

"I know, I know. We shouldn't have left her there. We should have gotten her out."

"What are you talking about? We were kids."

"I mean when we were grown up. We could have done something."

"Like what? Drop out of college and take care of her?"

"No, afterwards."

"Did you forget what happened when I tried? After Daddy died? I couldn't handle it, remember?"

"Other families manage. We should have helped her."

"Other families have aunts and uncles, grandmothers and grandfathers—people we never had. Besides, Mama doesn't like to be around people. You can't just move her in with a family. She'd be afraid to come out of her room."

The whole exchange caught me off guard. I felt blamed. I wanted to say, "How does this get to be my fault? Where have you been all these years? I'm the one who visits every month." But I held back. I was afraid we would spiral into accusations, and she would pack up and go home, and we would never speak again.

After a long silence, she spoke. "Well, you did keep a relationship going with her all these years. I guess that's something." It felt like a crumb to pacify me. We ended our exchange of words, but a change had occurred. I would never fall back into the little sister who accepted her word as truth. We were each on our own now, making our way as best we could. I felt a terrible loneliness.

After that, Eveli didn't come back. Our phone calls and letters were sporadic. I thought telling her about Mama's foot sore would be futile, but I didn't want her saying, "Why didn't you tell me?" so I wrote a letter explaining the situation.

Several months later, I had still gotten no response. I had given up hope of hearing from her when she called to say she was coming and bringing Lucy, her youngest daughter. Eveli wanted Lucy, who had just graduated from high school, to meet her grandmother. I understood her need. It was no different than my own need to have Mama acknowledge and bless my own two sons. But I knew it wouldn't work. Mama was not open to acknowledging any grandchildren.

I reminded Eveli of how Mama had treated Brian and Evan, but she didn't pay attention, almost as if she didn't believe me. Perhaps she only chose to remember the good times I had told her about, when Mama actually got in the car with Brian and Evan to come to our therapy sessions with Carl.

Eveli was determined to get Lucy and Mama together. I could only stand back and watch, wondering if perhaps she would succeed where I had failed. We decided to drop Lucy off at the restaurant before picking Mama up, hoping it would go better if we didn't bring Lucy into Welbourne Hall. We were tricking Mama, and I felt like a traitor. As soon as I steered Mama toward the table where Lucy sat, I could feel her freeze. I pulled out a chair, and Mama sat down lightly, refusing to look at Lucy, who was trying hard to smile and look friendly.

"Mama, this is my daughter, Lucy." Eveli tried to sound natural, but I could hear the tension in her voice.

Mama looked like an animal caught in a trap.

"Hi," Lucy ventured bravely. Mama refused to answer.

"Let's order lunch, shall we?" Eveli's determination amazed me. We all escaped into our menus except Mama, who stared down at her place mat as if in shock.

"What's decent here, anything?" Eveli asked.

I fumbled an answer, my eyes on Mama who seemed to be sliding under the table. When the waitress came, Mama refused to order. Then she grabbed her purse and fled towards the ladies room.

I followed and found her standing before the mirror, combing her hair with long hard strokes. I sat on a chair, waiting. Finally, she said, "I can't go back there."

"It's okay. She's Eveli's daughter. She won't hurt you."

"No, take me back." I tried to imagine being eighteen and having my grandmother refuse to eat lunch with me.

After Lucy flew back to California, Eveli took on the project of healing Mama's foot. She rented a room close to Welbourne Hall and twice daily soaked Mama's foot, then air-dried it. She had managed to get Mama to a doctor who prescribed this. A doctor? Why would Mama go with Eveli and not me? I was the baby, so she needn't take me seriously. Eveli was the smart one, the bossy one. And now Eveli was bossing me, acting as though what I had gone through all these years didn't matter. The only thing that mattered was her plan.

Eveli's plan went from curing the foot sore to finding Mama a better place to live, one with nice, normal people. She insisted that in a normal environment, Mama would behave more normally. As she checked assisted living homes for the elderly, my anxiety grew. It was just like Eveli—a big project, *her* project. I feared she would move Mama to a new place where they would expect her to make conversation at dinner, and when Mama refused to come out of her room, the director would call me: "We can't keep your mother here. You'll have to come get her." Eveli would by that time be back in California, and Welbourne Hall would be full. Then what? Bring her home? Right back where I was when I wanted to drive off the parking ramp?

We couldn't discuss it without fighting. Eveli saw me as the enemy, someone unwilling to fight the system for Mama. It was true. I wasn't interested in more sacrifices.

I had hoped that together, taking care of Mama would be easier, that we could even laugh and reminisce. But we only made each other feel more guilty, more angry so we stopped talking.

Before Eveli returned to California, she called to tell me she had given up on trying to move Mama. "You were right. It's too hard for her to be around people."

I felt relieved, but still guarded. I wished the tension between us could be erased, and we could go back to the easy relationship we used to have, when we were kids. There was so much I'd never said, that I was afraid to say. I longed for the courage to open my mouth and say what was in my heart, to tell her how she had been the idol of my childhood, how I had longed for her approval for as long as I could remember. I wanted to reminisce about our childhood, to tell her my earliest memory of her—when I was four and Mama was spoon feeding me in my high chair. She was only eight, but she stormed into the kitchen and yelled, "This has got to stop. She's four years old, and you're feeding her like a baby. She's going to kindergarten next year, and she doesn't even know how to tie her own shoes."

Mama, intimidated, just replied meekly, "Oh, she's little yet. I can take care of her a little bit yet." She kept right on feeding me, but I felt ashamed. I knew Eveli was right. I was amazed at her bravery. I couldn't imagine how she found the courage to stand up to Mama. I thought she was disappointed that I didn't jump out of the high chair, rip the bib off and join her in protest. But I couldn't. I had to play the baby because that's what Mama wanted.

I was glad Eveli had been part of my childhood, demanding I grow up, showing me it was possible to be more than Mama allowed me to be. I had ached for her praise, her approval, her affection. I thought she could give it to me if she only wanted to. I didn't understand that she couldn't have given what she had never received herself.

37

Finding Home

◆

1989

Eveli succeeded in healing the foot sore, but Mama continued to decline. Walking became harder and harder until she had to give up her daily shopping trips. Once, in the drug store, she had to ask a clerk to get her a chair. After that, I persuaded her to use a cart so she could lean on it like a walker.

I filled with dread as I imagined Mama aging and dying. She didn't have to tell me she feared death. It leaked out in many ways. She refused fresh flowers. Fresh flowers die. Once, I brought her a pot of mums. "Take those away," she said. "They're for a funeral." How would she live once she couldn't walk or shop? How would she spend her days, already so empty?

When the social worker called to tell me Mama was in the hospital, that she was on a catheter and couldn't urinate, a chill went through me. I remembered how Mama smelled on our last visit. She had always been so fastidious. Was it the smell of death? Cancer? Would I soon live out my worst fantasy?

Mama looked small and weak in her hospital bed, tubes running liquid in and out of her body. She seemed strangely content, surrounded by nurses and aides. She was very glad to see me. Her requests were simple: a sweater, hand lotion. These I could give her. She even said, "Thank you." I felt relief. Then I realized she had been saying, "Thank you," often lately—"Thank you for coming. Thank you for the money. You are so good to me." The mother I feared existed only in the past.

There was no cancer. Within a week, Mama mysteriously regained her ability to urinate. She was sent back to Welbourne, where she lost her balance and fell, unable to get up until staff found her three hours later. She was sent back to the hospital, where she fell again, trying to go to the bathroom without help. This time she broke her hip.

Now in a wheel chair, she was sent to Lakeland Nursing Home near Lake Geneva. On my final drive to Welbourne for her belongings, I felt strangely unsettled. Why would I care that someone else had moved into the small room where she had lived for the last fifteen years? Mama never got confused into thinking that it was her "home." But I considered that room where I dependably found her for fifteen years and which held all her belongings her "home."

The social worker joked as he helped me load my van. We barely managed to cram everything in. "This stuff is all your fault, you know. You bought it for her," he teased. I knew it would have made more sense to him if Mama had spent her money on cokes, cigarettes, and candy. Then there would be nothing to deal with.

What difference does it make to you anyway, I thought angrily. What right do you have to pass judgment on her?

Here it was, in my van, the final harvest of years of shopping: polyester suits, pearl-trimmed sweaters, beaded purses, and fake gold chains, all she had dreamed of, the only thing that gave her purpose and meaning.

Okay, I'm angry she cared more about a pile of polyester than about me, angry she never asked one more question about my life, angry she didn't want to know me, except as I served her.

I thought I was over my anger. Maybe I had been fooling myself, lulling myself into something I could live with. Maybe I compromised too much. Perhaps I should have insisted on being more of myself. Maybe she would have told me not to come back unless I could be "nice." So what? Perhaps I wouldn't have lost much.

A part of me, I knew, was relieved that little was required of me on our visits. I could slip into passivity as I had as a child. Mama didn't want to know my thoughts, so I made no effort. All I had to do was smile when she looked at me.

The hardest moments came at the end of our afternoons of shopping—after she put away her purchases, after her excitement subsided, after she cut the pastry and handed me my portion on a paper plate. We ate, sharing a brief, silent communion. I dreaded only the final moment when she sat staring into my face, and I could no longer hide from the yawning emptiness between us.

What would we do on our visits now, now that she could no longer shop? I dreaded the emptiness that being with her in the nursing home would mean.

The first time I walked into Lakeland Nursing Home to visit Mama, I wasn't sure what to expect. Then I saw a long line of gray-haired ladies silently slumped in their wheel chairs, waiting to go into the dining room. The sight depressed me more than Welbourne's smoke filled lounges.

We sat in a dreary dayroom, Mama slumped in her wheel chair, silent as usual. I felt her persistent plea: stay with me, comfort me, love me. I sorely missed the distractions of stores and restaurants. I felt the limits of my own caring and felt ashamed of my inability to love her enough.

I imagined a dozen righteous nurses, middle-aged ladies in white uniforms worn with years. They had fulfilled their female obligation of caring for the young, the old and the sick. They shouted in unison: "She's your mother! How can you neglect her? Who will visit her if you don't? She took care of you when you were a baby, now it's your turn! You're always thinking about yourself!"

"I don't care what you think," I shouted back. "You don't understand."

"Oh, we understand all right. You'd rather have fun than take care of your mother. But we sacrificed to take care of others. And that's what you should do. You ought to visit your mother every chance you get."

"I can't give up my life for her. Why doesn't anyone else see how hard this is? I don't exist just to take care of her."

"Cry baby. You've got a happy marriage and a wonderful husband. Isn't that more than she ever had? You've got a nice house with a beautiful garden and a well-respected job that pays well. Isn't that what she wanted? What did she get? A lifetime in an institution, that's what!"

"But it's not my fault that her life has been so unhappy. It's not my fault that my life is better than hers. She didn't want me to be locked up like she was. She did her best to protect me. My life is what she hoped hers would be. She just doesn't want to hear me talk about it."

It was true, I realized. She wanted a good life for me. But hearing about it was more than she could bear. I needed to accept that.

I expected Mama to protest being in a nursing home. In the hospital, she had pleaded, "I want to stay here, no nursing home." But at Lakeland, she thought she was in a different hospital. Evidently, it didn't match her idea of a nursing home.

It didn't match mine either. It was both worse and better. I compared it with the *Altersheim* in Switzerland where Bob and I visited my Uncle Fritz, Mama's brother. Bob and I had visited Switzerland for our honeymoon, my first visit there and my first meeting with cousins and my uncle.

The *Altersheim* had the ambiance of a pleasant hotel. My uncle's room was furnished with his own oriental rugs, leather chairs, and oil paintings. We drank tea and ate cake in the cafeteria on wooden tables set with lace doilies and fresh flowers while we gazed out at a landscaped garden.

I was surprised at how at home I felt in Switzerland. White curtains, embroidered tablecloths, fresh flowers on every dining table, fresh salads with neat mounds of grated vegetables—just the way Mama had things in our home. The parks with flower gardens and lakes with white passenger boats reminded me of Lake Geneva, the town where I grew up. I understood at last why Daddy chose that impractical, expensive town. He tried so hard to make Mama feel at home in America.

Most of all I was surprised by the feeling of being with my family. I had been afraid to write my cousins to tell them I was coming to Switzerland. I didn't know them, and they didn't know me. I feared they wouldn't want to see me.

"Why bother us after all these years?" I thought they might say.

"But, but I was busy.... I was in school, then I had children ..."

"Your father had to get after you to write us at all, even thank-you notes to your Tante Grete after she scrimped and saved to send you presents. You've even forgotten how to speak our language. How do you expect to talk with us?"

I wasn't sure I was worthy of having a family. But my fears were unfounded. My cousins welcomed us warmly, and, at last, I tasted the feeling of belonging. We stayed with my cousin Bethli, on Daddy's side. Her taste, her home, her values were surprisingly similar to mine. Even though we grew up five thousand miles apart, never knowing each other, we connected with no special effort.

I was more nervous about meeting Uncle Fritz, Mama's only sibling. Daddy had tried to keep in contact with Fritz. But when Fritz accused Daddy of trying to get Paula's inheritance, Daddy gave up. Uncle Fritz's son, my cousin, Fritz, and his wife, Renata, invited us to their home in Ruti, where Mama grew up. We gathered there along with my other cousin, Erich, Fritz's younger brother, to meet my uncle.

I felt embraced and welcomed by Fritz, Renata and Erich, but Uncle Fritz studied me with disbelief. He turned to Erich and mumbled something in *Switzerdeutsch*. I didn't understand, but I knew it wasn't positive. My cousins laughed and chided him. Renata explained that he didn't think I could be his niece because I didn't look like his sister. I was a big disappointment to him.

Without actually slipping across the chasm that divides sane from insane, Fritz was Mama's twin. He, too, was humorless and off in his own world. He showed no interest in me other than answers I could provide about his sister. He demanded an accounting. Renata translated his questions. "What caused her breakdown? Why hadn't we found doctors who could help?" I stammered, trying to satisfy an old man who wanted reasons. He didn't seem to realize that when these things happened, I was an eight-year-old child. It didn't occur to him to sympathize.

Uncle Fritz had invented his own answers years ago, and whatever I said made no difference. "My sister married a scoundrel," he announced with finality. As my father's daughter, I was also guilty by association. We had committed the crime of driving his sister crazy.

Later, as we sat around the supper table, our spirits warmed by wine, he pressed a bundle of Swiss francs into my hand and told me with tears in his eyes that he had been saving this money for his sister. I should take it and buy something for her. Then he announced that perhaps I did look like Paula after all, around the eyes.

I wished Mama could live in a room as elegant as the one Uncle Fritz enjoyed. Unlike the *Altersheim,* Mama's nursing home looked and smelled like a hospital, not a hotel. It was clean, hard, and practical. No lace doilies here, no fresh flowers. However, the staff did their best. They hung bright tinsel and plastic decorations for holidays. On Halloween, costumed children paraded through the halls calling out, "Trick or Treat." Friendly dogs roamed the corridors looking to be petted, while community volunteers passed out coffee and cookies from hospitality carts. Yet a depressive gloom hung in the air.

I sat with Mama while she ate supper on a tray in the day room. As I pushed her wheelchair down the halls, so reminiscent of pushing my infant sons in their stroller, she seemed strangely content. That night, I dreamed:

> I am with my family in a dimly lit hospital corridor, waiting. Daddy sits by Mama on an old worn couch. Her long white hair hides her face. Her belly is round and large and pushing against the buttons of her coat. Astonished, I realize she's pregnant. I wonder how it's possible at her age. I worry she isn't strong enough. I feel frantic, but there is nothing I can do. This sibling will be twelve years younger than I, so I must be twelve. But I'm also an adult.

> I am both child and adult, both young and old. This is my family, then and now. This man is both father and husband, these who wait with me, both sisters and sons. We focus on the patient, Mama. We sit in dreary institution halls, quietly worrying, waiting for something to happen. A lady in a white uniform with long blond hair smiles from the door of an examining room. Why is she so cheerful? Holding a clipboard, she takes charge of keeping this production on schedule. I dart back to my chair for my book. I dread long hours of waiting without something to read. I worry I'll be left with nothing to do but wait.

When I awoke, I reflected on this strange dream. Why would I[?] eighty-two-year-old mother was pregnant? Why this dream no[w?] pushing out with new life is a hopeful image. What else could hap[pen ...er life] now? Or did the dream call me to look again for new life in the least hopeful of places, the dreary corridor of yet another institution, the final institution of Mama's life? Did the dream call me to do something, something I was afraid of? I didn't want to be swallowed up in her emptiness, her silent yearning, she who never saw or heard me. Was I afraid of having nothing in my own life but waiting like the ladies in wheelchairs?

I didn't want to be disappointed once again. I refused to hope for a real conversation before she died, a conversation about her, me, what our life has been like.

I had reached the limits of what I had to give her. I could go through the motions of love, but I couldn't will the feeling. Was I being stubborn? Had I ever felt real love for her? I had felt pity, fear, concern, frantic worry, anger, longing, hopeful waiting, and deep disappointment, even respect and appreciation, but had I ever felt pure, simple love? Or had I protected myself from being swallowed? I waited now for her death. I longed to be released from my life sentence of dutiful daughterhood.

"How dare you dream, you who come and tease me now! You make me feel the weight of my life with her. How dare you suggest hope! Hope of what? Who are you? What are you, now growing in my old mother's womb and waiting to be born? How can you ever expect to be born alive, you who chose an eighty-two-year-old womb? I can see your tiny curled form. You're an old, wrinkled infant with long white hair floating inside Mama's stomach. What do you want from me now?"

"I am the story. The story of this life, the life of this woman who carries me heavily and with great effort. I am almost ready and almost complete. I await the final labor."

38

A Final Visit

❖

1993

Four years later Mama was alive, but barely. She had become completely passive, closer to death than I thought possible for a living person to be. She had lost all interest in shopping, even being pushed through the mall to browse. Eating was managed only with effort. She seemed to enjoy nothing. She seemed to want only to gaze at my face.

I visited every three weeks or so and took her for a drive, since she no longer had interest in the mall.

The aide helping Mama was young and gentle. She called Mama "honey" and caressed her hair. Her tenderness touched me. She helped Mama with her coat, kissed her on the cheek. I was surprised Mama endured the kiss without protest. The last time I tried to kiss Mama good-bye, breaking her rule against mouth contact, she reminded me urgently, "No kissing, no kissing, just touch faces."

Two aides together lifted Mama into my car. I drove into Lake Geneva by the same route Daddy had brought me to the rooming house on Main Street, our first home in Lake Geneva. As we approached the house, I slowed down. It hadn't changed. The view of the lake was just as grand. I drove slowly past the beach and parked in front of the Riviera Dance Hall so we could look at the lake. Soft shadows rested on the snow in the warm February sun. The dark blue ice looked ready to melt. Mama seemed content, so we sat in silence for a long time. Then I drove through Lake Geneva, past each house we had lived in, all eight of them, stopping in front of each one, remembering what had happened there. Washed clean by tears, memories of childhood shimmered before me. I embraced them all, so dear to me now, and felt the peace of reconciling with my past.

Mama made no protest as we lingered in front of each house. I wondered if she, too, was remembering. The quality of our silence suggested she did.

I ended our tour at the corner where we had once dreamed of building our own house. A modest house stood there now, amid the oaks, just right for a small family. I couldn't help but ache for what might have been.

Back in her room at the nursing home, we ate lemon meringue pie in silence.

"A nice day for a ride," I said.

"A good ride." Saying this much was an effort for her, and I was gratified.

"A good ride. What part did you like the best?"

Her words were slow and slurred, but I understood.

"Lake Geneva."

"Me too."

Epilogue

Mama turned eighty-six on March 19, 1993, the age at which her brother, Fritz, died. I wondered if she, guided by some unseen clock, would also die at eighty-six, though I had never told her of his death. She had become as helpless as an infant, bathed, diapered, clothed, lifted, and fed by others. She communicated with shrugs, gestures, and occasional slow words. Even the small pleasure of riding in the car and gazing out the window had faded. She had survived the shrinking of her life until hardly any was left.

After our last ride that spring, she took my hand as I said good-bye and replied, with effort, "Thank you." Only later did I understand she meant thank you, not just for that ride, but for all my visits over the years.

A week later, the nursing home called to tell me she had stopped eating. They tried to stimulate her appetite with changes in her medications, but I knew Mama had decided it was time. Eveli and I had agreed years before not to use feeding tubes or artificial resuscitation. We talked on the phone, reconfirming this decision. Eveli, I guessed, had been out to visit Mama, but I didn't know how often or when since she didn't call or visit me when she came. I only knew about these visits when Mama mentioned them or showed me something Eveli had given her.

Bob, my husband, went with me to see Mama. I was afraid to look death in the face alone. When I saw Mama's shriveled body, curled semi-conscious on her bed, an oxygen tube in her nose, I was grateful he was with me. I took her hand, and she struggled to open her eyes. She made an effort to speak but didn't succeed. Only the first moment was hard. As I sat next to her bed, I grew more peaceful.

The next day, I returned alone. She died the following night. I waited to be overwhelmed by a great sense of loss as when Daddy died, but I felt only a wistful sadness. I had lost her years before.

I called Eveli. I wasn't surprised when she said she wouldn't come to the burial. She had no use for ceremonies especially of a religious nature. She didn't have to explain to me that it felt pointless to make the trip now that Mama was dead. I felt a sense of loss but knew we would not be good at providing each other comfort. We remained divided, each still wounded from our long battles over Mama.

I had always dreaded Mama's funeral. I imagined Eveli and me standing alone at an open grave, like abandoned orphans. Since I never could bear to hear Daddy out when he tried to tell me about plans for Mama's burial, I knew only that he had made arrangements with a funeral home in Monroe. I didn't even know the headstone had already been erected on the burial plot, all ordered and paid for by Daddy.

In Mama's final years at the nursing home, I recoiled at the thought of bringing her back to Green County. I didn't want her final resting place to be so close to the hospital that had imprisoned her and stripped her of dignity, where she had suffered for twenty-three years. Why not bury her in Lake Geneva, the place where our family was whole? Or Delavan, where I still had happy memories?

When I shared my idea with Eveli, she persuaded me to give up this idea in favor of honoring the arrangements Daddy had made. Now that the dreaded time had arrived, I was glad she had. I had no idea how comforted I would feel to follow the steps laid out by him, to be carried through this last ritual of grief by his long arms reaching out one last time.

The morning was green and tender as Bob and I drove down to Monroe for our small ceremony. Mr. Steussy, with whom Daddy had made these arrangements twenty-five years before, met us at the cemetery. Mama's coffin, holding her body and Daddy's ashes, stood raised over the grave they were to share. The simple stone, which I saw for the first time that day, was already engraved with both their names.

Mr. Steussy, a comforting man, a minister as well as a funeral home director, read a poem about cemeteries as places of remembrance, repositories of history, places of celebration of individual lives. I read a poem I had written at her bedside on the last day I spent with her. After I placed it in the coffin, Bob, my former-priest husband, said prayers, and the three of us recited the Twenty-third Psalm.

As we drove to Lake Geneva for lunch, I shook the bracelets Mama had given me years before. Their sound connected me to the happy part of my childhood. Afterwards, we walked along the lakeshore. I gazed out at the lake, fresh and eager, newly released from winter captivity under thick black ice.

978-0-595-41227-3
0-595-41227-0

Printed in the United States
107160LV00004B/65/A